Governor
Theodore Roosevelt

The Albany Apprenticeship, 1898–1900

Governor Theodore Roosevelt

The Albany Apprenticeship, 1898–1900

BY G. WALLACE CHESSMAN

1965   Harvard University Press   Cambridge, Massachusetts

to Oscar Handlin

Preface

This study of Theodore Roosevelt's governorship of New York was first begun in 1948, when scholars were just beginning to reappraise the historical position of the Republican Roosevelt. By 1950 the manuscript was acceptable as a doctoral dissertation, but as Elting E. Morison remarked, it said "too much about too many things." The pruning for publication proved to be a lengthy process, interrupted again and again by teaching duties and other research. To all those who prodded and encouraged me to finish this book, I wish now to express my warm thanks.

The work owes much to other historians: Richard W. Leopold first directed me toward Theodore Roosevelt; Frederick Merk and the late Hermann Hagedorn approved the particular topic for the initial award of a Theodore Roosevelt Memorial Association Fellowship at Harvard University (1948–1950); Elting E. Morison and John M. Blum gladly shared their knowledge of Roosevelt's letters, which they were then assembling for publication; Oscar Handlin patiently directed the dissertation, and has since given unsparingly of his counsel and skill in revision; William H. Harbaugh has reviewed the whole manuscript in constructive fashion; my colleague, William Preston, Jr., advised me on the labor section. To them all, and to the Theodore Roosevelt Memorial Association for its generous assistance, I am most grateful.

Librarians in Massachusetts, New York, and the District of Columbia also contributed. The late Nora Cordingly was a gracious guide through the Roosevelt Collection. The curators of manuscripts at Houghton Library, the Library of Congress, Low Library, Columbia University Library, the New York Public Library, the Russell Sage Foundation, Rundel Memorial Library, and the New York Regional Library at Cornell University were cooperative and helpful. The public librarians at Buffalo, Rochester, Syracuse, Utica, Binghamton, and New York City opened their newspaper files, and so did the Library of Congress, Cornell University Library, the New York State Library, the Harvard College Library, and the New England Deposit Library. To them all I am indebted.

Particular individuals aided me in various ways and should be thanked. Blake McKelvey gave a new dimension to my knowledge of Rochester's past, and James T. Rogers, Jr., graciously opened his home and the scrapbooks of his father. Mrs. John K. Huckaby read the entire manuscript and made most helpful editorial suggestions. Miss Mary Graeff and Mrs. Robert W. Alrutz accepted the more onerous typing chores. Miss Ann Orlov was an able and exacting editor, and my wife, Eleanor Osgood Chessman, assisted me in compiling the index. The trustees of the Denison University Research Foundation granted financial aid in the final preparation of the manuscript.

However, the greatest debt owed by anyone who studies Theodore Roosevelt is to the Association that assembled the Theodore Roosevelt Collection at the Harvard College Library. This extensive collection of primary and secondary sources expedites every research task. It supplies a depth and a breadth that any study of Theodore Roosevelt otherwise might lack. It is a resource worthy of a great American who often wrote for posterity himself, and who was always content to rest upon the full record.

I am of course solely responsible for errors of fact or interpretation that may remain in this work. Those who may desire a fuller treatment of some aspect of the governorship should consult the manuscript dissertation, "Theodore Roosevelt, Governor" (1950), copies of which are in the Harvard University Archives, the Roosevelt Collection, and the William Howard Doane Library of Denison University.

Finally, I must express my deep gratitude for the understanding support of my wife and children through these many years.

G. W. C.

Granville, Ohio
September 1964

Contents

Governor
Theodore Roosevelt

The Albany Apprenticeship, 1898–1900

Introduction

Historical appraisals of Theodore Roosevelt have gone through a familiar cycle. The earliest studies, heavily influenced by his dynamic personality, were generally favorable, often adulatory. Then in the late 1920's, came a sharp reaction climaxed by Henry F. Pringle's Pulitzer-Prize-winning biography in 1931; a man as compromising yet self-righteous as Roosevelt was a perfect target for a debunking generation which found a domestic program of cautious adjustment to modern industrial conditions almost as unfashionable as a foreign policy based on empire and power. It was only in the aftermath of World War II, marked by its conservative trend at home and its deep involvement against Communism abroad, that historians shifted back to a more realistic view of the Republican Roosevelt's stature and achievement.[1]

Today, with his selected letters published in an excellent edition; with a multi-volume biography begun and several major ones completed; and with more detailed analyses of important aspects of his career newly available, Theodore Roosevelt has finally taken his rightful place among American political leaders of the first rank.[2]

[1] Contrast William R. Thayer, *Theodore Roosevelt* (Boston, 1919), or Joseph Bucklin Bishop, *Theodore Roosevelt and His Times*, 2 vols. (New York, 1920) with Henry F. Pringle, *Theodore Roosevelt: A Biography* (New York, 1931).

[2] Morison and Blum, eds., *Letters*; Carleton Putnam, *Theodore Roosevelt: The Formative Years* (New York, 1958); John M. Blum, *The Republican Roosevelt* (Cambridge, Mass., 1954); William H. Harbaugh, *Power and Responsibility: The Life and Times of Theodore Roosevelt* (New York, 1961);

The main interest in his career, understandably, has centered on the Presidential years. A man of large capacities and broad conceptions, he found his most adequate theater of action in the White House. There he could grapple with the giant trusts and combinations that were dominating national development. There he could chart America's course through the perilous waters of international diplomacy. It was only there that, in the fullest sense, he could promote the general welfare of the American people.

Roosevelt was so well suited to this preeminent position that in retrospect it seems almost inevitable that he came to fill it. In his early years in politics he performed capably at a variety of tasks—member of the state assembly, United States civil service commissioner, president of the New York City police commission, Assistant Secretary of the Navy—but it was that fabled charge up San Juan Hill in 1898 that first distinguished him for high elective office. Out of that incident, in large part, came his nomination and election as governor of New York. Yet only one predecessor, Grover Cleveland, had stepped from that position into the Presidency, and in 1900 the G.O.P. simply sidetracked Governor Roosevelt into the Vice-Presidency, from which the supreme accident of an assassin's bullet rescued him.

Beyond the fateful occurrences there were the risks of political life—the chance that he would split with the Republican leaders over some reform issue, or that he would antagonize the independents by siding too much with the machine, or that some scandal or error would estrange every element in the party. In his private correspondence Roosevelt always refused to look too far ahead as to political place; almost instinctively he sensed the foolhardiness of trying to plan one's way into the nation's top office, and besides,

Howard K. Beale, *Theodore Roosevelt and the Rise of America to World Power* (Baltimore, 1956).

he was always too absorbed in the immediate dangers of his present position. To close friends like Henry Cabot Lodge he often referred to "the rocks" ahead; his favorite description of what he was doing was "sailing round and round and to and fro between Scylla and Charybdis." [3]

The chance of shipwreck was particularly menacing after the Cuban adventure of 1898, as the hero home from the war contemplated the probability that the Republican party in New York, led by Senator Thomas Collier Platt, would nominate him for the gubernatorial race that fall. In his only major canvass up to that time, the New York City mayoralty contest in 1886, Roosevelt had gone down to defeat. And even if he won the governorship, there was the chilling prospect of having to work harmoniously with Boss Platt and other machine leaders to accomplish anything at Albany. There were moments when the Rough Rider Colonel almost wished that he wouldn't get the G.O.P. nomination; at the same time he flirted with a third-party independent ticket that would free him somewhat from Platt's clutches and assure victory at the November polls. In September 1898, Theodore Roosevelt was a troubled and confused man, uncertain of his proper course.

And once safely past the election, his troubles had but begun; as one machine lieutenant put it, "everybody is expecting so much . . . so many impossible things and from such conflicting points of view." An Easy Boss, Platt would allow this reform politician a certain freedom of action, but where important corporate interests were at stake, or the machine's functioning endangered, he would quickly intervene. The reformers and independent Republicans, on the other hand, looked to Roosevelt not only to frustrate the organization's schemes but to battle for the right, whether Platt liked it or not. The more extreme independents, represented by the New

[3] Roosevelt to Thomas Brackett Reed, July 1, 1899, TR MSS.

York *Evening Post*, even argued that if Platt disapproved, so much the better: their real aim was to destroy the Boss's power.[4]

For Roosevelt to escape criticism, under these conditions, was manifestly impossible: the most he could hope for was to fend off the most damaging blows. And since he had to act, he inevitably sought a middle way among the alternatives, a compromise that would command as much support as possible among diverse factions. More than that, he inevitably sought a position that was above party or special group, a stand that he could defend as in the broad public interest. The genesis of the idea of the neutral state, the state that "must be severely neutral among all the special interests in society, subordinating each to the common interest and dealing out evenhanded justice to all," was rooted in the hard facts of day-to-day politics in a state such as New York. It was a concept vital to Theodore Roosevelt's leadership of the progressive movement.[5]

Albany did not mean dangers solely: it offered great opportunities. If, as governor, Roosevelt managed to avoid a crippling blow, he had a magnificent chance to show that he was of Presidential stature. Already the most populous of the states, with the largest port and city and the most diverse production, New York afforded a scope for executive leadership unsurpassed outside the national capital. Here was a premier place to explore the problems disturbing the urban-industrial society, and to advance solutions that might mark the way for others. Here was that rare rostrum assured of national prominence and attention.

It would be misleading to suggest that Roosevelt calculated every move with an eye to its national impact. The only major

[4] Lemuel E. Quigg to Roosevelt, September 10, 1898, Quigg MSS.
[5] On the concept of the neutral state, see Richard Hofstadter, *The Age of Reform: From Bryan to F. D. R.* (New York, 1955), ch. vi.

instance in which he consciously did so was in his proposal of publicity as an initial answer to the trust problem. To this the machine leaders quickly objected, and the public conspicuously failed to respond, with the result that the governor gained nothing beyond an airing of his personal views. His one bid for the nation's attention failed.

Yet Roosevelt was well aware that his actions were under close surveillance in the Empire State. When he took up a matter of general import, such as the taxation of corporate franchises, or the improvement of the Erie Canal, or the enforcement of the labor law, he knew that interested parties beyond New York would be attending the result. Everything he did would go into the record, to be used for or against him in the future. This was a real testing time.

And it was a time to test himself, all the ideas, all the talents that he possessed. Never before had he had so much responsibility in the legislative process, where he had to work out an acceptable program with his advisers and the party leaders; to guide bills through the assembly and the closely divided senate; to investigate and stop measures that were not in the public interest. Nor had he ever been in charge of such a large and varied administrative establishment, where he had to oversee the enforcement of the laws; to recommend reappointment or replacement of the many officials whose terms would expire; to try to institute new policies as needed in the management of state agencies and institutions. In so many areas the clash of reformer and machine, of state and local interests, and of different theories of proper practice demanded the utmost skill of a chief executive. Roosevelt was to learn much in this challenging school.

The ideas which Colonel Roosevelt brought to the governorship were for the most part simple, direct rules of conduct: complete honesty in public affairs, an equitable sharing of privilege and responsibility, the subordination of party and local concerns to the interests of the state at large. What remained was the far more demanding task of defining their application. On honesty there might be no dispute, but what was a corporation's fair share of the burden of taxation? Or where was the true public interest in a struggle between the railroads and the canal men, or between an employer and a striking union? Or what was the legitimate concern of a municipality or a party or a private individual over against that of the state?

The answers to these and other questions, worked out over a series of specific instances, were the best evidence of Roosevelt's devotion to the ideal of the honest broker in the neutral state. In fact, it is the contention of this volume that at Albany, in implementing this ideal, he developed the more important positions that he would take later as President. Insistence upon the public responsibility of large corporations; publicity as a first remedy for trusts; regulation of railroad rates; mediation of the conflict of capital and labor; conservation of natural resources; and protection of the less fortunate members of society from exploitation—all these were parts of Roosevelt Republicanism as it emerged in his two years as governor.

But in the late summer of 1898 it was the danger rather than the opportunity of the governorship that absorbed the Rough Rider's attention. The Republican party in New York was plainly in difficulty; otherwise, Platt would not even entertain the possibility of nominating so independent a man for the gubernatorial office. The question was: was the situation so desperate that the senator had no choice? For an Easy Boss understood the dangers, too.

CHAPTER I **Boss Platt**

It was August 1898. A light breeze off the Atlantic danced over the breakers, curled around the minarets of the fashionable Oriental Hotel and blew past Sheepshead Bay into Long Island. Down toward Coney Island a Sunday afternoon throng swarmed along the shoreline. Here and there a daring bather in black hose and a puff-sleeved knee-length suit attracted appreciative glances. Some residents were departing for Victor Herbert's concert with the 22nd Regimental Band, while others lounged on the Oriental's broad veranda, content to relax from the heat. Here, observed the London *Times* correspondent, was "the resort of the New York business man, whose business will not suffer him to be at Newport, which is practically a day's journey distant, or the Adirondacks or other remoter haunts of leisured classes." Here, too, was the summer abode of Thomas Collier Platt, the junior United States senator from New York, the man who held the key to Theodore Roosevelt's immediate political career.[1]

That well groomed man of slight frame who stepped slowly toward his accustomed chair on the Oriental veranda might have been any vacationist bent upon an afternoon's relaxation. The marked stoop to his shoulders, the whitening beard which partially hid a standing collar, emphasized his sixty-five years of age. The lined face was ascetic, thoughtful, full of patience and reflective calm, the face of a scholar or a philosopher. Only the touch of

[1] London *Times*, August 10, 1899 (RS); New York *World*, August 15, 1898.

watchfulness, of keen shrewdness about the penetrating eyes betrayed the politician. That elderly gentleman was "Easy Boss" of the Empire State's Republican machine, Thomas Collier Platt.[2]

His was a familiar figure at the seaside hotel. For the past fifteen summers he and his wife had forsaken their stuffy apartment in Madison Square's Fifth Avenue Hotel for cool Manhattan Beach. Their arrival transformed a corner of the piazza into an informal business office. Seated there in a wooden porch chair Platt received the party faithful, some with a particular issue to present, some in search of patronage or place, a few just old friends desirous of companionship. Rarely did the senator speak; indeed an admirer once stated that Platt "could not conduct a conversation, much less make a speech." His callers received a bored, listless handshake, a faint smile of recognition. The casual observer would have wondered how this unpretentious man, seemingly so lacking in the magnetic qualities of leadership, had attained his preeminent position. Dynamic Roscoe Conkling, the previous Republican boss of New York, might have been surprised himself.[3]

Of course, Conkling had valued his successor's abilities. When they first struck up their alliance, back in 1870, the thirty-seven-year-old Platt was devoting his attention principally to banking and political pursuits in his native Tioga, an upstate rural county of the "Southern Tier" of counties served by the Erie Railroad. Thereafter, with Senator Conkling's backing, this quiet Tioga banker assumed more important responsibilities. He served two terms in the United States House of Representatives, and as chairman of the party's state committee. At the same time he gained a

[2] London *Times*, August 10, 1899 (RS); New York *Mail and Express*, September 6, 1898.

[3] Lemuel E. Quigg, "Thomas Platt," *North American Review* 191:668 (September 1910). See also Burton J. Hendrick, "Governor Hughes and the Albany Gang," *McClure's* 35:496 (September 1910).

more useful position as president of the United States Express Company, originally an Erie affiliate but by the late 1870's an independent concern strategically placed in the world of business and politics. T. C. Platt moved to New York City and grew a beard. He had arrived.[4]

But Platt's association with Roscoe Conkling bore bitter fruit in 1881, when in a patronage quarrel with the about-to-be-martyred President Garfield they blundered into the loss of their United States Senate seats. The next year, having lost more prestige in Grover Cleveland's astounding gubernatorial victory, Lord Roscoe abdicated leadership of the G.O.P. in New York. Tarred by the same brush as his mentor, Tom Platt did not appear a likely heir. Yet by 1888, in part for lack of a rival persevering enough to pursue the thankless task, the express company president had assumed direction of the faction-ridden state organization. After several bleak election days, fortune finally smiled on his efforts: the Republicans recaptured the state legislature in 1893, the governorship in 1894, and one of the two United States Senate seats in 1897. Ruler of the Empire State from Capitol Hill, Senator Thomas Collier Platt could declare himself the true inheritor of the mantle of Roscoe Conkling.[5]

Tall, handsome, domineering, a man whose very presence commanded attention, Conkling had distinguished himself in Washington by his oratorical power and brilliance in debate. For lack of such gifts, Platt exploited to their fullest his own simple virtues— patience, capacity for work, and a businesslike mind. His talent

[4] On Platt's career, see Platt, *Autobiography;* Harold F. Gosnell, *Boss Platt and His New York Machine* (Chicago, 1924); William Allen White, "Platt," *McClure's* 18:146 (December 1901).

[5] Platt, *Autobiography,* pp. 150–152; Gosnell, *Boss Platt,* p. 28; Alexander, *Political History,* IV, 11, 55–57, 158ff., 259; Donald Barr Chidsey, *The Gentleman from New York: A Life of Roscoe Conkling* (New Haven, 1935), p. 344.

was that of the behind-the-scenes manipulator, his best theatre the state committee rather than the senate floor. His political progenitor was Thurlow Weed, not William H. Seward or Conkling.[6]

Platt differed from his predecessor in a more significant way. In his day Conkling had relied chiefly on federal patronage to control the party organization, but as civil service reform began to undermine the spoils system, Platt cast about for a better means of political management. He discovered it in party financing by powerful corporations anxious for political protection and privilege. These companies were beginning to find the customary legislative "lobby" too cumbersome and expensive. Why not guarantee them an efficient legislative service for their campaign contributions, and with the funds thus collected maintain, despite declining spoils, a reliable political machine? Such was the "business government" Platt evolved.

Though the role of businessman's political agent had originated with Tammany chieftain Richard Croker in the early 1890's, T. C. Platt was an ideal man for the job. Highly placed in the commercial field, he enjoyed the confidence of the business community. Thoroughly schooled in the intricacies of Empire State politics, he commanded a loyal organization. As Theodore Roosevelt later described the situation:

> Big businessmen contributed to him large sums of money, which enabled him to keep his grip on the machine and secured for them the help of the machine if they were threatened with adverse legislation . . . When the money was contributed there was rarely talk of specific favors in return. It was simply put into Mr. Platt's hands and treated by him as in the campaign chest.[7]

[6] Chidsey, *Conkling*, pp. 39–40, 119; Platt, *Autobiography*, p. 55; Chauncey Depew, *My Memories of Eighty Years* (New York, 1922), p. 79.

[7] Roosevelt, *Autobiography*, pp. 298–299. See also Gosnell, *Boss Platt*, pp. 281–282; Joseph Bucklin Bishop, "The Price of Peace," *Century* 48:668–671 (September 1894).

In further contrast to his mentor, the senator was familiarly known as the "Easy Boss." Roscoe Conkling had been "intolerant of any exercise . . . of independent judgment" by his subordinates, Chauncey Depew once asserted, but Platt "was always ready for consultation . . . sought advice, and was tolerant of large liberty of individual judgment among his associates." The hold Platt maintained upon the party was not harsh and dictatorial; if he obtained his way in vital matters, he usually took care to do so tactfully. The Easy Boss was "often arrogant, pre-emptory, irritable," remarked a trusted lieutenant, "but when he faced a crisis . . . he was quiet, conciliatory, open to suggestion, ready for any concession that did not compromise or embarrass the ultimate at which he was aiming." [8]

The easy methods to which he naturally inclined were admirably suited to political conditions in the Empire State. Within the party Platt always had to contend with an antimachine element substantial enough to decide close contests; these independent Republicans bulked largest in New York City, where the Union League Club and individuals like Elihu Root, Chauncey Depew, Cornelius N. Bliss and Joseph H. Choate wielded much influence. Then within the organization itself there were powerful local leaders who could successfully defy dictation. Conclaves of these chieftains on state matters had long been regarded as indispensable; in seeking their advice Boss Platt only followed an established custom. [9]

And this August of 1898 the senator needed good advice, for Empire State Republicans were at odds over the gubernatorial choice for the fall election. Upstate adherents of the incumbent

[8] Depew, *My Memories,* p. 85; Quigg, "Thomas Platt," p. 672.
[9] Philip C. Jessup, *Elihu Root,* 2 vols. (New York, 1938), I, 171–172; Gosnell, *Boss Platt,* p. 56.

governor, Frank S. Black of Troy, were already championing his claim to renomination. Downstate and in the Buffalo area, on the other hand, machine leaders were increasingly critical of Black's candidacy; a few of them were even beginning to assert that his record so imperiled G.O.P. prospects that only by naming a war hero like Theodore Roosevelt, Colonel of the Rough Riders, could the party hope to prevail in November. Of this Platt was not yet convinced, but he had to concede one thing: the past two years had endangered the organization's hold on the state government.

In 1896 at the state convention, Platt had found much to commend Black's first bid for the governorship. A lawyer and congressman who had achieved prominence for his prosecution of the Troy election frauds, Frank Black was then regarded favorably both by reform elements and by the organization. He had a most potent backer in the notorious lobbyist Louis F. Payn, Republican boss of Columbia County and a longtime political associate of Senator Platt. According to one authority, Payn's best argument for his man was that Black would approve a bill consolidating the five boroughs into Greater New York—a project cherished by Platt but reportedly opposed by the other leading contender for the nomination, Congressman Benjamin B. Odell, Jr., of Newburgh. In any case, Platt passed over the near unanimous endorsement of Odell by other party lieutenants to swing the convention vote to Payn's candidate. Though that decision rankled, the campaign went off without a hitch; Black's plurality exceeded Cleveland's colossal 1882 margin, and the legislature was overwhelmingly Republican in both branches.[10]

The new governor's policies soon disillusioned independent

[10] On Payn, see Charles Francis Adams, *A Chapter of Erie* (Boston, 1869), pp. 70–71; New York *Evening Post*, January 13, 1900; Gustavus Myers, "'Boss' Platt," *National Review* 38:221 (October 1901). On the convention of 1896, see Platt, *Autobiography*, pp. 329–330; Alexander, *Political History*, IV, 256–259.

Republicans. He rewarded Lou Payn with a nomination for superintendent of insurance, and pressured the senate into confirmation.
Over the protests of reformers he also reappointed George W.
Aldridge, a Payn confederate and the burly boss of Rochester,
as superintendent of public works. Then, as if to give these avowed
spoilsmen freer rein, Black initiated a civil service law amendment
which added to the board's written test of "merit" an examination
for "fitness" conducted by the appointing official. This "starchless"
amendment permitted gross favoritism in the selection of subordinates, as Governor Black himself admitted when he refused
to extend it to the normally Democratic city of New York. Nor
were reformers fooled when the next year Black acceded to the
attorney general's opinion that the "fitness" examination did not
apply to municipalities but only to the state government: he was
merely recognizing that most of the larger cities had gone Democratic in the fall elections of 1897!

Equally destructive of the bond with independent Republicans
was the organization's reluctance to cooperate with antimachine
forces in the first mayoralty contest under the new Charter of the
Greater City of New York. Though Platt yearned for more control
of elections and police in the metropolis, and though he had
selected Black over Odell to insure approval in 1897 of this new
charter consolidating Manhattan, Brooklyn, Queens, Richmond,
and the Bronx into the greater city, he was not so enamored of
victory in the fall of 1897 as to accede readily to the plans of the
Citizens' Union, the nonpartisan reform group which had secured
100,000 signatures to petitions sponsoring Columbia College president Seth M. Low for mayor. Platt's cooperation with these "good
government" disciples in the anti-Tammany coalition of 1894 had
brought triumph in that year, but once in office Mayor Strong had
broken pledges to the senator and had alienated the G.O.P.
machine with sweeping reforms of the street cleaning and police

departments. This time Boss Platt wanted to have a firmer grip on the candidate. This time he wanted any combination with the independents to be more definitely under Republican leadership.[11]

To this end he proposed that if Seth Low would withhold acceptance of the Citizens' Union candidacy until after the local Republican convention, then the machine would make an effort in Low's interest so that he could accept both nominations simultaneously. But this matter of punctilio made little impression upon President Low, who was forming an ever stronger attachment to the principle of municipal nonpartisanship. Well before the Republican meeting convened, the Columbia College head announced that he would run under the Citizens' Union standard.

Those independents who expected Platt's desire for success to force an endorsement of Low soon learned otherwise. The senator, whose devotion to party was basic, believed that Low had severed all Republican ties and might do positive harm to the organization. Moreover, the city machine adherents who preferred Tammany to reformers pressed for a separate ticket. All the signs Boss Platt understood pointed toward the nomination of another Republican, ex-Secretary of the Navy Benjamin F. Tracy, as the regular G.O.P. candidate.[12]

That November the party harvested the fruit of the disastrous split. Less than half the votes cast went to Tammany's pliable nominee, "an obscure judge" of old Dutch family, Robert W. Van Wyck, but he garnered a plurality of more than 80,000 over his closest contender. Nor did the state at large escape the effects

[11] Allan Nevins and John A. Krout, eds., *The Greater City: New York 1898–1948* (New York, 1948), ch. ii; Quigg, "Thomas Platt," p. 675; Platt, *Autobiography*, p. 303; Alexander, *Political History*, IV, 248; Everett P. Wheeler, *Sixty Years of American Life* (New York, 1917), pp. 358–360; Benjamin R. C. Low, *Seth Low* (New York, 1925).

[12] Platt, *Autobiography*, pp. 356ff.; Alexander, *Political History*, IV, 292–296.

of the mayoralty contest, as the Republican majority in the assembly plummeted from 78 to 8, and Alton B. Parker, a future Democratic Presidential nominee, won the chief judgeship of New York's highest court. Theodore Roosevelt pronounced a verdict shared by many Republicans when he wrote Henry White that "the result in New York has been an overwhelming disaster, partly because the reform or Citizens' Union element behaved with much perversity, but infinitely more because the Platt machine people were equally stupid, and a great deal more immoral." [13]

In the months following this defeat Governor Black sought to mend the breach with the independents. There were no more bad appointments, the civil service was partially redeemed, and a bill governing primaries approved by antimachine Republicans received his support. His opposition to undesirable legislation also merited nonpartisan praise. Frank Black clearly intended to seek renomination in the fall.[14]

But clouding the political horizon was yet another thunderhead, one of sufficient magnitude to place the party itself in jeopardy. When Platt expressed doubt in April 1898 about whom he would back for governor, he acknowledged the storm signals. The legislature prepared for the blow by passing a law which would enable a Republican senate to protect state officials from being replaced by a Democratic governor. For a scandal over the administration of the nine million dollar canal-improvement project was about to break.[15]

[13] M. R. Werner, *Tammany Hall* (Garden City, 1928), pp. 452–458; Alexander, *Political History*, IV, 299; Roosevelt to White, November 8, 1897, TR MSS. See also Roosevelt to Henry Cabot Lodge, September 29 and October 16, 1897, in Lodge, ed., *Selections*, I, 283–284, 287.

[14] Gosnell, *Boss Platt*, pp. 85–88; *New York Tribune*, October 13, 1898; *Nation* 66:256 (April 7, 1898).

[15] Platt, *Autobiography*, pp. 364–368; New York *World*, December 7, 1898.

This costly enlargement program, the first of its kind in the long history of the Erie Canal, was the outgrowth of a decade's agitation by the Canal Improvement Union founded in 1885 by the grain traders of New York and Buffalo. The Constitutional Convention of 1894 at last had adopted an amendment for improving the canals in whatever way the legislature should decide. Hampered by a shortness of time and by inadequate surveys, the state engineer had estimated that to deepen the seven-foot Erie channel to nine feet would cost about $12,500,000. With this figure as a guide, the people had approved the constitutional amendment. The 1895 legislators, motivated by expediency and without engineering advice, had set the appropriation at $9,000,000, and a popular referendum had given final sanction to the work in November of that year.[16]

Once underway, the work had quickly exceeded cost estimates, necessitating slashes in less vital features. Even then the appropriated funds were exhausted before the essential conversion was two-thirds completed. With press and public aroused over the disappearance of the original appropriation, Governor Black had no choice but to appoint a special investigative committee.

Released to the public on August 4, 1898, the commission's report quieted some of the worst Republican fears. Superintendent of Public Works Aldridge and State Engineer Adams did not appear to have profited personally, and the total project received praise, the investigators recommending that $13,000,000 more be allotted to complete it. But there was much evidence of "improper expenditures" upon the work, especially in the reclassification of excavated material as "rock" when the specifications contracted—

[16] Frank S. Gardner, "The Canal Improvement Union," Buffalo Historical Society *Publications* 13:1 (1909); Noble E. Whitford, *History of the Barge Canal of New York State* (Albany, 1922), pp. 17–25.

at a far lower cost—for "earth." The commission estimated that a million dollars had been spent improperly, "exclusive of moneys paid out for ordinary and extraordinary repairs which amount to not less than $1,500,000." [17]

Of course, the *Troy Times,* a staunch Black supporter, whistled bravely that the "explosion" hadn't been as big as the Democrats had hoped, but the silence of the organization press generally showed the serious proportions of the exposure. Independent journals, concluding that Black's chances had suffered a damaging blow, speculated on the prospective nominee. On the other hand, calling Black "The Inevitable Candidate," the Democratic *Albany Argus* was maliciously solicitous of the incumbent's renomination; to substitute another at this juncture, it declaimed, would be a confession of "hopeless political bankruptcy." [18]

Among Republican politicians Lou Payn resorted to a similar argument as he maintained that to reject Black's candidacy would only lend credence to opposition charges of fraud and thievery. But a number of those who had been neutral or even friendly toward Black now doubted the expediency of renomination. The young leader of the Erie County Republicans, Judge John R. Hazel, expressed the view privately that the investigation had so influenced sentiment in his area that the governor could not be reelected. Reports from other county leaders confirmed this testimony. The anti-Black elements needed some other candidate; and events in Cuba came to their assistance.[19]

[17] *New York Tribune,* August 4, 1898.

[18] *Troy Times,* August 6, 1898; New York *Evening Post,* August 8, 1898; New York *Commercial Advertiser,* August 11, 1898; *Albany Argus,* August 8, 11, 1898.

[19] New York *Commercial Advertiser,* August 10, 1898; *New York Press* (Black supporter), August 7, 21, 1898; Lemuel E. Quigg to Roosevelt, April 23, 1913, Quigg MSS.

John Hay's "splendid little war" produced a hero prepared to reap full political advantage of his fame, the dashing Colonel of the Rough Riders. Born and brought up in New York State, member of a well-known Dutch family, Theodore Roosevelt had served the Republican party as member of the state assembly, New York City mayoralty candidate, United States civil service commissioner, president of the New York City police commission, and Assistant Secretary of the Navy. His had been a notable career well before he resigned from the Navy Department to organize and lead the First Volunteer Cavalry. But the charge of the Rough Riders up what became familiarly known as San Juan Hill had catapulted Roosevelt almost overnight into national prominence.[20]

Newspaper gossip at once had singled him out as a possible gubernatorial candidate. And the very day the commission published its report of the canal investigation had come word that the Army, alarmed by the yellow fever peril, planned to rush several regiments, among them the Rough Riders, north from Cuba to Montauk Point, Long Island. With an early end to hostilities predicted, it seemed certain that the Colonel could be available for the fall campaign. Here, concluded many Republicans, was the answer to the party's distress.[21]

The "boom" to nominate the Rough Rider had no single source; it was spontaneous, "in the air." Newspaper editors from far and near reflected the pervasiveness of the demand, as did the poli-

[20] Actually "Kettle Hill," a spur of San Juan Hill. Roosevelt never tried to deceive anybody about the charge, a fact which Secretary of War Alger admitted in his *The Spanish-American War* (New York, 1901), pp. 164–165, but for a malicious commentary see J. J. Chapman to Elizabeth C. Chapman, February 21, 1929, in M. A. DeWolfe Howe, *John Jay Chapman and His Letters* (Boston, 1937), pp. 423–424.

[21] Lodge to Roosevelt, June 29, 1898, in Lodge, ed., *Selections*, I, 316. For an amusing argument in Roosevelt's behalf, see Depew, *My Memories*, pp. 161–162.

ticians who plagued the Colonel in Cuba with numerous letters of inquiry or advice. In New York State, a resolution endorsing the hero of San Juan was approved on July 20 by the First Assembly District convention in Chautauqua County. Meantime at the extra legislative session in July a number of Republican state senators agreed that they would "personally urge Platt to nominate Roosevelt for Governor as the only hope of success." [22]

The first organized demonstration in New York City occurred the evening of July 25, 1898, when a hundred anti-Platt Republicans composing the general committee of the "Swayne-Brookfield faction" gathered at Mott Memorial Hall to consider their program for the fall campaign. After a stormy session in which a minority group led by Colonel Lovell H. Jerome clamored for consideration of Roosevelt's name, General Wager Swayne abruptly adjourned the proceedings. Twenty-seven "bolters" answered Jerome's call to remain, but their rump meeting was suddenly interrupted when the janitor, dismissed by a Black adherent, threw the main light switch. Not to be dismayed, Jerome rehired the hall and restored the current, only to discover that the more cautious members of his group did not yet approve a Roosevelt resolution. The upshot was a petition to Swayne for another meeting to consider "the Roosevelt demand." [23]

Within the regular Republican organization Roosevelt sentiment had the backing of a highly placed Platt lieutenant, Lemuel

[22] Philadelphia *North American*, January 3, 1899 (RS); *Chicago Times-Herald*, July 10, 1898 (RS); Joseph I. C. Clarke, *My Life and Memories* (New York, 1925), p. 368; *Binghamton Weekly Herald*, July 27, 1898; New York *World*, July 22, 1898; John Ford, "Theodore Roosevelt's Feet of Clay," *Current History* 34:679 (August 1931).

[23] Interview of Lovell H. Jerome by J. H. French (RHP); *New York Press*, July 26 and August 10, 1898; Victor Hugo Paltsits, "An Unrecorded Chapter in the Political Life of Roosevelt" (MS. in Roosevelt Collection); *New York Press* and New York *Mail and Express*, July 25, 26, 1898.

Ely Quigg, chairman of the New York County Republican Committee, who first began to talk up the Colonel after the battle of San Juan Hill. For some time the thirty-three-year-old Quigg had been at odds with the Black faction, but he championed Roosevelt primarily on the basis of friendship and the best interests of the party. No prominent figure in New York politics could approximate young Quigg's long acquaintance—first as a *New York Tribune* reporter and later as congressman from New York's Fourteenth District—with Theodore Roosevelt.[24]

Quigg found an ideal ally in the newly elected chairman of the Republican state committee, Benjamin B. Odell, Jr. Odell undoubtedly nursed his own resentment against Payn and Black, over the 1896 convention, but what mainly interested the forty-one-year-old state chairman was a successful election campaign in his new post, possibly with the eventual purpose of supplanting the infirm Platt as G.O.P. leader. In late July or even before, Odell had requested Congressman Lucius N. Littauer to write Roosevelt "suggesting to him that if he would put himself wholly in the hands of his friends, under the Organization standard, he could be nominated for Governor." Encouraged by the reply, Odell had set to work to win over delegates to the state convention.[25]

The enthusiasm of Quigg and the quiet determination of Odell did not readily impress the rest of the organization. As a state assemblyman just out of college, Roosevelt had consorted with the independent Republicans, and he had been in that camp ever

[24] Quigg to Roosevelt, June 30, 1899, in TR MSS. (LC); Quigg to Roosevelt, March 19 and April 30, 1913; September 10, 1898, Quigg MSS.; *New York Press*, July 15 and August 20, 1898.

[25] Interview of B. B. Odell, Jr., by J. H. French (RHP). This letter is not in the Roosevelt papers, which are quite incomplete in this period, but confirmatory evidence is in Alexander, *Political History*, IV, 304. Odell grossly exaggerated when he testified that "I received back word that he [Roosevelt] would follow my advice as to his course implicitly, and by the time he reached Montauk Point I had succeeded in winning over every one of the delegates to the coming convention."

since. Recollections of his civil service commissionership, and especially of his nonpartisan activities on the New York police board, were still fresh. Black had shown some independence as governor, observed the New York *Commercial Advertiser*, but the Rough Rider would be "even more intractable." And though he admitted that the Colonel would be a "formidable vote-getter," the *Albany Evening Journal* editor, William A. Barnes, could not believe "that if Colonel Roosevelt should be nominated and elected Governor the Republican organization of this state would continue to be the powerful factor in politics which it had been in the past." Grandson of Thurlow Weed and Republican leader of Albany County, Barnes well represented the typical machine viewpoint; he had quarreled with Black over patronage and over the biennial sessions amendment the governor sponsored, yet he awaited Platt's decision before coming out openly for Roosevelt.[26]

Odell and Quigg therefore concentrated their campaign upon Senator Platt, to whom they came this Sunday afternoon in mid-August 1898 for the last of several conferences prior to the state committee meeting the following Saturday. As they sat on the veranda of the Oriental Hotel, Odell "dark, saturnine-looking . . . with black hair, black eyes, black moustache and a parchment white complexion," young Quigg with his "prematurely gray locks parted abruptly near the center," and the venerable senator, the three could easily recall their many past arguments.[27]

Platt agreed that the situation was serious. He still remembered how the Stanford canal investigation of 1867 had crippled the Republicans, and how effectively Tilden had used John Bigelow's committee in the 1875 election. When the reaction to the investiga-

[26] New York *Commercial Advertiser*, August 11, 1898; *Binghamton Weekly Herald*, August 10, 1898; *Albany Evening Journal*, August 19, 1898. On the *Journal's* apathy toward Black, see the *Albany Argus* (Democratic), August 20, 23, 1898.
[27] New York *World*, October 1, 1898.

tion of the $9,000,000 improvement set in across the state, Black could not be reelected.[28]

But the senator refused to conclude that that meant Roosevelt. For one thing, there was question whether even the Colonel could win in November. Many of Black's adherents would drag their feet during the campaign, as would machine men antagonized by a reform Republican of Roosevelt's stature. Nor would the liquor interests and the Germans support a former police commissioner who had relentlessly enforced the Sunday closing law.

Granted that he might pull through, what would he do in office? Platt had "a little mite of apprehension" about the Rough Rider's "impulsive nature"—would Roosevelt bear out his reputation for "off-the-cuff" statements and rash action without consultation? The senator feared even more that this reformer "might fight those who put him in office, just like that fool of a Mayor Strong." War on the organization would be a heavy price for even as important an election as this. And such a result might ensue if, as governor, Roosevelt disregarded the senator's legitimate requests and responded to the clamor of the antimachine element.[29]

Beyond these obvious questions, Platt had at the back of his mind two reservations, at least one of which he had expressed to his lieutenants. As Quigg long afterwards informed Roosevelt, Platt

was still unwilling to bring your name before the convention . . . because, in his heart of hearts, he had opposed the Spanish War. He often talked to me, when I was urging your nomination, of the expensive responsibilities which would result to the United States from our success in the Philippines and Cuba, and he held you personally as much responsible

[28] Alexander, *Political History*, III, 182–184; A. C. Flick, *Samuel Jones Tilden: A Study in Political Sagacity* (New York, 1939), ch. xii; *Syracuse Herald*, September 4, 1898.

[29] Platt to Roosevelt, May 6, 1899, in *Barnes v. Roosevelt*, p. 2368; Ferdinand C. Iglehart, *Theodore Roosevelt: The Man As I Knew Him* (New York, 1919), pp. 131–134; *Albany Argus*, September 5, 1898.

for our declaration of war with Spain as the destruction of our battleship in Havana Harbor. I remember his saying to me . . . "if he becomes Governor of New York, sooner or later, with his personality, he will have to be a candidate for President of the United States . . . I am afraid to start that thing going." [30]

The second reservation did not bulk as large perhaps in the summer of 1898 as it did later on, but for a practitioner of "business government" it merited more than passing concern.

The thing [wrote Platt to Roosevelt] that did really bother me was this: I had heard from a good many sources that you were a little loose on the relations of capital and labor, on trusts and combinations, and, indeed, on those numerous questions which have recently arisen in politics affecting the security of earnings and the right of a man to run his own business in his own way, with due respect, of course, to the Ten Commandments, and the Penal Code.[31]

Against these arguments the two lieutenants stood firm. Their long gun was Roosevelt's popularity, and the ground swell of sentiment throughout the state daily supplied fresh ammunition. It was true that a part of the machine might sulk, but the independent Republicans would in all likelihood return to the ranks. The liquor interests and the Germans who were not already Democrats would be balanced by the church people and by those who had admired Police Commissioner Roosevelt's honest enforcement of the law. As for Roosevelt's future course as governor, Odell and Quigg could not give positive assurances. But since Roosevelt's attitude toward the organization was of such great concern, why not sound him out on that when he returned from Cuba?

The old man stared out over the breakers. Even now, far out at the tip of the island, the *Miami* with the First Volunteer Cavalry embarked was nearing the Montauk Point anchorage. An interview could not be kept secret; Governor Black's jealous adherents would

[30] Quigg to Roosevelt, March 19, 1913, Quigg MSS.
[31] Platt to Roosevelt, May 6, 1899, in *Barnes v. Roosevelt*, p. 2369.

at once charge that Senator Platt had deserted their candidate. Moreover, Colonel Roosevelt too hastily might conclude that he had the boss's support.

Yet the information gained would be most useful at the meeting of the state committee the next Saturday, August 20, 1898. Platt knew that politician after politician would come there inquiring about the possibility of drafting the Rough Rider. In fact, the senator was already being "pestered" by county leaders who were telling him that their assemblymen were in danger; that Black could not be reelected; and that Roosevelt sentiment was rising. If the Colonel's attitude was unsatisfactory, this grass-roots sentiment might still be choked off. If his reply was promising, then the question of his nomination could be explored further in party councils. And when word of Quigg's visit got back to Black's supporters, Platt could simply deny (as he later did) that he had even known about it.[32]

At last the senator sent his lieutenants away satisfied: at the first opportunity Quigg was to sound out Colonel Roosevelt. As he waved goodbye to them from his seat on the Oriental veranda, Platt no doubt had lingering misgivings about taking on a Rough Rider. But as the *Mail and Express* said, the express company president had "the habit, when two unpalatable alternatives were presented to him, of choosing the less nauseous, smacking his lips over it and declaring that he [had] always liked it." The field had not yet narrowed to two alternatives, but if need be Platt was prepared to live up to his reputation as an Easy Boss.[33]

---

[32] Quigg to Roosevelt, April 23, 1913, Quigg MSS.

[33] New York *Mail and Express*, August 22, 1898. The evidence that this decision was reached on Sunday, August 14, 1898, though circumstantial, is still compelling. Quigg implies that he, Odell and Platt decided as a group, and this is the last time before the Quigg trip to Montauk Point that the three men definitely can be placed together.

CHAPTER II **Colonel Roosevelt**

At 11:15 the next morning, August 15, 1898, as he followed General "Joe" Wheeler of Fifth Army Corps down the transport *Miami's* gangplank onto the railroad pier at Montauk Point, Theodore Roosevelt gave little thought to his political future. Only the evening before he had written Brander Matthews that he expected to return shortly to Cuba with the Rough Riders for "the great Havana campaign." Now when reporters pressed him for some political comment he brought his right fist down resoundingly on his left palm: "I don't know anything about politics, not at present, and I don't care about it either." What absorbed his interest was the war—"bully time and a bully fight"—and about that he talked so well that the correspondents carried away a vivid account of the First Volunteer Cavalry's experiences. This thirty-nine-year-old soldier still might be the old Roosevelt, "jolly, genial, free-for-all, a happy, simple man, exactly as he was before he went away," yet the aura of battle smoke about him made a difference, and gave him an aspect to be reckoned with, the glamor of a hero.[1]

Within twenty-four hours the prospect of a siege of Havana was less certain. An armistice had been signed on August 12 and on Tuesday, August 16, came word of Dewey's great victory at Manila. That morning General Wheeler departed posthaste for Washington, at the summons of President McKinley. Meantime the Rough

[1] *New York Tribune, New York Press* and New York *Commercial Advertiser,* August 15, 16, 1898; Roosevelt to Brander Matthews, August 14, 1898, Brander Matthews MSS., CUL.

Riders and the rest of the corps went into detention camp on the treeless, windswept expanse of Montauk Point. Camp Wikoff was still in a chaotic state, with hospitals under construction, troops coming in daily, and supplies disorganized; but it was good to be home—and off that ship.

Having received an advance discharge from quarantine the next day, August 17, Roosevelt soon had several callers at Camp Wikoff's "Second House," where he was to spend the night. One was Lovell H. Jerome, who since the serio-comic episode at Mott Memorial Hall on July 25 had continued to promote the Rough Rider within the Swayne-Brookfield faction. At Montauk Point he told the Colonel "things were in good train and begged him for God's sake to say nothing—not to talk to anybody." [2]

Roosevelt could hardly follow that advice with his other two visitors, Isaac H. Klein and John Jay Chapman, members of the reformist City Club and of the Central Committee of the Citizens' Union, and since 1897 the anonymous proprietors of a political journal published in New York City entitled *The Nursery*. Though Klein was an experienced organizer on the municipal level, in conversation he deferred to Jack Chapman, Harvardman and fellow Porcellian of Roosevelt's, whose talk was "notoriously spontaneous, brilliant, and exciting." Chapman's most distinctive physical feature was a missing left hand, a grim reminder of his first love affair; in a sudden frenzy of repentance over a thrashing administered to a rival, he had thrust that offending member into a bright fire and burned it so badly amputation was necessary. Passionate, exuberant, tender, Chapman lived intensely, and in the 1890's the energies he later poured into criticism and poetry flowed into politics.[3]

[2] *New York Press*, August 10, 18, 19, 1898; *New York Tribune*, August 17, 1898; interview of Jerome by J. H. French (RHP).
[3] *New York Times*, October 22, 1895 (RS); Julius H. Cohen, *They Builded Better Than They Knew* (New York, 1946), p. 348; M. A. DeWolfe Howe,

Uncompromising foes of the Boss system in either party, Chapman and Klein had regarded Seth Low's defeat in the mayoralty contest of 1897 as a great victory—just "181,700 victories, in fact"— because the Platt machine had failed to capture the independent vote. They now feared that the Republican organization would seek to retrieve its position by drafting the hero of San Juan for its gubernatorial candidate. If Roosevelt's popularity was to be exploited, they reasoned, it must not be to save Platt but to destroy him. This they proposed to do by extending the nonpartisan municipal campaign of 1897 into state politics and putting the Rough Rider at the head of an Independent party ticket. The senator would then be forced to accept Roosevelt also, which would practically assure election. But Platt would not be able to claim any credit for the victory, and the rest of the machine's candidates would probably go down in defeat. Roosevelt was thus "to be the instrument of the citizen destroying the boss." [4]

The framers of this ambitious scheme did not regard Roosevelt merely as a means to an end; indeed, Klein accused his colleague of "being in love with" the Rough Rider, and Chapman later admitted that "I never before nor since have felt that glorious touch of hero-worship which solves life's problems by showing you a man." Chapman thought that Roosevelt had the very quality "most needed in State politics today—moral courage." He sincerely believed the Republican leaders would ruin Roosevelt; they would force him to compromise, to give evasive answers on the canal scandal, to commend the national administration for the conduct

---

John Jay Chapman and His Letters (Boston, 1937), pp. 1–9, 59–60, 465. Howe mistakenly places the first meeting on the twenty-fourth, as do Morison and Blum, eds., *Letters*, II, 1496. For a somewhat different account of this whole incident with the Independents, see *ibid.*, pp. 1474–78.

[4] John Jay Chapman, *Practical Agitation* (New York, 1900), *passim; The Nursery* (New York), January, September, 1898.

of the war. The man he sought to "save" was the fearless enforcer of police regulations, the Navy's protector from "rascally contractors," the soldier with the temerity to prod Secretary of War Alger into action with the "round robin" letter. As an Independent, the Colonel could speak his mind, preserve his integrity against the machine. And he could gain the support of many decent citizens who would not vote for even a Rough Rider if by doing so they strengthened "the hands of Platt, Quigg, Aldridge and the ring." [5]

Yet few of the Independent leaders shared Chapman's enthusiasm for his friend; "the reform group was not nominating him because they loved him, but because they desired to make use of him." The more level-headed Klein remembered the 1895 election, when Roosevelt, supporting the Fusion ticket, had labelled the Klein-managed nonpartisan campaign "the conscience vote gone silly." Klein, and possibly Chapman, realized that Roosevelt set up common sense as a concomitant political virtue with conscience. No, he was not an ideal candidate; he was too inured to political expediency. But even absolutists have to compromise, and at the moment this war hero was their only hope.[6]

Roosevelt's answer to all this was noncommittal. He had been out of close touch with New York politics and knew the situation only from secondhand reports. He had yet to learn from Quigg—whom he had invited to Montauk by a wire on August 17—how matters stood in the Republican camp. Anxious though they were to launch a state organizational drive, Chapman and Klein gave

[5] Memorandum of J. J. Chapman, December 21, 1919, in Howe, *John Jay Chapman*, pp. 142–143; *The Nursery*, September 1898.
[6] Memorandum of J. J. Chapman, December 21, 1919, in Howe, *John Jay Chapman*, p. 143; Roosevelt to Preble Tucker [n.d.], in *New York Times*, October 23, 1895 (RS).

him "a week to think it over." At a City Club meeting to which they reported that Thursday evening, one newspaperman gathered that things were in a "chaotic condition" but might "bear fruit in the future." [7]

Roosevelt did not exhibit such indecision when Quigg arrived at Camp Wikoff the next day. The New York County leader brought the Colonel up to date on political developments. Then Quigg said that he wanted, as Roosevelt put it, "a plain statement as to whether or not I wanted the nomination, and as to what would be my attitude toward the organization in the event of my nomination and election." Roosevelt replied that he would like the nomination. He assured Quigg, furthermore,

that I should not make war on Mr. Platt or anybody else if war could be avoided; that what I wanted was to be Governor and not a faction leader; that I certainly would confer with the organization men, as with everybody else who seemed to me to have knowledge of and interest in public affairs, and that as to Mr. Platt and the organization leaders, I would do so in the sincere hope that there might always result harmony of opinion and purpose; but that while I would try to get on well with the organization, the organization must with equal sincerity strive to do what I regarded as essential for the public good; and that in every case, after full consideration of what everybody had to say who might possess real knowledge of the matter, I should have to act finally as my own judgment and conscience dictated and administer the State government as I thought it ought to be administered.[8]

Though he secretly feared Platt might balk at the condition that Roosevelt "must have direct relations with everybody" and must

[7] Roosevelt to Quigg, August 17, 1898, Quigg MSS.; Chapman to Roosevelt, September [20?], 1898, in Howe, *John Jay Chapman,* p. 469; John DeWitt Warner in New York *World,* August 20, 1898.

[8] Roosevelt, *Autobiography,* pp. 294–296. See also Quigg to Roosevelt, April 23, 1913, with enclosures, and April 28, 1913; Quigg MSS.

not have "one man speaking for all," Quigg pronounced himself well satisfied with this statement, which he said was "all anybody could expect." All in all, the county chairman was pleased with the results of his mission; now he and Odell could answer the senator with assurance. That evening Lem Quigg was seen talking earnestly with Platt at the Oriental Hotel.[9]

On his part, Roosevelt had misgivings. If he was nominated and elected he would surely have difficulty with the organization on "a matter like the Canal, or Life Insurance, or anything touching the Eighth Commandment and general decency." On the other hand, when as governor he would "see and consult the leaders—not once, but continuously—and earnestly try to come to an agreement on all important questions with them," he would alienate his friends among the antimachine Republicans and the Independents. The latter, claiming a superior moral position by their refusal to do business with men like Platt, were particularly annoying to Roosevelt. He also loved to be moral, but he had long ago decided that it had to be morality within the party.[10]

The 1884 campaign had been his own personal crisis on this issue. As a reform assemblyman imbued with the ideals of George William Curtis and E. L. Godkin, he had gone to his first national convention that year wholeheartedly committed to Senator Edmunds of Vermont against James G. Blaine. When the prize went to Blaine, Roosevelt suffered most acutely. But though Godkin and Curtis in protest turned Mugwump, this twenty-five-year-old New Yorker refused to desert to Cleveland and subsequently took part in the Blaine campaign. As he stated at the time, one "cannot

[9] Quigg to Roosevelt, April 23, 1913, Quigg MSS.; *New York Tribune*, August 20, 1898.
[10] Roosevelt to Leupp, September 3, 1898, in Francis E. Leupp, *The Man Roosevelt: A Portrait Sketch* (New York, 1904), p. 30.

act both without and within the party." He decided right there to become a politician.[11]

Over the years he devised a justification for political expediency. Morality alone was not enough, he preached; the twin gospel of the reformer must be "efficiency." If a man "goes into politics he must go into practical politics, in order to make his influence felt."

He must be prepared to meet men of far lower ideals than his own, and to face things, not as he would wish them, but as they are. He must not lose his own high ideal, and yet he must face the fact that the majority of the men with whom he must work have lower ideals. He must stand firmly for what he believes, and yet he must realize that political action, to be effective, must be the joint action of many men, and that he must sacrifice somewhat of his own opinions to those of his associates if he ever hopes to see his desires take practical shape.

The party, in other words, was the only way in which a man could make his influence felt. A "conscience vote" might occasionally be necessary, but not ordinarily. "As a general rule a man ought to work and vote for something which there is at least a fair chance of putting into effect." [12]

Roosevelt practiced what he preached, though his position at times caused him personal embarrassment. In the state campaign of 1895, for example, Police Commissioner Roosevelt was chagrined because the Republican organization discountenanced the effort he had made for honest enforcement of the Sunday-closing liquor law. On the other hand the Good Government advocates, who had supported him with rallies and speeches through all his struggles that thirsty summer, were in Roosevelt's estimate wrong to run a

[11] Interview of Bernard Biglin by J. H. French (RHP); Henry F. Pringle, *Theodore Roosevelt: A Biography* (New York, 1931), pp. 85–89.

[12] Theodore Roosevelt, "The Manly Virtues and Practical Politics," *Forum* 17:551–557 (July 1894), reprinted in T. Roosevelt, *American Ideals and Other Essays Social and Political* (New York, 1897), pp. 35–46.

third ticket. He was "gunning for the Goo Goos," he explained to Seth Low, "in what has proved the vain hope of getting them . . . to support the fusion ticket." Though he termed Platt's influence "poisonous," Roosevelt could not refuse to play on the team when the opponent was Tammany.[13]

Roosevelt's preachments and practice could mean only one thing in August 1898. Despite the trials that he might have to undergo with Platt, despite the antimachine friends he might alienate, he had to be the organization candidate or nothing. But Jack Chapman had dangled before him the intriguing possibility of accepting the Independent nomination as well. That would remove the stigma of the Platt brand. It would practically assure him the Republican nomination. And with his name on two tickets he would obtain votes that might be a deciding factor at the polls.

Independent votes for Roosevelt, of course, would not go to the rest of the Republican ticket—that was John Jay Chapman's plan. And at this point Roosevelt's reasoning becomes obscure. Perhaps he entertained the notion that with the Independent "club" he could secure such strong Republican candidates that the Independents would drop their separate slate. Or possibly he imagined that a merger of the two tickets could be effected; he had advocated a similar procedure in the New York City mayoralty race the year before. Or most likely he simply didn't think of the rest of the candidates; he merely saw how the Independents could strengthen his own hands. For whatever reason, Roosevelt made a miscalculation that would cause him grief.[14]

[13] Roosevelt to Lodge, October 18, 1895, in Lodge, ed., *Selections,* I, 188; Roosevelt to Low, October 15, 1895, Low MSS.

[14] Cf. John W. Bennett, *Roosevelt and the Republic* (New York, 1908), p. 104. See also J. J. Chapman to Elizabeth C. Chapman, September 24, 1898, and Chapman to Roosevelt, September [20?], 1898, in Howe, *John Jay Chapman,* pp. 139–140, 469; Roosevelt to William Dudley Foulke, November [?],

About one thing, though, he wanted no mistake: he would accept the Independent indorsement *only* if he became the Republican nominee. And inasmuch as the Independent state party would have to publish its program well in advance of the Republican Convention, he wanted "his exact position in the matter . . . covered by a statement to be given to the press . . . at the time the ticket was announced." [15]

In making these stipulations Roosevelt clearly was thinking of Seth Low's troubles in the 1897 mayoralty contest; on August 27 he was to write Low that "like you I have a fire on both flanks." In 1897 the then Assistant Secretary of the Navy had urged Low to satisfy the organization's pride "by the trivial concession of letting them nominate you first." When the chance for that had passed, Roosevelt still had sought to effect some coalition. The machine should realize that Low was "not a mere doctrinaire," he had written the Columbia president, but the Independents were equally at fault in denouncing any sort of compromise with Platt and Quigg:

For heaven's sake, don't let them shut the door upon the possibility of an alliance with the republican party . . . We want to win, and we don't want to be scared by people condemning as "deals" what they would heartily back if called "understandings."

To make sure that an Independent nomination did not foul relations with the machine in 1898, that no question of priority arose again, Roosevelt would have his own attitude carefully explained when Chapman's group revealed its plans.[16]

1898, in W. D. Foulke, *A Hoosier Autobiography* (New York, 1922), pp. 112–113.

[15] Howe, *John Jay Chapman,* p. 465.

[16] Roosevelt to Low, August 27, 1898; to Low, June 23, Sepetmber 4, 11, 1897; all Low MSS.

Within the week allotted him "to think it over," the Colonel notified the Chapmanites of his decision. With Quigg also he had set conditions, but these were more drastic ones, so drastic that less determined men might have given up on his candidacy altogether. Certainly Roosevelt thought himself well protected against misunderstanding. He did not see the difficulties ahead. "I am 'running' in the same kind of a way you did," he wrote Seth Low on August 27, "I am just letting events take their course." [17]

Among Republican leaders sentiment was swinging definitely in his favor. At the state committee meeting on August 20, Governor Black had supporters from the central and eastern sections of the state, but Roosevelt's backing in western New York was "surprisingly strong." One informal poll of twelve out of the thirty-four committeemen showed nine in favor of the Rough Rider. In his own political soundings, Platt paid especial heed to Judge Hazel's report from Buffalo and Erie County; for according to Quigg, the senator always operated on "the theory that on election day the forces between Democratic New York City and its environment and the Republican country counties were so evenly balanced that Buffalo and Erie would decide the issue." Quigg later declared that it was "Hazel's urgency" plus the reassurances of the Montauk Point statement which finally convinced Senator Platt that Roosevelt had to be the candidate.[18]

Still Platt delayed an outright commitment, in the hope that he could persuade Black to forsake a fight. The senator recalled perfectly how Governor Cornell, seeking a renomination in 1882, had battled Roscoe Conkling's candidate right onto the convention floor;

---

[17] Roosevelt to Low, August 27, 1898, Low MSS.
[18] *Albany Evening Journal,* New York *Mail and Express,* New York *Commercial Advertiser,* August 20, 1898; *Buffalo Express,* August 21, 1898; *Syracuse Journal,* August 23, 1898; Quigg to Roosevelt, March 19, 1913, Quigg MSS.

only by extreme measures had Conkling prevailed, and the consequent loss of harmony had contributed much to Cleveland's victory. To avoid the risk of another such struggle, Platt conferred personally with Black at Washington, D.C., on August 27, but the governor was not to be dissuaded. Upon his return, the senator informed callers at 49 Broadway that he intended to pursue a strictly neutral course—the "strongest candidate" would prevail. But behind the scenes he prepared to remove the wraps that had cloaked the Roosevelt movement within the organization.[19]

The first intimation of this change came on September 1, 1898, when convention delegates from Kings County reported that Odell, perhaps with Platt's support, had come out for Roosevelt. Lou Payn at once stormed into Platt's office to protest this breach of neutrality, but the next day Barnes' *Albany Evening Journal* announced the new departure in a bold headline: "ROOSEVELT CAN HAVE IT; NOTHING CAN STOP HIS NOMINATION NOW BUT HIS REFUSAL TO RUN; A WAVE OF ENTHUSIASM." Platt organs like the staid *Buffalo Commercial* shortly observed that the party's choice was a "foregone conclusion," while such antimachine papers as the *New York Tribune* ("ALL SEEM FOR ROOSEVELT") and the New York *Mail and Express* were pleased with the senator's concession to purer politics. All these signs were not lost on Boss Croker, who declared that "by nominating Colonel Roosevelt the Republicans are trying to escape the consequences of the canal frauds and the other glaring acts of maladministration." [20]

Though the Black faction refused to admit defeat, Platt cut away at the governor's strength in such vital areas as Kings County, where dapper Lieutenant Governor Timothy L. Woodruff con-

[19] Alexander, *Political History*, III, ch. xxxvi; *Albany Evening Journal,* August 23, 29, 1898; *New York Tribune,* August 29, 30, 1898.

[20] *New York Press,* September 2, 1898; *New York Tribune,* September 2, 4, 1898; *Buffalo Commercial,* September 7, 1898.

trolled about one hundred delegates. After a conference at the Oriental Hotel and an interview in the executive chamber, Woodruff announced that to keep the Brooklyn organization from splitting, he would not run for renomination with Black. Rumors of a Roosevelt-Woodruff ticket immediately arose—and later proved well-founded. On September 8 Quigg confidently predicted that "no further doubt" existed about the nomination, that Roosevelt would receive over 800 of the 971 votes at the Saratoga convention.[21]

Two days later the Independents demonstrated that they also had been busy. As early as August 22 the Citizens' Union executive committee had all but decided to support a state party, and after further meetings of the City Club and a final interview with Roosevelt, a group headed by Chapman and Klein had undertaken a quiet canvass of the principal upstate cities. Their task had been made easier by the progress Good Government forces had already made there; in Albany, for example, a nonpartisan third ticket in the mayoralty elections of 1895 and 1897 had so cut the Republican vote that the Democrats had won easily, while in Rochester the reformers headed by Joseph T. Alling and Baptist minister Clarence A. Barbour had beaten Boss Aldridge at his own game in 1897 by throwing their support to an anti-ring Democratic candidate for mayor. Utica, Binghamton, Syracuse, Buffalo, Auburn—in each city the Chapmanites had found prominent advocates of civic reform who would circulate the necessary petitions and organize the local effort. By the close of the five-day canvass the foundations of the new party had been established; the Independents were ready to publish their plans.[22]

[21] *New York Tribune,* September 8, 1898.
[22] *New York Tribune,* September 7, 1898; Clement G. Lanni, *George W. Aldridge: Big Boss, Small City* (Rochester, N.Y., 1931), pp. 68–71.

In the morning papers of September 10, the party organizers put forward an imposing slate of seven "tried and sturdy opponents of the boss system in politics," headed by Theodore Roosevelt. The promoters explained that they were impelled to this action by all the evils of state and national politics, which also dictated the choice of the leading candidate.

Our reasons for nominating him are plain. We think that the evils of our public life can be traced to the exclusive control over nominations by the party bosses and their creatures. While Roosevelt is a party man, he is one in whom the masses of the people of both parties feel a confidence amounting to devotion, and who in his person represents independence and reform . . . The feeling for Roosevelt . . . has been growing so uncontrollably strong that we feel that we shall be doing a public service by giving the people a chance to vote for him as Governor.

Having hinted thus that "the party bosses" would reject Roosevelt unless he was "forced" upon them in this manner, and that only through a third party would a number of admirers feel free to vote for their hero, the Chapmanites then admitted that "We do not know that when nominated by us, in case he should be opposed by the regular Republican organization, he would find it his duty to run." They simply expected Roosevelt "to be free to deal with that situation if it ever arises with absolute freedom." [23]

From Chapman's point of view this statement was a masterpiece. It committed Roosevelt to nothing, yet his unmentioned "duty" in case he *was* the Republican candidate was taken for granted. This negative approach was intentional, and indeed essential, for a simple assertion that if Roosevelt received and accepted the G.O.P. nomination he would like the Independent indorsement would have placed the new ticket in the back seat at once. Again there was the

[23] Text from *New York Tribune*, September 10, 1898. Howe, *John Jay Chapman*, p. 466 leaves out a very important "not."

implication that Platt must be prodded, with the added and hardly justified threat that the Rough Rider might decide to run without his party's seal of approval. Despite Roosevelt's carefulness, in other words, Chapman's adroit sentences resurrected many of the features of the 1897 Low fiasco.

Editorials from New York to Buffalo immediately drew the parallel with Low's case, and before the day passed, Roosevelt himself appeared to take exception to the Independent announcement. Returning from Montauk Point on September 10, Colonel Jerome issued a statement through the Associated Press which he claimed Roosevelt had authorized. The Rough Rider had not been seeking but would gladly accept the Republican nomination, Jerome asserted, and should he be nominated and elected "he would be a Republican Governor—a Governor of the entire party; and he would most earnestly hope to receive the support of the Republicans throughout the State irrespective of faction." Beyond that, Jerome stated, an "indorsement from the Independents would be most flattering and gratifying" to Roosevelt, "and he would certainly hope for their loyal support toward his election should he be honored with the nomination." Republican headquarters at the Fifth Avenue Hotel at once questioned Jerome's authority, but out at Camp Wikoff Roosevelt assured reporters the statement was "substantially as I told him and several of the other Independents who spoke to me as to whether or not I would accept an Independent nomination if I were not nominated by the Republicans." [24]

The Independent Party leaders, fearful that the Jerome statement endangered their whole effort, hurriedly dispatched Meyer D. Rothschild to Montauk Point. On September 12 he wired back the reassuring news that "Roosevelt stands where he did when Chapman and Klein saw him." That same day Roosevelt confirmed that

[24] *New York Tribune,* September 11, 1898.

to Preble Tucker: "That address was all right; I have just seen Rothschild." [25]

To Roosevelt, obviously, there was no inconsistency between his statement to Jerome and the Independent address. But he was giving his own interpretation to the latter, an interpretation which the Chapmanites had taken care to disguise. He might have done better to insist that the new party reword its address in order to make his position perfectly clear, but he may have imagined that the Jerome incident rendered that awkward step unnecessary.

The flurry of excitement quickly subsided. The Chapmanites went back to work, now speeded in New York City by the indorsement of the Citizens' Union campaign committee. The Republican press pointed to the Jerome statement as evidence that Roosevelt was a regular but welcomed the support of the Independents. And at Montauk Point the Colonel resumed his concentration upon the affairs of his regiment. Back in August he had had a "pleasant" but "fairly quiet" leave of four days at home in Oyster Bay, but otherwise he had been preoccupied with camp routine and the many details of demobilization. Somewhat to Roosevelt's chagrin, the War Department wanted the Rough Riders deactivated as soon as possible.[26]

The First Volunteer Cavalry mustered out at Camp Wikoff on September 14, 1898. The men were disappointed not to have a regimental parade in New York City, but they had had their share of adulation. Wall Street brokers had lavished food and money

[25] *New York Press,* September 11, 1898; Jerome interview (RHP); the Independent summary in *New York Tribune,* September 26, 1898. See also Roosevelt to Chapman, September 19, 1898; to Preble Tucker, [September 12, 1898]; Meyer D. Rothschild to Chapman, September 12, 1898; all Chapman MSS., Houghton Library, Harvard University.

[26] *New York Tribune* and New York *Commercial Advertiser,* September 13, 1898; *Albany Evening Journal,* September 12, 1898; Roosevelt to Quigg, August 28, 1898, Quigg MSS.

upon "Teddy's Terrors," girl excursionists had captured their crossed sabre insignia, press correspondents had fully recorded their adventures, the President of the United States had even given them a personal inspection. And now the parting was at hand. One final gallop past Newspaper Row to the shore for a swim, a presentation of Remington's bronze of "The Bronco Buster" to their Colonel, an evening's "grand jollification" followed by a morning's blanket-tossing, and the unit broke up. Roosevelt stayed on one more day with his staff to complete arrangements for the disposition of 1,400 horse and mules, a mascot dog, a mountain lion, and a big eagle named "Teddy." The morning of September 15, with the zoo-bound eagle in tow, he departed for Sagamore Hill.

Two days later the corridors of the Fifth Avenue Hotel were crowded with expectant reporters and politicians. Word of Roosevelt's coming had gone out the evening before, and on the sidewalks outside were many spectators eager to catch a glimpse of the war hero. The Fifth Avenue bore the excitement well. So many Presidents had stayed within its white marble walls since 1869 that someone had dubbed it "the White House of Madison Square." Countless political conferences had taken place on the two plush-covered benches in the niche near the desk—the famous "Amen Corner"—while from one step of the broad stairs the Reverend Samuel D. Burchard had addressed his "Rum, Romanism and Rebellion" speech to James G. Blaine. History came easily to this dignified old hotel.[27]

This conference with Senator Platt, to which Roosevelt had agreed two weeks before, did not shape up as one of great importance. But so concerned was Quigg that nothing go awry that he

[27] *New York Press* and *New York Tribune*, September 17, 1898; *Chicago InterOcean*, September 20, 1898 (RS); New York *Evening Post*, August 21, 1900; Platt, *Autobiography*, ch. xxiii.

had forwarded to Montauk Point an elaborate restatement of "precisely the report" he had made to Platt about Roosevelt's attitude toward the organization. Roosevelt had taken exception to the Quigg version: though it was "*substantially* right; that is, it gave just the *spirit*," still it bore too close a resemblance to a bargain and by its choice of verbs softened his insistence that he must be governor in fact as well as name. On both scores the Colonel had received immediate reassurance: Quigg "did not ask for any pledges" and the wording was no "Apostles' Creed." His sole aim, the New York County leader had asserted, had been to understand Roosevelt's "mental attitude towards the office." [28]

At the same time the circumstances of the prenomination meeting had worried Quigg. In the letter he had drafted originally to send to Montauk Point, he had explained that the senator saw "no occasion . . . for any particular secrecy about the visit" and thought "that the conference ought to take place at the Fifth Avenue Hotel at the regular party headquarters." But for some reason Quigg had not mailed this letter; he had used it instead to prepare another, dated four days later, September 10, and from this final version he had eliminated all references to the exact nature of the conference except to place it in New York City on September 14 or 15. This deletion lends credence to the story Roosevelt subsequently told of "mysterious negotiations" in which the machine leaders had "suggested that if necessary we could meet at some out of the way place in the evening." Moreover, it is not unlikely that, as Roosevelt later wrote, he had rejected this suggestion and notified Platt that he "would call upon him with the utmost pleasure in broad daylight

[28] Quigg to Roosevelt, September 10, 1898; Roosevelt to Quigg, September 12, 1898; Quigg to Roosevelt, September 14, 1898, and telegram same date; all Quigg MSS. Roosevelt to Douglas Robinson, September 13, 1898, Robinson MSS., in Roosevelt Collection.

at the Fifth Avenue Hotel." At any rate, the participants finally had agreed to meet without secrecy on the afternoon of September 17.[29]

Just before three o'clock Roosevelt and Quigg dodged through "a mob of enthusiastic citizens" into the Broadway entrance, avoided the crowd in the lobby and went directly to Odell's room on the third floor. At five o'clock reporters watching the central stairway espied Roosevelt, in civilian garb of black coat and gray trousers but wearing a soft felt hat of the wide-brimmed Army type. As he churned his way through the throng to the street, they learned that the talk had been "satisfactory." Once outside, he walked over to the Hoffman House to bid a promised farewell to some of his Rough Riders, and then departed for Oyster Bay.[30]

For several days prior to this conference it had been clear that the organization would oppose Roosevelt's candidacy on a third ticket; in fact, on September 13 Quigg had divulged the reason when he told reporters that "by nominating a full ticket with Colonel Roosevelt at its head they [the Independents] force him to decline their nomination out of loyalty to his associates on the Republican ticket." But the first evidence that Roosevelt accepted this argument in advance of seeing Platt appeared in the New York *Commercial Advertiser* (on which Lincoln Steffens was a reporter). In its news account of the meeting, the *Commercial Advertiser* asserted that when the Colonel entered the hotel room he had already decided to announce his intention of rejecting the Independent nomination. Whether such was the fact or not, it at least credited Roosevelt with elementary political judgment. It also countered any charge that the Boss had "forced" the Rough Rider

[29] Roosevelt to Bradley T. Johnson, May 10, 1899, TR MSS.
[30] New York *World* and *New York Tribune,* September 18, 1898; *Chicago InterOcean,* September 20, 1898 (RS).

to take this step. In short, it put the best face upon a decision that made Roosevelt most uncomfortable.[31]

Whatever the inside story of this conference, the results were plain.[32] Platt had openly declared himself for Roosevelt, so there was no further question about the nomination. And Roosevelt had agreed not only to run, but to decline the Independent indorsement. As Roosevelt wrote Cabot Lodge on September 19, the same day that he informed Jack Chapman of his decision,

Apparently, I am going to be nominated. I saw Platt the other day, and had an entirely satisfactory talk. Of course, I shall have great trouble in the governorship, but there is no use in shirking responsibilities. The first installment of trouble is already at hand, for I cannot accept the so-called independent nomination and keep good faith with the other men on the Republican ticket, against whom the independent ticket is really put up.

Roosevelt was to wish that he had foreseen this contingency, for the "first installment of trouble" proved drawn-out and bitter.[33]

Chapman was shocked. Not six days before he had joyfully

[31] *New York Tribune,* September 14, 1898; New York *Evening Post,* September 17, 1898; New York *Commercial Advertiser,* September 19, 1898. See also *New York Press* and New York *Commercial Advertiser,* September 20, 1898, and *Albany Evening Journal,* September 21, 1898.

[32] In the version of this conference which he first set down in an article in *Plain Talk* in 1928, and later incorporated into his *Autobiography,* Lincoln Steffens told a far different story. According to Steffens, Roosevelt "sneaked over" to see Platt and was furious afterwards because he thought no one had seen him yet " 'the news of it has leaked out. How? How? How?' " With Steffens' aid Roosevelt then concocted a denial that he had seen Platt which the papers subsequently published. Needless to say, no such denial was ever needed, let alone appeared. The only service Steffens, as a reporter on the *Commercial Advertiser,* may have done for Roosevelt is the one indicated—to announce that Roosevelt had decided, before meeting Platt, to reject the Independent nomination. For Steffens' account, see Steffens, "Roosevelt as a Politician," *Plain Talk* (September 1928), pp. 273–278; *The Autobiography of Lincoln Steffens* (New York, 1931), pp. 344–348.

[33] Lodge, ed., *Selections,* I, 346.

informed a friend that "he got up the whole Roosevelt independent movement and never had so much fun in his life watching others in convulsions of fear lest it was a blunder." Now a triumphant campaign threatened to crumble into futility. At once he refused to consider withdrawal final; "I am satisfied," he replied to Roosevelt's letter of September 19, ". . . that you misapprehend the situation and that you never will decline." In a talk with Preble Tucker on September 21 Roosevelt reportedly did promise to think the whole matter over.[34]

On the other hand Roosevelt received encouragement from Seth Low and other independent Republicans. In rejecting a request from the Citizens' Union for support for the Independents, the Columbia president replied that he could perceive "absolutely no benefit to accrue" from the nonpartisan state campaign, which he thought was "the one thing that can cause the defeat of Colonel Roosevelt, and the possible loss of a sound money Senator, as well as a sound money representative in Congress." Low forwarded a copy of this reply to Roosevelt, who took the liberty of letting it get into the hands of the press for publication on September 21, 1898. It created a small sensation, for few people knew that following his defeat in 1897 Low had resolved never again to endorse the separate-ticket policy of the Citizens' Union. The bulk of the reform Republican papers heartily approved Low's stand, as did such prominent leaders as ex-Mayor Strong and Charles Stewart Smith. And General Wager Swayne revealed that for some time within the Citizens' Union he had been protesting against cooperation with the state party.[35]

[34] Entry of September 14, 1898, in Richard W. G. Welling diary, NYPL; Howe, *John Jay Chapman,* p. 469; New York *Commercial Advertiser,* September 23, 1898.

[35] *New York Tribune,* September 22, 23, 1898; Low to Arthur V. Briesen, March 30, 1898, Low MSS. See also Low's correspondence with Abner S.

Yet the final break with the Independents came with agonizing slowness. On September 22 Roosevelt prepared a formal statement declining their nomination, but for three days he carried it around in his pocket as he attended one Independent conference after another. He felt a compulsion to justify his action, to convince his friends that the next step was the only possible one. Chapman saw in Roosevelt "only a very muddleheaded and at the same time pigheaded young man, who needs to be shoved right at this crucial point." He failed to budge him. On the afternoon of September 25 the Independents conceded their candidate's withdrawal.[36]

Some of the Chapmanites believed that Roosevelt had acted in bad faith, others that he really hadn't understood the situation. The latter was the more reasonable explanation, but it did not say much for his astuteness. Chapman claimed that at Montauk Point he had explained the case fully, with "an almost brutal frankness," and "as it were with diagrams." Even if Roosevelt hadn't taken in the scheme then, he should have foreseen the organization's reaction to the third-party ticket. For a politician of his experience it was a serious error.[37]

The days before the Republican convention at Saratoga were among the most trying ones in Roosevelt's experience. So disturbed that he was "hardly able to eat or sleep," at one conference at Klein's house he was said to have "cried like a baby—I don't mean in a babyish way." The Independents' slurs upon his character and intelligence naturally tormented him. But he was equally agitated

Haight, the Citizens' Union treasurer, Low MSS., over the release of this reply to the press.

[36] J. J. Chapman to Elizabeth C. Chapman, September 24, 1898, in Howe, *John Jay Chapman*, pp. 140–141.

[37] Chapman to Roosevelt, September [20?], 1898 and memorandum of J. J. Chapman, December 21, 1919, both in Howe, *John Jay Chapman*, pp. 143, 469.

over the "peculiarly ugly business" which had just arisen regarding
his eligibility for the governorship. The question whether he had
dodged payment of personal taxes in New York was as embarrassing
as it was dangerous. It helped to explain why he appeared "broken
up" at the last few meetings with Chapman and his friends.[38]

It was on Thursday, September 22, that Odell and Platt first
learned about the damaging document Tammany had put into the
hands of the Black adherents: an affidavit executed by Assistant
Secretary of the Navy Theodore Roosevelt for the New York City
board of taxes and assessments on March 21, 1898, declaring that
he had been a "resident of Washington" since October 1897, and so
was not liable to taxation upon the $50,000 assessment of his per-
sonal estate by the City of New York.[39] Since the state constitution
required a continuous residence of five years or more in New York
to be eligible for the governorship, the Black faction charged that
this affidavit disqualified Roosevelt. But when the Colonel dug out
old letters to show how he had protested to his lawyers at the time
that he did not wish to endanger his New York residence, Senator
Platt determined to brazen the matter through. While Roosevelt
retired to Sagamore Hill under an injunction of strict silence, Elihu
Root and other Republican lawyers would construct the legal defense. As Boss Platt departed for Saratoga on September 24, he
assured reporters that the Rough Rider was eligible.

Root found the matter exceedingly complicated. Only the year
before, in August 1897, in reaction to a "perfectly absurd" increase
of $10,000 (to $12,000) in his personalty assessment by the Oyster

---

[38] Roosevelt to Lodge, September 26, 1898, in Lodge, ed., *Selections*, I, 349;
Chapman to his wife, September 25, 1898, in Howe, *John Jay Chapman*, p.
140.

[39] For an extended study of the incident, see G. W. Chessman, "Theodore
Roosevelt's Personal Tax Difficulty," *New York History* 34:54–63 (January
1953).

Bay authorities, and on the advice of his uncle James Roosevelt, Theodore had declared by affidavit that he was not liable to personal tax at Oyster Bay because he lived in New York City. But his lease at 689 Madison Avenue expired on October 1, 1897, so when the City tax board (newly taken over by Tammany) notified ex-Police Commissioner Roosevelt in January 1898 that his personal estate for 1898 was assessed at $50,000, he had asked his brother-in-law, Douglas Robinson:

Could I not make an affidavit that on November 1st my interest in New York ceased: that I did not vote there and have no residence there; and that I then intended, and now intend, to make my residence in Oyster Bay, where I shall vote and pay all my taxes this year?

John E. Roosevelt (of Roosevelt and Kobbe) had replied that the proper step was to give Washington as a residence, and Theodore accordingly had signed an affidavit to this effect, but in returning it to John on March 25, 1898, had stated that

I do not want to lose my vote this fall and therefore I will just pay the penalty and pay those taxes in New York. Is it practicable to alter matters so as to have me taxed at Oyster Bay? Would this be practical or not? If not, then I will pay in New York anyway. I don't want to seem to sneak out of anything, nor do I wish to lose my vote two years in succession.

Thereupon John had informed him that the affidavit *would* cause him to lose his vote, to which Theodore had replied that he hadn't understood this.

This doubtless was stupidity on my part, and I ought to have expressed myself more clearly in the accompanying letter, where I meant to state that I did not want to take any step that would cause me to lose my vote this coming year in New York. Don't you think that I could fix the matter up at Oyster Bay? Can't I pay the taxes there now?

And there the matter had rested as the Rough Rider went off to war, John vacated the City's assessment, and James Roosevelt died before carrying out his supposed instructions to put his nephew's name back on the Oyster Bay rolls.

On this evidence the famed Joseph H. Choate reportedly was "unwilling to put himself on record sustaining" Roosevelt's eligibility, and Root himself was said to have been "extremely anxious and dubious about the position which he was expected to take." But with assistance from Judge George W. Ray, Elihu Root finally prepared a brief. It held that Roosevelt was eligible for the office on two counts, namely, that the Washington affidavit referred to the temporary type of residence, not to the permanent type, "equivalent to domicile," which governed questions of eligibility; and secondly, that Roosevelt could not be deprived of his residence against his will, which by evidence of his letters was to retain his domicile at Oyster Bay.[40]

Had this case ever gone to the courts—a possibility the G.O.P. leaders had considered, and dismissed as unlikely—it is difficult to say what might have been the result. But at Saratoga the judge and jury were over nine hundred delegates gathered in a flag-festooned hall. As soon as Black and Roosevelt had been placed in nomination, Elihu Root strode to the platform. He explained that Roosevelt had requested that the convention hear the facts on the eligibility question before anyone cast his vote. He then launched into the "dry details," which he cleverly embellished with apt references to the Colonel's war record. "I mixed my argument with a lot of ballyhoo and it went over with a bang," Root later asserted; "There was nobody prepared to answer—nobody had studied the question from the bottom up." Amid the cheers as he concluded, it was announced that the Black forces were perfectly satisfied that Roose-

[40] Platt, *Autobiography*, p. 372; unsigned memorandum in Loeb MSS., in Roosevelt Collection, dated July 31, 1902, and marked "Hold for Secretary Root." For the Root speech, see New York *Commercial Advertiser*, September 28, 1898.

CHAPTER III **A Rough Rider Storms Albany**

Nomination of a war hero by no means assured a Republican triumph in November. The Democrats entered this fray with a decided advantage on the issues, state and national. In Judge Augustus Van Wyck of Brooklyn, they found a gubernatorial candidate fully Roosevelt's match in probity if not in popular appeal. And at first the Republican strategy played into their hands, as Roosevelt's managers tried to restrict him to a dignified, respectable canvass. Only in mid-October, when Tammany made the mistake of rejecting Judge Daly's bid for renomination, and the Rough Rider launched his first whistle-stop foray into upstate New York, did G.O.P. prospects begin to improve. From then on it was a close contest. "I have had a very hard campaign," Roosevelt was to write Lodge on election eve, "but at any rate I have made the best fight I could, and if Blifil and Black George win, why win they must." [1]

Augustus Van Wyck was perhaps the ablest candidate the Democrats could have selected. Though "never heard of as a nominee till word came out of Croker's room that he was to be the man," this judge of the Supreme Court of New York had a remarkably clean record. At the same time, his connection with faction was vague enough to commend him to rival leaders. Boss Croker had originally backed Augustus' brother, Mayor Robert Van Wyck of

[1] Roosevelt to Lodge, November 4, 1898, in Lodge, ed., *Selections*, I, 362.

velt was eligible. The delegates then ratified the inevitable by a thumping 753 to 218 vote.[41]

"So the 'tax-dodge' bugaboo bursts with the eligibility scare," wrote the *New York Tribune* correspondent at Saratoga; "everybody here is glad of it now." Certainly Roosevelt was relieved, for he thought that his "probity and honor" had been vindicated. He was to blame, he informed Lodge, "for having left the whole matter, as I have left all my business affairs, to Douglas, Uncle Jim, and John." But the letters "left the thing pretty straight"—if the *New York Times* and the *Evening Post* refused to say whether he was truly eligible, they just did not "wish to be convinced." All that remained to be done was to pay the tax of $1,005 in New York City (the books in Oyster Bay already being closed) and the affair would be at an end.[42]

The fact that Roosevelt survived such episodes as the personal tax difficulty and the rejection of the Independent nomination affords a valuable insight into the nature of his career. The figure here revealed was a good deal less than a careful schemer with long-range ambitions; indeed, in both instances he was singularly short-sighted and confused. Mistakes like these might well have been fatal for other politicians, but in his case they were taken as signs of his ingenuousness. If men thought he had done wrong they assigned the blame to others, to his family advisers and to the Platt machine. Roosevelt was the simple and good man loose in an evil world, and the world was the better for it. The strength of that popular belief would bulk large in the fight ahead.[43]

[41] Root to Jessup, November 13, 1934, in Philip C. Jessup, *Elihu Root*, 2 vols. (New York, 1938), I, 200. See also Root to John M. Bowers, March 23, 1915, Root MSS.

[42] *New York Tribune*, September 28, 1898; Roosevelt to Lodge, September 28, 1898, in Lodge, ed., *Selections*, I, 350; Roosevelt to Nicholas Murray Butler, September 30, 1898, Butler MSS.; *New York Tribune*, October 4, 1898.

[43] Cf. Lewis Einstein, *Roosevelt: His Mind in Action* (Boston, 1930), p. 104.

New York City, while ex-Senator David B. Hill, the titular head of the party, had favored an upstate man; at the behest of Kings County leader Hugh McLaughlin they finally compromised upon his former legal adviser and fellow Brooklynite for governor, and Elliott F. Danforth, a Hill follower, for lieutenant governor. Given the striking advantage always afforded the party out of office when the incumbent regime has suffered the opprobrium of scandal, the Van Wyck ticket appeared formidable indeed.[2]

Among the state issues the Democrats relied heavily upon the canal fiasco. Here the Republican platform clearly hedged, pledging

a resolute and thorough continuance of the investigation so fearlessly begun by Governor Black into all alleged mismanagement of the canals. If there are errors in the system and the law, we will correct them. If there has been fraud, we will detect and punish the wrongdoers.

The Democrats replied that there was no "If" about it, and to back up their charges of "Thievery and Jobbery" they pointed to the canal commission report itself. Quoted time and again in speeches and newspapers, this document made first-rate campaign material throughout New York, and particularly in the rural, anti-canal counties upstate, where traditionally the G.O.P. was strong and the Democratic program was less attractive.[3]

In urban areas the Democrats also directed their fire against the Raines liquor law, a Republican-sponsored measure which had placed excise enforcement under state supervision, set uniform

[2] New York *Evening Post,* September 30, 1898; Alexander, *Political History,* IV, 312–315; *New York Tribune* and New York *World,* September 29, 30, 1898.

[3] *New York Tribune,* September 28, 30 and October 23, 25, 1898; Binghamton *Democratic Leader,* September 30, 1898; New York *World,* October 9, 14, 1898; *Rochester Union and Advertiser,* November 3, 1898. See also *Utica Herald,* October 28, 1898; *Broome Republican,* October 22, 1898.

saloon license rates that increased proportionately with population, and continued with few amendments the proscription on Sunday opening. Country districts welcomed the reduction in drinking places and the lower tax rates resulting from this legislation, but not so the brewers, the saloon vote, and those German citizens who cherished their "personal liberties." Roosevelt's candidacy only abetted the Democratic call for repeal of the Raines law in favor of a "just and reasonable" statute enforced by local authorities. His enforcement of the dry Sabbath while New York City's police commissioner still rankled. And though the *New Yorker Zeitung* published a statement that Roosevelt was impressed with the "law-abiding orderliness" and "good fellowship" of the German-Americans, Oswald Ottendorfer of the *Staats-Zeitung* expressed the more prevalent opinion that the ex-police commissioner was "a narrow-minded, egotistic and unreliable man" who had "enforced the Sunday law in such a tyrannical manner that he practically put Tammany Hall in power again." [4]

The Democrats further cultivated "home rule" sentiment in New York City by opposing the Metropolitan District Elections Act of 1898. This new state law supplemented the local bureau of elections, which the Republicans claimed was corrupted by its connection with the police department, with a state superintendent in command of 700 deputies empowered as sheriffs; they could arrest without warrant and possessed extensive control over lodging houses, registration lists, and election-day polling places. Tammany promptly labelled this law the "Metropolitan 'Force Bill'" and painted a fearful picture of the "self-cocking pistols and bludgeons" with which these officers would try to intimidate good Democrats. The fact that at least 300 of the deputies were themselves Demo-

[4] *New York Tribune,* September 28, 30 and October 7, 20, 24, 1898; *Albany Evening Journal,* October 7, 1898; New York *World,* October 5, 9, 11, 1898.

crats was a mitigating circumstance for informed voters, yet they still resented state interference in the city's affairs.[5]

And, finally, the Democrats denounced Adjutant General Tillinghast's administration of the New York national guard. The state troops had entered the late conflict ill-prepared in equipment and training. In the field the performance of some units had been conspicuously poor. Now that hostilities were over the guardsmen were anxious to return home, yet several regiments remained in Southern camps, from which came reports of sickness, dissatisfaction, and incompetency. On all counts the blame fell upon the Adjutant General; "Tillinghastism" was just as bad as "Algerism."[6]

Secretary Alger's inefficient direction of the War Department was the one "national issue" the Democrats raised. It had a strong appeal; when Senator Lodge expressed fear that the G.O.P. was going to lose a "great many votes" in the Bay State if Alger remained in office, Roosevelt replied that the "anger and dissatisfaction here are quite as great as you describe in Massachusetts—indeed I think greater." This issue particularly embarrassed the Rough Rider Colonel. Ever since the publication of the "round robin" the public had regarded Roosevelt as the Secretary's foremost critic, yet now as the Republican candidate for governor he patently ignored the topic. Such evasion only antagonized those independents who decried political expediency.[7]

[5] *New York Tribune,* September 30, 1898; New York *World,* October 1, 9, 14, 1898.

[6] *New York Tribune,* September 30, 1898; New York *World,* October 14, 1898.

[7] Lodge to Roosevelt, September 1, 1898; Roosevelt to Lodge, September 4, 1898; both in Lodge, ed., *Selections,* I, 338, 341. *New York Tribune,* September 30, 1898; *Buffalo Express,* August 6, 1898; New York *Commercial Advertiser,* August 5, 1898; *Binghamton Weekly Herald,* August 17, 1898; *Auburn Daily Advertiser,* October 29, 1898. See also *New York Tribune,* October 15, 1898.

To offset their disadvantage on state affairs and Algerism the Republicans brought up another national issue: expansion. The islands wrested from Spain could not be turned back, affirmed the Saratoga platform, for "wherever our flag has gone, there the liberty, the humanity and the civilization which that flag embodies and represents must remain and abide forever." Wholeheartedly committed to this doctrine, Roosevelt opened the campaign at Carnegie Hall on October 5 with a ringing appeal to the voters to show their approval of the war by sustaining the McKinley administration in November. America, he asserted, had "entered upon a new career" and must now accept the great responsibility of world power with all it entailed in the way of a strong Navy and a far larger regular Army.[8]

Though militant expansionism may have prodded some Republicans to a greater effort, it further alienated many independents. Directly after the conventions Roosevelt had been "the choice of all friends of honest government," asserted the New York *Evening Post,* but his imperialistic stand "chilled the zeal of thousands in his cause and made them hesitate about voting for him." Despite a conciliatory letter from Roosevelt, anti-imperialist Carl Schurz publicly avowed his intent to vote the Independent ticket. And though Jacob A. Schiff replied ably to Schurz's argument, Roosevelt admitted that his maiden effort at Carnegie Hall "was not received with any particular favor here; neither by the mugwumps on one side nor the practical politicians on the other." [9]

Among other charges against the Republican candidate was the

[8] *New York Tribune,* September 28 and October 6, 1898.
[9] New York *Evening Post,* September 30 and October 10, 1898; Roosevelt to Schurz, October 14, 1898, Schurz MSS. (LC); *New York Tribune,* October 23, 1898; Schiff to Schurz, October 24, 1898, in *New York Tribune,* October 25, 1898; Roosevelt to Lodge, October 11, 1898, in Lodge, ed., *Selections,* I, 354. See also Richard W. G. Welling diary, October 7, 8, 1898, NYPL.

contention that he was anti-labor. Unable to deny that as an assemblyman in the mid-eighties he had opposed abolition of the convict-contract labor system or the regulation of working hours, Roosevelt maintained that over the years his views had changed; he had come to recognize the "very great good" that unions could accomplish, he approved of state factory inspection and anti-sweatshop legislation, and as governor he would bring about better enforcement of the labor law. The Democratic press nevertheless continued to exploit the issue. To the *Buffalo Courier*, expediency alone dictated Roosevelt's "conversion" to labor's side, while the New York *World* merely repeated its biased recital of his assembly record.[10]

Democratic papers alleged further that the Republican nominee had belittled the prowess of the national guard when he wrote Alger on July 23, 1898, that "the cavalry division, including the Rough Riders" was "three times as good as any State troops." Republican sources replied that the Colonel obviously had based his judgment on respective arms, for in the more complete text of this much-publicized letter he had gone on to state that "this cavalry division, close to 4,000 men . . . would be worth, easily, any 10,000 National Guards armed with black powder Springfields and other archaic weapons." Yet Alger spitefully had called down Roosevelt for this "invidious comparison," and the Democrats eagerly adopted the worst interpretation. "It is evident that the National Guard will give a majority against me," wrote Roosevelt to Lodge, "partly on account of my letter to Alger, but more on account of the fact that

[10] *New York Tribune*, October 6, 18, 1898; *Buffalo Courier*, October 26, 1898; New York *World*, October 19, 1898. The *World's* account neglected several items favorable to Roosevelt's record. On Roosevelt and labor, see Howard L. Hurwitz, *Theodore Roosevelt and Labor in New York State, 1880–1900*, Columbia University Studies in History, Economics, and Public Law, no. 500 (New York, 1943).

they were really not very good soldiers and are sore and angry and mortified about the hardships they have encountered." [11]

And naturally the Democrats contended that tax-dodger Roosevelt was either ineligible for the governorship or "morally disqualified" because of perjury. Actually the Democratic press made little use of this issue, but in a matter of this nature a word spoken in conversation was as important as an address or an editorial. The Republicans at least took it seriously; the larger dailies published their own rebuttals of the charge, while the campaign committee gave wide distribution to a full statement of Roosevelt's position. When they were so clearly at a disadvantage on the canal scandal and other issues, the G.O.P. leaders did not propose to take chances.[12]

Had the Democrats continued thus to keep Roosevelt on the defensive, he probably would have gone down in defeat, whistle-stop campaign or no. But in mid-October Boss Croker made a move that exposed his flank to counterattack. His decision to nominate another man than Judge Daly for the Supreme Court in the First Judicial District violated a principle which the Republicans in all righteousness could rise to defend: the independence of the judiciary. Before they were done, they would make boss rule in the person of Richard W. Croker a vital issue.

Some time before the nominating conventions in New York County convened it was reported that Supreme Court Judge Daly, a Democrat who had served two terms of fourteen years each on the bench, would not receive a renomination from Tammany. He

[11] For Roosevelt's letter and Alger's reply, see *New York Press,* August 5, 1898. Conflicting interpretations are in the *New York Tribune* and the *Rochester Union and Advertiser,* November 5, 1898. Roosevelt to Lodge, November 4, 1898, in Lodge, ed., *Selections,* I, 361–362.

[12] *New York Tribune* and New York *World,* September 30, 1898; *Rochester Herald,* October 4, 1898; *Albany Argus,* October 31, 1898; *Auburn Daily Advertiser* and *Ithaca Daily Journal,* October 28, 1898; *Steuben Courier,* October 14, 1898.

and his Republican colleague, Judge Cohen, had honorable records, and the Bar Association of New York, in its resolution reaffirming the principle of nonpartisanship in judicial elections, had plainly indicated that it favored their renomination by both political parties. But the rumor was that the Democrats would turn down Daly "because he has not obeyed Mr. Croker and appointed one of his [Croker's] henchmen to a clerkship in his court." Roosevelt heard about it, for on October 10 he asked Quigg: "Don't you think we ought to nominate Daly? I think it would be a great card for us." The next evening the Republican County Convention did nominate Daly, Cohen, and Henry W. Taft for the three Supreme Court candidacies. On October 12, true to advance forecasts, the Democrats passed over both Daly and Cohen to name a straight party ticket.[13]

Protests against Tammany's action, which in normally Democratic New York County virtually assured Daly's defeat, were immediate and vocal. "Mad, indeed," declared Daly, "is the brain that conceives the punishment of a just judge." The judicial nominations committee of the Bar Association agreed that Croker's action was calculated "to destroy the independence of the judiciary, and is a menace to public safety." At the same time the committee labelled one Democratic nominee unsuitable because his "professional and moral standards are low." Never, concluded the *New York Tribune*, had there been "a more barefaced, patent and undisguised exhibition of boss rule in a political convention." [14]

Admitting that the machine had requested Daly to appoint one Michael T. Daly a clerk in his court, and that the judge had refused to do so, Croker brazenly contended that "Justice Daly was elected

---

[13] *New York Tribune*, September 20, 21, 1898; Roosevelt to Quigg, October 10, 1898, Quigg MSS.
[14] *New York Tribune*, October 13, 14, 16, 1898.

by Tammany Hall, and Tammany Hall had a right to expect proper consideration at his hands." The Bar Association, he asserted, was a "partisan machine annex of the Republican party," and this whole affair was just a "false issue." [15]

But Croker's opponents were not to be diverted. The Bar Association countered the charge of partisanship by showing that more than half the lawyers who had signed the Daly-Cohen petitions were nonmembers. At a mass protest meeting under Bar Association auspices at Carnegie Hall on October 21, moreover, four of the five speakers were well-known Democrats. Other rallies "FOR THE UNSULLIED ERMINE" followed, while the Republicans incorporated "Croker and the Judiciary" into their campaign material. From a book entitled *Boss Croker's Career: A Review of the Pugilistic Activity of Bill Tweed's Pupil and Successor,* which had seen service in the election campaign of 1894, campaign manager William A. Barnes compiled a condensed, up-to-date version. Together with Raines law figures and a defense of Roosevelt's tax difficulties, country weeklies and small upstate dailies gave this canned document full billing.[16]

The onetime bully boy of the Fourth Avenue tunnel gang punched back so wildly that the New York *Evening Post* termed him Roosevelt's "most effective campaigner" and Joseph H. Choate recalled how Balaam's ass—"until the ass spoke, nobody in the world imagined what a perfect ass he was"—broke silence for fright at the sight of "a young man with a flaming sword in his hand." Croker swung at the Bar Association by raking up Elihu Root's

[15] *New York Tribune,* October 15, 16, 17, 25, 1898.

[16] *New York Tribune,* November 1, 4, 1898; *Albany Evening Journal,* October 14, 15, 1898; Rochester *Post Express,* October 18, 1898; *Prattsburgh News,* November 3, 1898; *Ithaca Daily Journal,* October 25, 26, 27, 1898; *Steuben Courier,* October 28, 1898; *Auburn Daily Advertiser,* October 29, 1898; *Harper's Weekly* 42:1051 (October 29, 1898).

old legal connection with Boss Tweed and dismissing the Daly case as "an attempt by Tweed's lawyer to re-elect Tweed's Judge." Then a *Harper's Weekly* article picturing New York as a "wide-open" city under Tammany's rule provoked Croker to recall that publisher Harper had attended "the scandalous Seeley dinner" at Sherry's where "Little Egypt" had danced while police protected Commissioner Roosevelt's "high-toned friends." Boss Croker wanted no discussion of current conditions on the police force; instead he jabbed at Roosevelt for putting policemen in "hired dress suits," for using infants as "stool pigeons," and for a poor record on apprehension of criminals. "Our real opponent is taking his place in this campaign," Roosevelt responded, as he devoted more and more of his speeches to Croker's bossism.[17]

By projecting boss rule into a prominent issue the Daly affair strengthened the Republican cause. Fear of Tammany rule revived among rural voters. Roosevelt's standing also improved among the independent element, for though the Democratic press played up his subservience to Platt, few believed in light of the Rough Rider's record that he would be as amenable to dictation as would Van Wyck. At last Roosevelt had a target to attack when he took the stump. "There are several State issues of importance," he declared on October 17 at West Nyack, the first stop on his upstate journey, "but none more important than the judiciary."

Before Roosevelt launched his spirited canvass in mid-October, the Republican campaign had lagged miserably. State Chairman Odell initially had opposed the Colonel's speaking at all, believing

[17] New York *Evening Post*, October 25, 1898; *New York Tribune,* October 25, 27, 30 and November 2, 3, 1898; Corinne Roosevelt Robinson, *My Brother Theodore Roosevelt* (New York, 1921), pp. 184–185; Franklin Matthews, " 'Wide-Open' New York," *Harper's Weekly* 42:1045–46 (October 22, 1898). On Root and Tweed, see P. C. Jessup, *Elihu Root,* 2 vols. (New York, 1938), I, 92–93.

that he was a poor orator, that he might muff heckler's questions or misrepresent organization views, and that a "Rough Rider campaign" in any case would be undignified and highly inadvisable. By October 10 Odell had been talked into accepting an expedition upstate, but inexperience soon again manifested itself. On October 13 Odell suddenly decided to demonstrate Republican harmony by having Roosevelt appear the next day at an agricultural fair in Governor Black's home county of Rensselaer. The quick trip north proved an utter fiasco. Black's organization had not been forewarned; the cold, rainy weather kept down crowds and enthusiasm along the way; and at the fair grounds barely two hundred people huddled in the stands to watch the last day's harness race. In a huff, Roosevelt sped back to New York to speak at a Lenox Lyceum rally of Negro voters, only to find that because several morning papers had said he would not return from Troy in time, only two hundred people had turned up. Roosevelt preserved his sense of humor at the ludicrous coincidence, but the *Troy Times'* cry of "Bad Management" cast gloom over the Republican camp.[18]

The two-car campaign special that chugged north along the West Shore Road out of Weehawken three days later carried a war party. Roosevelt was in civilian garb, but his light-colored wide-brimmed hat was unmistakably similar to the service one. If anyone missed the resemblance, the former Minister to Spain, Stewart L. Woodford, and six Rough Riders in full uniform were there to remind him. Even lawyer John Proctor Clarke (who along with Lieutenant

---

[18] Interviews by J. H. French with Odell and Lafayette B. Gleason (RHP); Joseph I. C. Clarke, *My Life and Memories* (New York, 1925), p. 369; Roosevelt to Lodge, October 16, 1898, in Lodge, ed., *Selections,* I, 356–357; Roosevelt interview in *New York Tribune,* October 3, 1898; New York *World* and *New York Tribune,* October 14, 15, 1898; *Albany Evening Journal,* October 14, 1898; *Troy Times* and New York *Evening Post,* October 15, 1898; *Broome Republican,* October 22, 1898; Robinson, *My Brother Theodore Roosevelt,* p. 183.

Governor Woodruff, secretary-manager Billy Youngs and the news-paper correspondents completed the trip's complement) had pol-ished up his inimitable "Only a Soldier" speech for delivery as needed.[19]

At most of the fifteen stops that first day out, Bugler Emil Cassi blew a blaring call for a cavalry charge to announce the train's arrival. Then flanked on either side by his men, Roosevelt made a short impromptu talk from the rear platform. At times he spoke of the simple virtues needed in government: "courage" and "honesty." Often he was more specific. He assured Haverstraw brickmakers and the ironworkers at Cornwall of his sympathy with labor's prob-lems. To over 4,000 people at Newburgh he pledged that he would put "the National Guard on a thoroughly soldierly and effective basis." "If elected Governor," he promised a sea of 5,000 faces at Kingston, "I shall have the most searching investigation made into the administration of the canals." He made only passing comment on the war, but after he finished, one of the Rough Riders usually said a few words about the Cuban battles. Except at Cohoes and Mechanicsville the crowds were sizable and interested; according to the *World* reporter's estimate, as many as 20,000 citizens along the Hudson's west bank attended Roosevelt's appearances.[20]

After a major speech on the "interests of labor" that night at Glen Falls, the expedition continued north the next day along Lake Champlain into New York's northeastern county of Clinton and then west to Ogdensburg on the St. Lawrence River. Emil Cassi bugled valiantly, and more and more Roosevelt touched on national

[19] Newspaper accounts and photographs refute Alexander's statement (*Politi-cal History*, IV, 317) that Roosevelt "wore the Rough Rider uniform including the long-legged boots" throughout the campaign. See also John Proctor Clarke, "Random Recollections of Campaigning with Colonel Roosevelt" (MS. in RHP).

[20] *New York Tribune* and New York *World*, October 18, 1898.

themes: sound money, the war, and the peace. That night at Ogdensburg the Colonel gave a clear exposition of Raines law tax benefits, but on Wednesday, as the railroad car *Wanderer* bumped southward through the rain on the third and final leg, he reverted to foreign policy. Paris dispatches had reported a "hitch" in the negotiations of the Peace Commissioners; with that fact as his inspiration, Roosevelt exhorted enthusiastic audiences at Potsdam and Canton to demonstrate to Spain at the polls that America endorsed McKinley's policy.

No summary of his talks could convey their full impact. At Carthage in Jefferson County, for example, there were 3,000 people standing in the mud and rain:

He spoke about ten minutes—The speech was nothing, but the man's presence was everything, it was electrical, magnetic,—I looked in the faces of hundreds and saw only pleasure and satisfaction—When the train moved away scores of men and women ran after the train waving hats and handkerchiefs and cheering trying to keep him in sight as long as possible.[21]

The reporter of this incident was William T. O'Neil, a Roosevelt admirer since their assembly days together, who for two days had accompanied his campaigning friend. Before boarding the train he had been admonished to tell Roosevelt "to stop his self adulation and talking about himself so much." But after watching the crowds at the stations Billy O'Neil advised Roosevelt to "continue to follow your own inspirations."

For the most part men are as nearly alike as peas—once in a while Nature produces a new type which she never duplicates—an original which sets at naught all our previous standards—These are the fellows who win the world, who can say and do things when and how they

[21] W. T. O'Neil to Jonas Van Duzer, November 1, 1898, Van Duzer MSS., NYRL.

please. You belong to this order. Don't attempt to change to suit the notions of critics.[22]

Of course, the Democratic press professed to be disappointed at Roosevelt's appearance. "Ungainly in figure, awkward in pose and gesture, crude in dress, and with a sharp metallic, monotonous voice," ran a typical comment, "there is absolutely nothing attractive in the personality of the Rough Rider." [23]

Such a view ignored the friendliness of broad grin and flashing teeth, the determination of squinting bespectacled eyes and bulldog jaw, the vigor of staccato speech accented by fist on palm. It failed to mention that the sincerity of his whole demeanor—"sincerity 'six feet high'" in the words of Billy O'Neil—made a powerful, lasting impression. It discounted a keen sense of showmanship which treated a political audience "as one coming, not to see an etching, but a poster," which realized that a politician had to have "streaks of blue, yellow, and red to catch the eye, and eliminate all fine lines and soft colors." It omitted, in sum, the very things about Roosevelt that so appealed to the popular imagination.[24]

The end of the first swing through the state meant no rest for Roosevelt. The night of his return he addressed four Brooklyn meetings of "unprecedented" size, the next day there were three large Manhattan rallies, and on Friday he was off again, first to Poughkeepsie and then into the Mohawk Valley—Little Falls, Gloversville, and Johnstown. With him went a new recruit of Barnes' campaign committee, Mason Mitchell, an ex-Rough Rider and vaudeville actor who had been earning over five hundred

[22] O'Neil to Roosevelt, October 21, 1898, TR MSS. (LC).

[23] *Rochester Herald*, October 28, 1898; see also *Buffalo Courier*, October 26, 1898; *Albany Argus*, November 4, 1898.

[24] O'Neil to Roosevelt, October 21, 1898, TR MSS. (LC); Lawrence F. Abbott, ed., *The Letters of Archie Butt* (Garden City, 1924), pp. 143–144. See also William A. Behl, "The Rhetoric of Theodore Roosevelt," unpub. diss., Northwestern University, 1942, *passim* (in Roosevelt Collection).

dollars weekly in Chicago theaters for his stirring "lecture" on the Rough Rider battles. New York City was too sophisticated for Mitchell's dramatic account of the charge up San Juan Hill, but by campaign's end his was a familiar anecdote throughout the central part of the state.[25]

Van Wyck meantime had begun a state tour "marked by Jeffersonian simplicity"; he traveled by regular trains, lived in hotels, and delivered set speeches only. His austere example may have caused the Republicans to tone down the "Wild West" features of Roosevelt's second whistle-stop expedition into the hinterland; bugler Cassi was left behind, and cavalrymen Sherman Bell and Buck Taylor were in civilian garb. But that didn't stop local enthusiasts. In Buffalo, for instance, one hundred mounted men in Rough Rider uniform escorted Roosevelt's carriage, and a bugle call for "Charge!" signalled his arrival at the Music Hall. The Colonel's quick response to the shrill notes had a familiar ring: "I have heard the trumpets tear the tropic dawn on the day that we marched to battle at Santiago, and I know what it means." [26]

In its general tenor this five-day swing west through Buffalo and Rochester was a triumphant progress before large, appreciative crowds. On a sidetrip up to Cortland a heckler raised the inevitable question about the "Oyster Bay incident"; by his able defense Roosevelt effectively dissipated fears that his tax difficulties would prove an embarrassment. Desperate for copy, the Democratic

[25] For Mitchell's speech, see the *Utica Press,* October 29, 1898. John Proctor Clarke remembered Mitchell once saying: "And then out of the woods darted the Colonel with a revolver in each hand and waving his sword in the air he shouted 'Come on, boys' and led the charge up the hill!" Clarke remarked: "Mason, if the Colonel had a revolver in each hand how did he wave his sword, with his teeth?"

[26] New York *World,* October 20, 1898; *New York Tribune,* October 22, 1898; *Buffalo Commercial,* October 26, 1898. Cf. the Port Henry opening, *New York Tribune,* October 19, 1898.

press finally alleged that Lieutenant Governor Woodruff had been hissed into silence midway through a speech at Rochester in defense of the canal administration; the fact was that he was suffering from a cold which had kept him from speaking at all in Buffalo.[27]

Nor did the Democrats profit from Buck Taylor's slip. This plain-spoken Rough Rider had been spoiling to make a talk on behalf of his colonel, but Billy Youngs had never let him get any further than "Mah fellar citizens—this is the proudest moment of my life—" before the engineer started the train. At Port Jervis Youngs had relented, so Buck had proceeded to recount in detail how Roosevelt "kept ev'y promise he made to us and he will to you." "He told us we might meet wounds and death and we done it," the recital concluded, "but he was thar in the midst of us, and when it came to the great day he led us up San Juan Hill like sheep to the slaughter and so he will lead you." Opposition papers gave this remark the widest circulation, but Roosevelt later observed that "it delighted the crowd, and as far as I could tell did me nothing but good." [28]

Returning to New York City on October 29, Roosevelt continued upon a throat-wearing schedule through the final week of the campaign. By now he seldom mentioned national affairs; instead, he stressed the importance of an upright judiciary—"an issue of fundamental right and wrong"—and the need for honesty in government. "There is not an issue they have raised on which we have not met them fair and square," he declared at Chickering Hall the Friday before election.[29]

[27] *Albany Evening Journal,* October 25, 1898; *Buffalo Express,* October 26, 27, 1898; *Buffalo Commercial,* October 26, 1898; *Rochester Union and Advertiser,* October 27, 28, 29, 1898.

[28] Clarke, "Random Recollections," p. 2; Roosevelt, *Autobiography,* p. 136.

[29] For Roosevelt's energetic progress, see *New York Tribune,* October 30–November 6, 1898.

Though optimism waxed ever greater in Republican councils, the outcome still seemed so debatable that this last weekend the managers dispatched Roosevelt on a whirlwind tour through the extreme southwestern section of the state, an anti-canal area he had missed on the first western swing. Between stops on Monday a tired Roosevelt read *Die Studien des Polybius* and rested his throat, but as the day progressed the entourage turned into "so many romping boys." That night in Dunkirk the venerable Stewart L. Woodford cavorted through the crowds arm in arm with Roosevelt's friend Jacob Riis shouting "Yi! Yi!" And at the Opera House trooper Sherman Bell convulsed the Colonel by bellowing in a voice "like a roaring bull of Bashan":

Who is this Dick Croker? I don't know him. He don't come from my State. Let him take thirty of his best men, I don't care how well they're heeled, and I will take my gang and we'll see who's boss. I'll shoot him so full of holes he won't know himself from a honeycomb.[30]

Back aboard the train about midnight, homeward bound, talk gravitated to the size of the majority the next day would produce. Jake Riis wanted a hundred, but Roosevelt guessed at ten to fifteen thousand. In the early morning the campaigners awakened as the cars jolted through Albany. Just then Roosevelt stepped from his room, and three cheers went up for "The Governor." Their confidence was warranted. That evening Odell telegraphed Oyster Bay that Van Wyck had been beaten by close to 20,000 votes.[31]

Analysis of the returns revealed the vital areas in what the *New York Tribune* called this "creditable victory." G.O.P. perform-

[30] Interview of L. B. Gleason by J. H. French (RHP); William J. Youngs, "A Short Resumé of Theodore Roosevelt as Governor" (1904), MS. in Roosevelt Collection; *Buffalo Express,* November 8, 1898; Jacob A. Riis, *Theodore Roosevelt The Citizen* (New York, 1904), pp. 203–207; Clarke, "Random Recollections," p. 2.

[31] The final plurality was 17,786.

ance had been below standard in Kings County and in the upstate cities of Buffalo, Rochester, and Troy. In the rural communities, however, the Republican vote generally had turned out in force. And New York County had been about 25,000 votes shy of its expected Democratic plurality.[32]

It was not difficult to explain why the Republicans had fared poorly in certain areas. Opposition to the Raines excise law, coupled with Van Wyck's popularity in his native Brooklyn, accounted for the defeats in Kings and Erie counties. The weak showing in Rochester and Troy, on the other hand, probably represented a protest against the leaders in these cities, Public Works Superintendent Aldridge and Governor Black. Some observers charged that the Black faction had deliberately sabotaged the ticket, but that was unlikely. In Albany County the Barnes organization had also been singularly ineffective, which showed that effort alone did not always produce pluralities in the 1898 election. It was unfortunate that this suspicion of treachery remained to plague the incoming administration.[33]

To account for the G.O.P. strength in country districts and in Manhattan was not as simple. In both areas Roosevelt's candidacy no doubt exerted an influence. But the rural showing was attributed as well to the fair weather and good roads on election day, to the fact that farmers feared repeal of the Raines law, to an unexpected disregard of the canal issue, and to the general dislike of Crokerism upstate. As for the result in New York County, the *World* and a number of prominent citizens blamed Croker and the Daly affair,

[32] The New York *World's* predicted plurality (October 24, 30, 1898) was 85,000, against the actual one of 60,670.

[33] *New York Tribune, New York World, Buffalo Express, Buffalo Courier,* Rochester *Post Express* and *Rochester Union and Advertiser,* November 9, 10, 1898; *Troy Times,* November 9, 12, 1898; *Buffalo Express,* November 11, 1898; interview of G. W. Aldridge by J. H. French (RHP).

while the "wide-open city" charge was also thought to have carried weight.[34]

Appraisals of Roosevelt's part in the verdict had a partisan complexion. Democrats did not hesitate to credit him with a major share in their defeat, but the Republican organization was reluctant to echo Chauncey Depew's opinion that "the personality of the candidate . . . neutralized all the discouraging conditions of Republican success," or Boss Platt's statement that Roosevelt was "the only man who could have carried our standards to victory this year." The regular party press often preferred to credit other factors. William A. Barnes declared that the Republican party, and no issue, had elected Roosevelt, while Odell attributed the result to the hard work of the organization.[35]

The most praise of the Rough Rider came from independent Republican sources, which went so far as to declare that Roosevelt's victory was "one of the most wonderful political achievements on record" and that he had "only himself to thank." The anti-machine press believed that the Republican candidate had prevailed because his sincerity and his reform record had won the decisive independent vote. And the fate of the Chapmanites lent support to that verdict, for in the tally they did not even hold the 3,050 voters who supposedly had indicated an intention to back their ticket. Though "deeply wounded" by Roosevelt's rejection of the third-party nomination, concluded the *Binghamton Herald,*

[34] *Buffalo Courier* and *Syracuse Journal,* November 9, 1898; *Utica Herald,* November 12, 1898; Roswell B. Flower in New York *World,* and Odell in *New York Tribune,* November 10, 1898; Rochester *Post Express,* November 9, 1898. Among those who claimed that Croker mismanaged the campaign were John D. Crimmins, John DeWitt Warner, William B. Hornblower, and Frederick R. Coudert.

[35] *Albany Argus* and *Buffalo Courier,* November 9, 1898; *New York Tribune,* November 10, 11, 1898; *Syracuse Journal,* November 9, 1898; *Utica Herald,* November 12, 1898; New York *World,* November 10, 1898.

the "vast majority" of independents had cast their ballots for him in the confidence that he would not submit to machine dictation.[36]

In the final analysis the decisive combination in this election was the judiciary issue and Roosevelt's record and campaign. The Raines law had helped in the rural districts, but the city vote had nullified this effect. The important issue upstate was the canal scandal, and "Crokerism" and Roosevelt had counterbalanced that. In the other vital area, New York County, Judge Daly's influence on the reduction of Democratic pluralities was undeniable. Had every vote he received gone to the state ticket as well, Roosevelt's over-all majority would have been twice as large. As it was, Roosevelt's reform record and the way in which the Daly affair had emphasized it swung enough independent voters to the Republicans to insure success.[37]

Roosevelt himself regarded his own aggressive campaign and the issue of the Daly nomination as the principal factors in the victory. And when Justice O'Brien announced on December 1 that he intended to resign from the Supreme Court of New York County two years before his term was up, Roosevelt prevailed upon the Republican organization to pass over Cohen in favor of Daly as the appointed replacement. At Croker's undoubted instigation, O'Brien soon afterward declared that the stir his action had aroused had caused him to reconsider and that now he intended to remain in office. But Roosevelt had successfully dramatized Daly's contribution and the importance attached by the Republicans to the prin-

---

[36] *Syracuse Herald* and *Binghamton Herald,* November 9, 1898; *Buffalo Express, New York Tribune,* New York *Commercial Advertiser,* and Rochester *Post Express,* November 10, 1898; *New York Press,* November 11, 1898.

[37] In New York County, Van Wyck's 173,476 was eight to nine thousand votes ahead of the Democratic judicial ticket; Roosevelt, on the other hand, polled 112,806 over against 122,102 for Daly, 116,788 for Cohen, and 110,384 for Henry W. Taft. *Manual for the Use of the Legislature of the State of New York, 1899* (Albany, 1899), pp. 868, 882.

ciple of an independent judiciary. As Cabot Lodge put it, he had gained "all the glory of the action without making the appointment."[38]

Still the contrast between the election verdicts of the regular and the independent Republicans was a warning for the governor-elect. He had drawn strength from diverse elements, and both machine and antimachine advocates thought they had him under obligation. As Quigg had prophesied, the road ahead was beset with difficulties, "for everybody is expecting so much . . . so many impossible things and from such conflicting points of view."[39]

[38] *New York Tribune,* December 8, 9, 11, 1898; Lodge to Roosevelt, December 7, 15, 1898, and Roosevelt to Lodge, December 6, 12, 1898, in Lodge, ed., *Selections,* I, 366–369.

[39] Quigg to Roosevelt, September 10, 1898, Quigg MSS.

CHAPTER IV **Governor and Machine**

The governor-elect faced a host of political decisions. He had to choose advisers and work out a method of conferring with Platt. He had to establish a policy on patronage and major appointments. He had to initiate action on reform legislation that would affect both machines. And in all this he could not in good conscience accept just the organization proposal; he had to consider independent views as well. The self-appointed mediator within the Republican party, Roosevelt was in for a hazardous time "sailing round and round and to and fro," as he often said, "between Scylla and Charybdis." [1]

He soon indicated that he intended to follow the course laid down in his Montauk Point statement to Quigg, namely, that he must be free to seek advice from other men than Platt. His first two post-election conferences with the senator were in each case preceded by a separate meeting with Root, Choate, and Low. By the end of November some members of the Republican organization were protesting that Roosevelt "doth confer too much," yet the next month his list of callers expanded even more. With a legislative message to prepare and numerous applicants for every available position, a certain amount of consultation was inevitable, but

[1] Roosevelt to Thomas Brackett Reed, July 1, 1899, TR MSS.

Roosevelt seemed to be taking pains to make up his own mind on any question immediately relevant to his administration.[2]

The selection of a new superintendent of public works provided the first major test of Roosevelt's determination. Reappointment of Aldridge was out of the question because Judge Countryman was about to recommend to Black a criminal investigation, so Boss Platt had another man all ready to step into the post. At their conference on November 22 he informed Roosevelt that the organization's choice was Francis J. Hendricks of Syracuse, in Onondaga County, who had just telegraphed his willingness to accept.[3]

To Platt's surprise Roosevelt did not take to this suggestion. Admitting that Hendricks was "clean and honest" and under ordinary circumstances might meet with favor as a "machine politician of a good kind," Roosevelt contended that the situation demanded a better-than-average nominee, "some man of high character and capacity who could be trusted to do the work not merely honestly and efficiently, but without regard to politics." As G.O.P. leader in a canal county Hendricks did not come up to this standard, for few "would believe that he intended to punish corruption in the Canal Department in any aggressive manner." To accept Hendricks at this stage, moreover, when Roosevelt's every move was under closest scrutiny to see whether he would truckle to Platt, would only confirm the worst fears of the independents. "It may be that I can do no better than take him," Roosevelt confided to Cabot Lodge, "but as yet I am not convinced of this." [4]

Time and again over the next few weeks "the really high-class men" he approached turned down the appointment. Still Roosevelt

[2] *New York Tribune,* November 13, 23, 1898; *Albany Argus,* November 28, 1898.

[3] Roosevelt, *Autobiography,* p. 308.

[4] *Ibid.;* Roosevelt to Lodge, December 1, 1898, in Lodge, ed., *Selections,* I, 365.

persevered, and once Platt realized the governor-elect was in earnest he stopped insisting on Hendricks and began to aid the search. "I continue to be on excellent terms with the Senator so far as I can find out," Roosevelt wrote Lodge on January 9. "He is treating me perfectly squarely and I think he is satisfied that I am treating him the same way; at the same time, I think everyone realizes the Governorship is not in commission." [5]

Shortly after the inauguration Roosevelt at last found a suitable and willing candidate, a Civil War veteran with engineering training and administrative experience, unconnected with the Republican organization yet endorsed by both the machine and anti-machine elements in his native city. Colonel John N. Partridge of Brooklyn, while not in Roosevelt's estimate the best candidate he had considered, was nevertheless a "very good man." Editorial opinion generally agreed with the *New York Times* that Partridge was "much above the level of excellence to which we have become accustomed under partisan and machine Governors"; the independent Democratic *Brooklyn Eagle* even called him "one of the best" choices Roosevelt could have made. [6]

The superintendent of public works appointment was hardly typical; only in filling the post of commissioner of labor statistics did the governor experience so much difficulty, and only in the nomination of a Democrat, West Pointer Avery D. Andrews, to be adjutant general of the national guard did he so disregard political considerations. Normally the selective process was briefer, the criteria more partisan. The appointments of Superintendent of

[5] Roosevelt to Lodge, December 1, 12, 27, 1898, *ibid.*, I, 365, 369, 376; *New York Tribune*, December 21, 30, 1898, and January 2, 5, 1899; Roosevelt to Lodge, January 9, 1899, TR MSS.

[6] *New York Times, New York Press* and *Brooklyn Eagle*, January 13, 1899 (RS). Roosevelt to Sherman S. Rogers, January 14, 1899; to Lodge, to St. Clair McKelway, January 9, 1899; all TR MSS.

Banks Kilburn and Commisioner of Agriculture Wieting were quickly renewed upon recommendations from leading bankers and state agricultural societies. Two Black supporters—Superintendent of Public Buildings Easton and State Inspector of Gas Meters Stewart—were to make way for candidates of Barnes and Quigg respectively. And Roosevelt's longtime political friend, Joe Murray, would have a place as first deputy in the department of public buildings.

Yet the Partridge appointment did exemplify the Roosevelt policy. He had given little consideration to any candidate whom party leaders would oppose automatically, but he had refused to accept a machine nominee without the proper qualifications. "I do not expect to appoint men as a rule (though I shall do so often) *purely* with regard to the interests of the service," he wrote one upstate Republican, "but I do expect to make these interests . . . the controlling consideration." Results, he clearly believed, depended upon the maintenance of harmonious relations with Platt; at the same time, results worth achieving demanded a vigilant and sustained effort to keep the machine on best behavior.[7]

Such a policy really supplied a comprehensive formula for political action, to which Roosevelt gave succinct expression the day of his inaugural. Waving gaily to his children in the balcony as he took the assembly rostrum before the impressive gathering of dignitaries and spectators, the new governor delivered a short message upon the responsibility of popular government to resolve antagonistic interests within the state. "Under no form of government is it so necessary thus to combine efficiency and morality . . . as in a republic," he asserted at one point, and then he spelled that out for Democrats and Republicans alike: "It is only through the party system that free governments are now successfully carried on, and yet we must keep ever vividly before us that the usefulness

[7] Roosevelt to J. S. Fassett, January 30, 1899, TR MSS.

of a party is strictly limited by its usefulness to the State, and that in the long run, he serves his party best who most helps to make it instantly responsive to every need of the people." That was a task befitting "an independent organization man of the best type." [8]

In his endeavor to run a responsive administration, Roosevelt found the newsmen invaluable allies. He could use them to improve his relations with the legislature, to help to quash undesirable bills, or to push pet projects. Through them he could test public reaction to his plans in advance of direct commitment. Most important of all, through them he could explain and justify his actions to the people, and in particular to the New York City reformers. Joseph Bucklin Bishop of the *Evening Post* editorial staff was especially valuable in this task; Roosevelt usually took care to inform him of the motives behind pertinent appointments and policies.[9]

Roosevelt's methods speedily "captured the Albany correspondents." They liked his friendly manner and the way in which he maintained his dignity without a trace of pomp. Above all they appreciated the frankness with which the new governor discussed state affairs at their twice-daily interviews. The fact that he openly revealed what had gone on each day, observed the *Brooklyn Eagle,* "should remove mystery from government, mummery from laws, secrecy from policy, and darkness from jobbery." Some of Roosevelt's remarks were "off the record," some were not for direct quotation. The reporters, who enjoyed "little innocent conspiracies against the public," seldom abused these confidences.[10]

From the moment he arrived in Albany Roosevelt enjoyed a "good press," but then, almost anything he did was newsworthy.

[8] *Public Papers* (1899), pp. 248–249.

[9] Roosevelt to Bishop, January 5, 12, 1899; to George McAneny, January 23, 1899; all TR MSS.

[10] *Brooklyn Citizen,* January 6, 1899 (RS); *Brooklyn Eagle,* January 14, 1899 (RS); *Albany Argus,* June 6, 1899.

It was no surprise, perhaps, to learn that he always walked from the executive mansion to his office in the Capitol building, or that he preferred the broad front steps two at a time to the Capitol elevator. Yet, it was interesting to discover that the governor arranged his day in a businesslike fashion, punctually alternating the hours for correspondence, appointments, and press interviews. It was of some moment to find that he had inaugurated a weekly "cabinet" meeting where all the elective state officers discussed their mutual problems. And it was most significant that he consulted frankly and openly with the Republican boss.

Roosevelt's conferences with Platt were the most celebrated part of the executive methods. From Monday through Friday his only contact with the senator was by occasional correspondence or through the visits Odell regularly made to Albany. Over the weekend, however, Roosevelt usually went to New York, Platt came on from Washington, and a consultation was held.

Democratic organs called these visits to the boss "practically unprecedented" in gubernatorial annals and depicted an imaginary sign on the door of the executive chamber: "CLOSED: GONE TO NEW YORK CITY TO SEE PLATT." Roosevelt ignored such jibes. New York City was the most convenient place to meet, for the senator was no longer robust and Roosevelt always had a quantity of other matters to attend to there. From the reports of what transpired at the conferences, moreover, it could be gathered that the governor had not forsaken his integrity in leaving Albany. The machine, in the words of St. Clair McKelway, had "neither been ignored nor enthroned." Roosevelt was candidly admitting that he was "not the whole thing, there is also the Legislature." [11]

[11] *New York Journal,* January 6, 1899 (RS); *Albany Argus,* January 23, 1899; *Brooklyn Eagle,* January 26, 1899 (RS); New York *Evening Post,* January 12, 1899 (RS). For a typically busy weekend see *New York Tribune,*

Platt's influence was most potent in the assembly, where the 88 Republicans had a safe majority of 26 votes. Most of the members had only a year's legislative experience; few would serve more than two terms, for local organizations generally believed that was enough for one man. As a result the leadership devolved upon several "old hands"—Platt men like Speaker S. Fred Nixon, majority leader Jotham P. Allds, and Otto Kelsey. They blazed the path through the maze of legislation, and the fledgling members, bound by party no less than inexperience, followed.

The senate was another story. The 35 Republicans who had controlled that body since 1896 had dwindled to 27, so that a shift of two votes to the Democratic side might effectively block any bill. Such a shift was entirely possible. Henry J. Coggeshall of Oneida County was notoriously independent, and such members of the Payn-Black faction as Henry S. Ambler of Columbia County and Benjamin M. Wilcox of Auburn in Cayuga County might also balk. The recalcitrant combination might vary with the bill under consideration, but a threat to party measures was always there. Roosevelt had good reason to consult with Platt; the question was, would even the boss's word hold good.[12]

Roosevelt's first aims in political legislation were reform of the civil service and of the New York City police. In his annual message he also recommended repassage of the constitutional amendment substituting biennial for annual sessions of the state legislature, but thereafter he preserved a discreet "hands-off" attitude toward this measure which Black had sponsored during his second or "reformist" year in office. Roosevelt realized that despite strong support from rural areas and independent Republicans, the amend-

January 21, 22, 23, 1899. The *Tribune* (January 22) declared: "There is not the slightest savor either of despotism or conspiracy about these consultations."
[12] On Coggeshall see *Utica Press*, November 9, 10, 1898.

ment was not likely to win final approval over the opposition of the party machines. This decision to husband his strength for more promising bills was wise, for eventually (and all too conveniently) the senate deadlocked and so defeated the biennial sessions proposal.[13]

Reform of the civil service was a different matter: from first to last Roosevelt displayed a paternal solicitude for the repeal of Black's "starchless" law. The fitness test introduced by this piece of legislation, he asserted in his annual message, was simply a "farce." At the same time there was "utter confusion" in civil service practice within the state, with "no less than three systems" in effect: the state government under the Black law of 1897, the cities other than New York under the 1898 revision which had dropped the fitness examination, and New York City with a municipal commission which claimed to function independently of the state civil service board's regulations. The legislature should remedy this situation, he declared, and the merit principle should also be extended to county officials.[14]

The bill framed by the Civil Service Reform Association to implement these recommendations contained merit features so rigid that few legislators would approve it, so its sponsor in the senate, Horace White of Syracuse, drafted a new measure. The secretary of the association, George McAneny, with whom Roosevelt had been cooperating closely, protested certain omissions from the original, and after a hearing on March 15 the senate judiciary committee restored all but the provision that required filing reasons for removal of competitive place holders. The bill which McAneny

[13] *Public Papers* (1899), p. 24; Roosevelt to Senator Brackett, March 1, 1899, TR MSS.
[14] *Public Papers* (1899), pp. 21–22.

was later to describe as "superior to any civil service statute here-tofore secured in America" was at last ready.[15]

At a Republican caucus on March 21 only Lou Payn's man, Senator Ambler, indicated that he would vote against the White bill, but there remained a risk that some other Republican might defect at the last minute. In Albany for a short stay during the latter part of March, Boss Platt urged doubtful senators to hold firm, and on the crucial ballot several days later they did so. The machine's attitude was a matter of wonder to the *New York Times*: surely Platt was on his best behavior.

More evidence of Platt's earnestness came shortly. The senate had always appeared to be the only obstacle to civil service reform, but at a party caucus in the assembly on April 11 only 61 Republicans showed up, too few to give a majority in the chamber. The next day, in an angry mood, Roosevelt complained to Odell that machine leaders in Brooklyn and New York City were advising their men to vote against the measure. At the same time, however, he wrote Platt that "I have just by accident seen the telegrams you have been sending, asking the members to support the Civil Service bill." Roosevelt "had never had more herculean labor" and had had "to interfere most actively," so he was properly grateful to Boss Platt for this unsolicited aid: "I am more touched than I can say, and I must just send you a line to express my very deep appreciation."[16]

[15] Roosevelt to McAneny, January 23 and February 16, 1899, TR MSS.; Senator White to McAneny, March 11, 1899, and McAneny to White, March 13, 1899, Civil Service Reform Association MSS., NYRL; *New York Tribune*, March 16, 1899; Executive Committee of the Civil Service Reform Association, *Annual Report, 1899*, p. 5.

[16] Roosevelt to Odell, to Low, to McAneny, April 12, 1899; to Bishop, April 14, 1899; to Platt, April 12, 1899; all TR MSS.

With Platt's backing the White bill passed the assembly, 83-59, only two Republicans voting with the Democrats. An amendment giving veterans preference required senate approval, but that did not provoke a crisis. Though Ambler continued in the negative and Coggeshall was unexplainably absent, the measure still gained the necessary 26 votes, for one Democrat—Senator Douglas of Albany—again broke party lines on the issue. Thus Roosevelt finally achieved one major reform.[17]

The next year the luster of this victory dimmed somewhat as Roosevelt signed a bill transferring from the surrogate courts to the state comptroller the power to appoint inheritance tax appraisers in New York, Kings, and Erie counties. There was much to be said for a measure substituting salaried officials for the more expensive fee system and curbing such abuses as the assembly inquiry into the surrogateship of New York in January 1899 had revealed. But reformers were angered at the machine stamp of the comptroller's appointees and at the fact that the state civil service commission, with the governor's approval, exempted the new appraiserships from any examination. The more independent editors maintained that it was impossible to disguise this "surrender to spoilsmen," while the Civil Service Reform Association officially condemned the governor's action.[18]

Viewed in the larger context of the progress of civil service reform under his administration, however, the inheritance tax appraisers law lost much of the importance its critics attached to it.

[17] "I do not believe it can possibly hurt you even with your party friends," Roosevelt had written Douglas on March 30, 1899 (TR MSS.), after his first vote. "In fact you are simply carrying out the provisions of the democratic platform."

[18] Roosevelt to Bishop, May 2, 1900, TR MSS.; *New York Tribune*, May 19, 1900; *Nation* 70:390–391 (May 24, 1900); Roosevelt to McAneny, May 25, 1900; to R. U. Johnson, May 29, 1900; both TR MSS.

Bills of which McAneny's group disapproved generally received a veto. The governor selected able civil service commissioners and worked closely with them. He approved the extension of the merit system to eleven of the larger counties. In the state government in the year 1899 alone there was an increase of 95 in the competitive and a decrease of 576 in the noncompetitive places as opposed to an increase of 59 in the exempt category. The fact was that Roosevelt's very identification with the cause of civil service reform only magnified for the association his neglect in this instance to champion it against the machine.[19]

Reorganization of the New York City police system was far more complex. Graft and politics undeniably pervaded the whole department, but there was no agreement on how to achieve administrative reform. The charter framers had set up the four-man bipartisan police commission because they preferred it to a more effective but perhaps overpowerful single head. And each party machine feared any change that might enhance the other's influence over the force. In his January message to the legislature Roosevelt tactfully avoided commitment to any specific solution: he merely called attention to the possible need for future action.

Roosevelt questioned the wisdom of the remedy which Platt and Quigg advanced, the creation of a metropolitan district with a commission appointed by the governor. Though not without precedent—the state had exercised such power over New York City from 1857 to 1870, and Massachusetts had inaugurated a similar relation with Boston in 1885—there were many objections to this scheme. It discriminated between Greater New York and other cities and was regarded as a flagrant violation of "home rule." No matter how

[19] Executive Committee of the New York Civil Service Reform Association, *Annual Report, 1899*, pp. 10–15; *Annual Report, 1900*, pp. 11–12; *Buffalo Express*, April 15, May 14, 1900; Roosevelt to Bishop, May 26, 1900, TR MSS.

efficient it might prove in practice, critics would charge that the Republicans merely sought greater political influence in this vital department. As Roosevelt informed ex-Police Commissioner Frank Moss, "I do not like to take part in any movement that may seem to be making a change for merely partisan purposes." [20]

On the other hand Roosevelt disliked "quite as much to set [sic] supine in the face of the hideous and brutal misconduct of the present Tammany police force." This counsel of "do nothing" came conspicuously from the Rev. Dr. Charles H. Parkhurst, of the Society for the Prevention of Crime, who blamed police short-comings on Platt's course in 1897 and so advised that New York City be left alone until the next election. Roosevelt considered this view "irrational" since Parkhurst and other good government advocates were equally responsible for Tammany's return to power. If the governor could find some legitimate basis he would interfere, for he agreed with the *New York Tribune* that there was a "genuine need" for state action.[21]

In late January, to Roosevelt's relief, Elihu Root "by a positive stroke of genius struck upon an excellent solution." Root's proposal took a middle course between state supervision and home rule. A single commissioner would replace the four-man board; his appointment would remain in the mayor's hands, but for misconduct in connection with elections the governor could remove him without charges or a formal hearing; and the bureau of elections would be taken from police control and placed under a bipartisan commission appointed by the mayor. Roosevelt was particularly pleased because he could defend this plan as nonpartisan and as "no de-

[20] Roosevelt to Moss, January 14, 1899, TR MSS. See also Raymond B. Fosdick, *American Police Systems* (New York, 1920), pp. 82–95.

[21] Roosevelt to Moss, January 14, 1899, TR MSS.; open letter of Parkhurst to Roosevelt, *New York Times*, January 28, 1899 (RS); Roosevelt to Moss, January 31, 1899, TR MSS.; *New York Tribune*, January 28, 1899.

parture at all" from home rule. By doing away with the old board, a change Roosevelt had long advocated, the Root draft would promote efficiency and responsibility throughout the police administration.[22]

Criticism of the provision giving the governor summary removal power persuaded Roosevelt to agree to an amendment giving him the power only to "suspend" the commissioner pending the outcome of a trial on charges of election misconduct.[23] Even so the possibility that this scheme would pass the senate was slim. Platt and Odell had approved Root's proposal (introduced on February 8 as the Raines-Mazet bill), but when Presiding Officer Ellsworth insisted on March 2 that it become a party measure, Coggeshall and Wilcox walked out of the caucus. Since another absentee—Willis of Schuyler County—was known to be hostile also, some Albany observers concluded that the matter was dead for the winter. Coggeshall based his opposition on the claim that the new commissioner would "Tammanyize" what was predominantly a Republican police force, whereas Wilcox reportedly acted out of friendship for one of the Republican police commissioners. Whatever the reason, the "Albany Hold-Up" called for remedial action.[24]

Sentiment for a full-scale investigation of "Mr. Croker's Punch and Judy Show Government" had meantime been growing stronger. The New York *World* had long contended that abnormal real estate

[22] Roosevelt to Low, to Moss, January 31, 1899, TR MSS.

[23] For criticisms of the removal power see New York *Evening Post*, February 8, 1899; *New York Herald*, February 10, 1899; *New York Times*, February 9, 1899 (all RS). Unqualified praise came from the *New York Tribune*, New York *Mail and Express*, *Brooklyn Times*, *Brooklyn Eagle*, New York *World* and New York *Commercial Advertiser* (all RS).

[24] *New York Tribune*, February 25, 28 and March 3, 4, 5, 1899; New York *World*, March 8, 1899; *New York Times*, April 1, 1899 (RS); New York *Evening Post*, March 6, 1899; New York *Sun* (RS) and *Troy Times*, March 17, 1899; Rochester *Post Express*, March 24, 1899.

evaluations by the boss's minions justified an inquiry; extravagant increases in official salaries, reports of lax law enforcement, and Tammany's latest assault upon the Manhattan Elevated Company further outraged the anti-Croker press. The attack upon Manhattan Elevated well illustrated the Tammany technique. Boss Croker was deeply involved financially in the New York Auto Truck Company; when Manhattan Elevated in mid-February rejected a contract permitting New York Auto Truck to attach a pipe to the elevated structure to carry compressed air around the city, the board of health, the park department, and the municipal assembly began a systematic attack upon its privileges. By February 28 Roosevelt was confiding to Frank Moss that he was "reluctantly coming to the conclusion that there must be an investigation along the lines you mention." A month later at a conference with Platt and Odell it was agreed that the G.O.P. should push through at once a bill authorizing an assembly committee investigation of the government of Greater New York. To one ex-Tammanyite as zealous for intervention as Frank Moss, the governor wrote, "I think we may be able to wake the voters up, after all." [25]

Coincident with the assembly's creation of the Mazet investigating committee, which with Frank Moss as chief counsel launched its first hearing on April 8, the Republican high command decided to drop the old Root proposal in favor of a much more drastic and sweeping measure. His interviews with rebellious senators at Albany in late March convinced Platt that the Raines-Mazet bill could not be put through, but only Coggeshall was reported to oppose the new "State Constabulary" scheme that Platt tentatively

[25] New York *World,* March 8, January 13, 1899; *New York Tribune,* February 19, 21, 22, 27, 1899; New York *Evening Post,* February 25, 1899. Roosevelt to Moss, February 28, 1899; to Henry Purroy, March 29, 1899; both TR MSS.

advanced. On April 13, just as the first revelations of the Mazet committee were capturing the headlines, the legislature received the latest reform bill.[26]

The new proposal contemplated a profound change in the police administration of the state's first- and second-class cities. It would abolish the police boards or commissions of New York, Buffalo, Rochester, Syracuse, Albany, and Troy, and transfer most of their supervisory duties to a new official whom the governor would appoint for a six-year term but whom he could remove upon charges and a hearing. These communities would retain their present police forces, but future admissions to the force would be under the state civil service law. The local chiefs would become chiefs of state police, empowered to make assignments and promotions subject to the state commissioner's approval; he could remove these chiefs on charges, with right of appeal to the governor; he could also appoint their successors, who would be chosen from among the deputy chiefs. Such was the main outline of the centralized police system which the Republican organization now put forward as a party measure.

Publicly professing to be "more than pleased" with this "most admirable bill," the governor informed Bishop that it fulfilled every condition he had laid down to the organization. He had always insisted that if there was to be state control it should not apply to New York City alone, nor "only to the democratic cities of New York, Albany, and Troy; that it must apply to the usually republican cities of Syracuse and Rochester, and to Buffalo (which is as often one as the other)." He had insisted also that the bill should represent "not an effort to get the police as tools of the republican

[26] *Assembly Journal* (1899), pp. 2006–07; New York *Evening Post*, April 14, 1899; *New York Herald*, April 17, 1899 (RS); *New York Tribune*, April 3, 1899.

party, but a genuine and honest effort to get them absolutely out of politics." He believed this would be the result of placing the police under civil service and bestowing administrative responsibility directly on the state commissioner and his chiefs. Of course, as he was to announce on April 19, Roosevelt would only appoint a nonpartisan to the key post of state commissioner.[27]

The press received the measure far more critically. The few Republican party organs that commented usually termed it a "good bill," but the influential *Troy Times* declared that to involve the upstate cities in the reform of the New York City police was "like dosing a whole family of children because the biggest boy has the colic." Naturally this "Irish Landlord Constabulary Bill" was anathema to Democratic papers, but independent Republican editors similarly regarded it as a radical invasion of the province of municipal self-government and felt it demanded the most careful scrutiny. Distrustful of any Platt-sponsored legislation, and especially of a bill introduced so late in the session as to render the "jamming" tactic necessary, many reformers shared the *Tribune's* feeling that "the Governor is misled by looking at the question too exclusively from the point of view of his own intentions . . . He does not give sufficient weight to the consideration that he could guarantee good results for only about eighteen months." [28]

Roosevelt defended the bill's infringement on "home rule." With a "semi-military organization" like the police force, he argued,

[27] *Brooklyn Times*, April 13, 1899 (RS); Roosevelt to Bishop, April 14, 1899, TR MSS.; *New York Tribune*, April 20, 1899.

[28] *Brooklyn Times* (RS) and Rochester *Democrat and Chronicle*, April 15, 1899; *Albany Evening Journal*, April 18, 1899; *Troy Times*, April 13, 1899; *Rochester Times*, April 24, 1899; *Buffalo Courier* and *Utica Observer*, April 15, 1899; *Brooklyn Citizen*, April 13, 1899; *New York Journal*, April 22, 1899 (RS); *Watertown Times*, April 17, 1899 (RS); *Buffalo Express* and Rochester *Post Express*, April 21, 1899; *Utica Press*, April 24, 1899; *New York Tribune*, April 14, 22, 1899.

there was "no more reason in abstract right for putting it under the city than for putting the National Guard under the city." And to Bishop he pointed out that good government advocates did not object to state interference with municipal civil service; why did they do so with the police? [29]

But in his correspondence with the party leaders Roosevelt increasingly questioned the political expediency of the measure. On April 4 he informed Platt that one of the upstate senators had just told him that the state constabulary scheme "would operate very much to our disadvantage politically"; indeed, the man was "so worked up over the matter" that the governor was going to sound out "a few of our other good friends in the State Legislature to find out what they think of it." The next day he relayed the information that Senator John Raines expressed similar fears about the popular reaction in Buffalo and Rochester. Though these representations left Platt unmoved, Roosevelt continued to be uneasy. On April 12 he wrote Odell that he hoped the bill would be introduced as soon as possible, for many of the state legislators were "very anxious, as I am, that there should be every chance for a full discussion and consideration." "I believe the measure is righteous," he added, "but I believe it would do us great harm to have it jammed through." [30]

For almost a week after the introduction of the bill on April 13, Boss Platt appeared to have the situation in hand; the Mazet committee's exposé of Tammany misrule was already impressing New Yorkers, and in the senate the vote of every Republican except

[29] Roosevelt to Bishop, April 17, 1899, TR MSS. See also his comments in *Albany Argus*, February 23, 1899; Frank Moss, "State Oversight of Police," *Municipal Affairs* 3:267 (June 1899).
[30] Roosevelt to Platt, April 4, 5, 1899, TR MSS.; Platt to Roosevelt, April 6, 1899, in *Barnes* v. *Roosevelt*, p. 2437. Roosevelt to Odell, April 12, 1899; to Platt, April 14, 1899; both TR MSS.

Coggeshall was said to be assured. But on April 20 Roosevelt, who had been more and more dismayed at signs of the machine's jamming tactics, suddenly discovered and revealed to the press that the two G.O.P. senators from Monroe County would oppose the measure unless it excluded Rochester. Their decision was popularly attributed to the influence of Boss Aldridge, who was determined to carry the city elections of 1899 and feared any step which might endanger his alliance with the good government faction. The Rochester Chamber of Commerce also disapproved of the plan. In any case, Roosevelt at last could breathe "a selfish sigh of relief" that the state constabulary bill was finished for the session.[31]

Thereafter Roosevelt remained ready to defend the constabulary bill's administrative merits. "If we can get the police fairly taken out of politics," he wrote Seth Low in November, "we ought not to hesitate." And to Nicholas Murray Butler, with whom he worked closely on educational reforms, the governor gave a revealing explanation of his position on police legislation. "Where I have so many fights with the Organization on points on which they are wrong," Roosevelt asserted, "I am in doubt how far to go in fighting them where I deem them right, and where they know I deem them right."[32]

Throughout the remainder of his term the governor continued to question the expediency of Platt's schemes for state supervision of the New York City police. Even if the boss did have "the legislature in shape," as he claimed the following November, Roosevelt considered it unwise to press reorganization over the protests of the independent Republicans. Deliberately he chose not to take

---

[31] Low to Roosevelt, April 18, 1899, Low MSS.; Roosevelt to Speaker Nixon, April 19, 1899, TR MSS.; *Albany Evening Journal,* April 19, 20, 1899; *New York Tribune,* April 21, 1899; Roosevelt to Bishop, April 14, 1899, TR MSS.
[32] Roosevelt to Low, to Butler, November 16, 1899, TR MSS.

a stand himself; rather he endeavored to bring the senator to appreciate the contrary view. If his representations proved less than convincing to Platt, they at least led to the abandonment of the constabulary bill without creating a disastrous break with the machine. In few other places was Roosevelt's mediating function so clear, the requirement that he exercise tact so great.[33]

One final task remained: to dispose of the findings of the Mazet committee. It was Platt's view that the committee itself should draft and introduce the amendments to the Greater New York charter which its investigation had revealed to be necessary. At the insistence of Charles Stewart Smith and other reform Republicans, however, Quigg had put through the county committee a resolution calling for a separate charter revision commission. This disagreement was thrashed out at a mid-December conference at which Roosevelt successfully supported the Smith-Quigg plan. Long under attack by the independent press for its partisanship, the Mazet committee would defer decision on all major changes to a nonlegislative commission appointed by the governor pursuant to a bill to be passed at the 1900 session.[34]

Aside from a fruitless attempt to have salaries provided for the commissioners, the governor left the resultant measure to the organization to put through over the futile protests of Tammany. His real job came with the selection of the members. In consultation particularly with Edward Cary of the *New York Times* and Joseph Bishop (now with the *Commercial Advertiser*), Roosevelt put together a group calculated to get by Platt, for the eight Re-

---

[33] Platt to Roosevelt, November 13 and December 1, 1899, in *Barnes* v. *Roosevelt*, pp. 2455–56, 2479; Roosevelt to Platt, November 27, 1899, TR MSS.; Odell to Roosevelt, November 27, 1899, TR MSS. (LC); Roosevelt to Lodge, to Mrs. Storer, December 2, 1899, TR MSS.

[34] Platt to Roosevelt, December 1, 1899, in *Barnes* v. *Roosevelt*, pp. 2459–60; *New York Herald* and *New York Times,* December 11, 1899 (RS).

publicans had a majority of one, and the Democrats were mainly of the anti-Bryan persuasion. On one important point, however, Boss Platt demurred; he thought at least one member of the old charter commission should be included, and for that spot he backed William C. DeWitt, a Brooklyn Democrat. Seth Low and Bishop both opposed this change, but Roosevelt finally agreed.[35]

The reason behind Platt's move became apparent once the nominations were announced. Roosevelt wanted Cleveland's former Assistant Secretary of State, George L. Rives, to be president of the commission and with that thought in mind had given his name first place. Platt, on the other hand, desired either a Republican or DeWitt to head the body, and not the more independent-minded Rives. On April 30 Roosevelt discovered that machine spokesmen were actually approaching the various commissioners to indicate the boss's wishes. That same day the senator wired the governor that unless a Republican—C. C. Beaman or Henry W. Taft—could be chosen president then action should be postponed because "defeat of amendments [was] liable to follow results of contemplated organization." [36]

In deference to Platt's wishes, Roosevelt did suggest to Beaman, Taft and others "that they wait as regards the organization of the commission until they could come up here Friday and all of them take lunch with me." Replying to the senator's wire, Roosevelt agreed "that we want to have such changes in the charter as a republican legislature will pass." But, he declared, "the first thing is to get a republican legislature," as he proceeded in typical fashion to present the case for compromise.[37]

[35] Roosevelt to N. M. Butler, February 17, 21, 1900, TR MSS.; *Barnes v. Roosevelt*, pp. 743–747; Roosevelt to Cary, April 10, 1900, TR MSS.; to Platt, May 1, 1900, TR MSS.; Bishop to Roosevelt, April 11, 1900, TR MSS. (LC).
[36] Roosevelt to Platt, May 1, 1900, TR MSS.; Platt to Roosevelt, April 30, 1900, TR MSS. (LC).
[37] Roosevelt to Platt, May 1, 1900, TR MSS.

"Nothing in my judgment would damage us more in New York among the elements whose votes have got to come to us if we are out to win the election," Roosevelt maintained to Platt, "than to have them get the idea that the charter commission was being managed as a republican adjunct." He recalled that the independent element had already "objected bitterly to the transfer tax appraisers bill, chiefly because of the appointments made under it." And he had "various other troubles with the independents, springing in every case because of their opposition to the organization." In the Republican organization's own interest, Roosevelt contended, he had not wanted to add to these troubles by giving the independents "a real cause of grievance," particularly when the charter commission was "eminently a body in which I could afford to recognize the independent element." Hence, he had indicated Rives as his choice for chairman, and he added, "you would be the last man to wish me to go back on my word where I had committed myself—it is not your style, Senator." [38]

In the end Roosevelt's view prevailed, for all the members present at the luncheon wanted Rives as chairman and the commission was so organized. Whatever the subsequent effect of this action, its immediate result was just what Roosevelt had intended. Already his slate of nominees had met with approbation in New York City. Now the selection of a Democrat of Rives' stamp further emphasized the nonpartisan approach for which the governor had always contended.[39]

Shortly afterward, in recalling the way in which Platt had tried to outmaneuver him, Roosevelt remarked that "the time had come when I had to show my teeth a little." So he had—but only a little. A master at adjusting his reaction to the demands of the issue

[38] *Ibid.*
[39] *New York Tribune,* April 26, 1900; Bishop to Roosevelt, May 2, 1900, TR MSS. (LC).

involved, Roosevelt reserved his best grimaces for the toughest fights. And in the political arena his most dangerous encounter with the machine was not over the civil service or the police or the charter commission. It was over the appointment of a superintendent of insurance to succeed Lou Payn.[40]

[40] Roosevelt to Bishop, May 3, 1900, TR MSS.

CHAPTER V **Speak Softly and
Carry a Big Stick**

The dispute over Lou Payn afforded Roosevelt an unparalleled
opportunity to exercise his political talents. He was as anxious as
any reformer to get rid of the ex-lobbyist whose three-year term as
superintendent of insurance was to expire in January 1900. At the
same time, though, he was determined if possible to avoid a rup-
ture of relations with Platt. In the interest of party harmony Boss
Platt might try to dissuade Roosevelt from supplanting Payn, and
failing that, could obstruct senate approval of the nomination of
anyone else. The governor's problem was to find some method by
which to bring pressure upon the organization. That endeavor
called for all his skill—and a bit of luck as well.

Roosevelt never questioned whether he would oppose Payn; he
wanted nothing to do with the Payn-Black coterie.[1] Had the new
governor possessed sufficient evidence he might have tried to remove Lou Payn at once; in any event, he tracked down every
derogatory clue. In May of 1899 he reminded his administrative
assistant to look up "that insurance matter" about which the insur-

---

[1] In refusing pleas that he do something about the removal of the capable
warden of Sing Sing, Roosevelt asserted that Superintendent of State Prisons
Collins, a Black appointee, was "just as independent as Superintendent Payn is,
and I shall have just as little to do with his administration." On this question,
see Roosevelt to John B. Devins, January 5, 1899; to Josephine Shaw Lowell, to
Rabbi Gustav Gottheil, January 16, 1899; to Bishop, February 16, 1899; all
TR MSS. *Albany Argus,* April 14, 1899.

ance editor of the New York *Evening Post* had inquired: "If there has been any iniquity I earnestly wish we could discover it." He also asked George McAneny about Payn's record on appointments, for the superintendent was an old foe of civil service reform; Roosevelt was disappointed to find that what Payn had done "in the civil service cases was only what the various other officers had done." It would not be easy to build a case, especially when the insurance companies discreetly would support the incumbent. "I shall pay no heed to the insurance people asking for his reappointment," Roosevelt confided to one reformer, "but I shall need . . . the help of every . . . good citizen when I send in the nomination of his successor, for I think it more than doubtful whether I can get him confirmed." [2]

Even if Platt sided with Roosevelt against Payn, the Republican majority in the senate was too slim to guarantee a successor's confirmation. If, on the other hand, Boss Platt refused to take sides, that would be tantamount to keeping Payn in office. In the summer of 1899 the senator was clearly moving toward neutrality—and beyond. In an August letter congratulating Roosevelt upon his reception at various agricultural fairs across the state, Platt casually suggested that "if you could shape your affairs so as to address the Columbia County Fair . . . it would be a good stroke of policy." By that he obviously meant that Roosevelt's appearance in Payn's county would help to unite the party for the fall election, but the senator hinted at something more. "You can see why I think it would be a good thing for you to go there," he concluded, "although in a recent conversation I had with Payn, I was surprised to find how favorably he talked about you; and he was not talking to me for effect." [3]

[2] Roosevelt to Youngs, May 27, 1899; to the Rev. Thomas R. Slicer, October 28, 1899; both TR MSS.
[3] Platt to Roosevelt, August 25, 1899, in *Barnes* v. *Roosevelt,* pp. 2450–51.

Though the governor tactfully avoided the suggested appearance at the Columbia County Fair, Platt served further notice that fall, through his conferences with Lou Payn, that the two of them had put aside their year-old differences. "Mr. Payn's reconciliation with Senator Platt will not affect me one least little particle," Roosevelt bravely asserted, but it certainly increased the odds against displacing the insurance superintendent. It was no wonder that Senator Feeter announced in November that the governor might as well give in because the upper chamber would never confirm another nominee.[4]

In this situation Roosevelt sought a candidate to whom Platt would not object. In Francis J. Hendricks of Syracuse, the banker-politician who had been Platt's first choice for superintendent of public works, the governor thought he had an ideal man. Not only might the Boss be willing to back Hendricks, but the organization might also relax its pressure upon the governor to jump Hendricks' man over another judge with a better claim to a vacancy on New York's highest court. At one blow Roosevelt might solve the two difficulties that were currently making his office worrisome.[5]

Such a coup was not to be. Platt and Odell did not protest when Roosevelt told them at a conference on December 9 that he thought Hendricks would make a good successor to Payn. But three days later, after premature publication of the news of his intention in the New York *Sun* had prompted Roosevelt to sound out his prospect without further delay, Hendricks declined "for business reasons" to

[4] Roosevelt to Platt, August 26, 1899, TR MSS.; New York *World*, October 25, 1899; New York *Evening Post*, October 23, 24, 1899; Roosevelt to Slicer, October 28, 1899, TR MSS.; *Brooklyn Eagle*, November 24, 1899 (RS).

[5] Roosevelt to Platt, December 13, 1899, TR MSS.; Platt to Roosevelt, December 16, 1899, in *Barnes* v. *Roosevelt*, p. 2463; Odell to Roosevelt, December 16, 1899, TR MSS. (LC); Roosevelt to State Senator Horace White, December 20, 1899, TR MSS.

stand for the nomination. The *New York Tribune's* Albany correspondent at once concluded that Platt had advised the Syracuse banker to decline, an allegation Hendricks denied and Roosevelt said he had never suspected. The fact probably was that Hendricks knew better than to agree to a nomination except at the senator's explicit request.[6]

Only the day before Hendricks' hurried trip to Albany to receive this offer, Lou Payn had called at the executive chamber to vouchsafe his support of Roosevelt's nomination; now he spoke out against the governor in a press interview. He asserted that he was confident of retaining his office, which he had administered well; that if Roosevelt were to follow the civil service principles he professed he could not legitimately make a replacement; that hate and prejudice should not enter the case; and that he, Payn, could not abide Mugwumps but respected Democrats. The fullest and most intemperate version of Payn's remarks was the New York *Sun's*, which noted, for example, that he identified Roosevelt as a Mugwump before stating "I have never trusted Mugwumps." But whatever paper one read, the fight was clearly joined.[7]

Although Payn wired Platt that "Ninety per cent of the pretended interviews with me . . . are garbled and in many instances have no foundation whatsoever," the incident made compromise more difficult.[8] The governor was as resolved as ever that the superintendent must go, while Payn had practically eliminated the possibility of graceful retreat. If Platt had ever imagined that he could persuade

[6] Roosevelt to Odell, December 16, 1899; to Platt, December 18, 1899; both TR MSS. Syracuse *Post-Standard,* December 13, 1899 (RS); *New York Tribune* and New York *Evening Post,* December 13, 1899; Hendricks to Roosevelt, December 14, 1899, TR MSS. (LC); Roosevelt to Hendricks, December 15, 1899, TR MSS.

[7] *Brooklyn Eagle* and New York *Sun,* December 3, 1899 (RS); *New York Tribune,* December 14, 1899.

[8] Platt to Roosevelt, December 16, 1899, in *Barnes* v. *Roosevelt,* pp. 2462–63; Roosevelt to Platt, December 18, 1899, TR MSS.

the Columbia County leader to leave office without a struggle, he now despaired of success. Instead he concentrated upon Roosevelt. "Platt does not want me to fight Payn and feels pretty bitterly about it," Roosevelt informed Lodge after a breakfast conference on December 28, "but here I could not compromise and I refused to alter my position." The price of refusal was nonetheless explicit. If the Democrats supported Payn, as Roosevelt supposed the great majority of them would, then "the attitude of the republican machine means that I will not get him out." The *New York Press* struck uncomfortably close to the truth with its report that the submission of another name to the senate would be "only a perfunctory act." [9]

The *New York Press* and the *Troy Times* were supporting Payn's right to reappointment. So were George F. Sheldon, vice president of the National Board of Fire Underwriters and president of Phoenix Insurance Company, John A. McCall of New York Life, James W. Alexander of Equitable Life, John R. Hegeman of Metropolitan Life, and numerous others who endorsed the "straightforward, vigorous and intelligent" record of the "splendid" superintendent. But from Lawrence Godkin, son of the *Evening Post's* editor and counsel for one of the insurance firms, came word that the officials of his company really didn't mean what they had stated publicly: "they had been obliged to write it for fear of the Superintendent," Roosevelt later noted in his *Autobiography,* "but . . . if they got the chance they intended to help me get rid of him." Since they thought they had influence with four of the state senators, the governor welcomed their assistance. [10]

[9] Brayton Ives to Roosevelt, January 1, 1900, TR MSS. (LC); Roosevelt to Ives, January 2, 1900, TR MSS.; to Lodge, December 29, 1899, TR MSS.; *New York Press,* December 29, 1899 (RS).

[10] New York *Sun,* December 25, 1899; *New York Press,* December 29, 1899; *Troy Times,* December 27, 1899 (all RS). Roosevelt, *Autobiography,* p. 316. Roosevelt to Lawrence Godkin, December 19, 21, 1899, January 8, 1900; Roosevelt to Lodge, January 8, 1900; all TR MSS.

The first requirement was to find a suitable Republican willing to stand for the nomination. Press estimates varied as to how many candidates were approached unsuccessfully, but by early January Roosevelt was concentrating on a man Lawrence Godkin had originally suggested, ex-Lieutenant Governor Charles T. Saxton, presiding judge of the court of claims and generally known as a higher type of organization member. Saxton was reluctant to consent because he felt indebted to Payn for keeping his son in office in the insurance department. However on January 8, just as the governor was writing to Godkin to "use every influence possible to persuade Saxton to stand," word came that the judge had thrust aside his qualms. "It's all right!" added Roosevelt in his postscript, "Saxton will stand. Now for the Democratic votes!" [11]

Roosevelt's best approach to the Democrats was through Francis B. Delehanty of Albany, member of the state board of mediation and arbitration and son-in-law of ex-United States Senator Murphy. By January 4 it was reliably reported that the state senator in Murphy's bailiwick, Rensselaer County, would vote "for any reputable Republican as successor to Mr. Payn." And Murphy told Roosevelt that he doubted whether Croker had ordered the Democratic delegation from New York and Brooklyn to stand by Payn; he advised the governor to get directly in touch with Senators Grady and McCarren, who were already pressing the Tammany boss to allow the legislators to vote independently. "Senator Grady practically told me he would support me," Roosevelt replied through Delehanty. "McCarren is doubtful," he added, but "I am

---

[11] For estimates and lists see *New York Press,* December 29, 1899; *New York Herald,* January 18, 1900; *New York Tribune,* January 5, 1900 (all RS). On Saxton see *Rochester Times,* January 8, 1900; Rochester *Post Express* and *Rochester Herald,* January 9, 1900 (all RS). Roosevelt to Saxton, January 6, 1900, TR MSS.; Saxton to Roosevelt, January 20, 1900, TR MSS. (LC); Roosevelt to L. Godkin, January 8, 1900, TR MSS.

greatly indebted to you and Senator Murphy for your courtesy." [12]

The governor did not neglect to quietly muster the forces of his own party. The more independent Republican senators—Horace White, Frank Higgins of Chautauqua and several others—he knew he could count on. To get at others he relied on the aid of men such as Representatives Lucius Littauer and James M. E. O'Grady, industrialist Frank S. Witherbee of Port Henry, and National Committeeman Frederick Gibbs of New York City. The influential Senator John Raines was strongly opposed to Saxton, but on January 11 Roosevelt tried to cheer up his candidate with the news that Hendricks had come in to say "that he thought we would surely win." [13]

That very day a new allegation about Payn's activities fortuitously did appear. Up to this time Roosevelt had relied most heavily on the *New York Press* investigation of 1894 for evidence against the superintendent's fitness. On that former occasion Elihu Root had represented the *New York Press*, so on January 6 Roosevelt had asked Root about the testimony taken on Payn's lobbyist activities. "While I do not intend to make an ugly fight unless they force me to it," the governor had concluded, "yet if they do force me the fight shall be had." Then to Albany on January 11 came Abram S. Kling, a disgruntled ex-director and stockholder in the State Trust Company, to make certain charges about illegal loans by that firm to several important individuals, one of whom was Lou Payn.[14]

According to Kling, the State Trust Company of New York City

---

[12] *New York Tribune,* January 5, 1900 (RS); Delehanty to Roosevelt, January 10, 1900, TR MSS. (LC); Roosevelt to Delehanty, January 11, 1900, TR MSS.

[13] Littauer to Roosevelt, January 17, 1900; Witherbee to Roosevelt, January 18, 1900; Fremont Cole to Roosevelt, January 10, 17, 1900; all TR MSS. (LC). See also Roosevelt to Saxton, January 11, 13, 1900, TR MSS.

[14] Roosevelt to Root, January 6, 1900, TR MSS. For Kling's petition, see *New York Tribune,* January 14, 1900.

had been a conservative institution down to December 1898, when the "Syndicate" composed of William C. Whitney, Thomas Fortune Ryan, R. A. C. Smith, P. A. B. Widener and Anthony N. Brady bought control in order to use the trust funds for their business ventures. The new directors disregarded the previous policy that loans to any one person were not to exceed 15 percent of the combined capital and surplus, which amounted in 1900 to $2,250,000. Instead, they made the following important loans:

Daniel E. Shea	$2,000,000
Moore and Schley	1,000,000
Anthony N. Brady	785,000
William F. Sheehan	412,800
Louis F. Payn	435,000
Metropolitan Traction Company	500,000

The Shea loan violated the state banking law forbidding loans in excess of one-half a trust company's capital stock and surplus. Loans directly or indirectly to any director or officer were legally prohibited also, yet Kling claimed that Daniel E. Shea represented Widener, Whitney, Ryan and Brady; that Whitney was indirectly interested in Moore and Schley; that the Sheehan loan was actually to a director, R. A. C. Smith; and that Metropolitan Street Railway was the Syndicate. As for the Payn loan, that was allegedly made on "various unsaleable industrial securities of uncertain and doubtful value, together with what purports to be a certified bank check for $100,000." State Trust's directors were endangering their $12,000,000 in deposits, concluded Kling, and the superintendent of banking should conduct an investigation.

Although Roosevelt strongly suspected that Kling's petition had a "sinister purpose," he decided to verify the allegations. Kling was "charging one of my own officials with misconduct," the governor explained to John Proctor Clarke, "and although I think this alleged misconduct was simply an excuse, I had to act at once." Roosevelt appreciated the fact that an investigation might assist his fight against Payn. But Kling and "the men who came to me evidently intend for their own purpose to make their accusations public." The governor had no choice, and rather than intrust the matter to Superintendent of Banking Frederick D. Kilburn, he detailed his former Adjutant General Avery D. Andrews as special investigator.[15]

Armed with the authority to examine the State Trust Company books, Andrews entered the offices at 100 Broadway the next day in company with Maurice Decker, a former secretary of the company who possessed extensive copies of the loan cards and was familiar with the bookkeeping system. It may be, though he afterwards denied it, that Roosevelt knew Decker would assist Andrews; in any case, State Trust President Walter S. Johnston was incensed at the presence of this former employee discharged "for cause." Knowing nothing about the banking business, Andrews made no attempt at a thorough accounting. But he did verify the loans mentioned in the Kling petition, and on that basis prepared two reports, one to Kilburn and the other to the governor, both of which he forwarded to Roosevelt on January 13, 1900.[16]

The report intended for Roosevelt confirmed his interest in Payn's connection with the case. Andrews pointed out that State Trust had close relations with a bonding and surety firm under Payn's jurisdiction, the American Surety Company, which occupied offices on

[15] Roosevelt to Clarke, January 12, 1900, TR MSS.
[16] *New York Times,* January 18, 1900 (RS); statement of W. S. Johnston in *New York Tribune,* January 14, 1900; Roosevelt to George R. Sheldon, January 19, 1900, TR MSS.; statement by Kling's attorney, Charles Bacon, in *New York Times,* January 18, 1900 (RS); W. S. Johnston to Root, February 20, 1900, Root MSS. The report to Roosevelt is in TR MSS. (LC).

other floors at 100 Broadway. The president of State Trust was also first vice president of American Surety, and nine directors—including Elihu Root—were on both boards. "The plain fact is that Mr. Payn has borrowed an enormous sum of money from a Trust Company which is under the same management as one of the companies in his Department," asserted Andrews, who then drew the inference that "he may have used his official position to obtain a loan at a time when the money market was in a very disturbed condition."

Meantime Kilburn, having been informed of what was afoot, hurried to New York on January 13 to conduct his own personal investigation. At its conclusion he hastily assured an anxious business world that State Trust was in "an entirely solvent condition, having a surplus of at least $1,000,000." Certain loans had indeed been excessive, but they had been "amply secured" and their holders were willing to reduce them to the legal limit at once. Kling's charge that the depositors' funds were endangered thus appeared false, and President Walter S. Johnston promptly so labelled the petition's allegations.[17]

Kilburn's report to the governor carried a somewhat different message. Not only were the loans cited in the Kling petition illegal, Kilburn asserted, but the $1,500,000 on deposit to the Metropolitan Street Railway Company's account was not connected in any way with its $500,000 loan, and the collateral Payn had put up was inadequate. The deputy banking official in the New York area should have caught these discrepancies when he examined the trust company on October 2, 1899, Kilburn confessed, but State Trust was now rectifying the situation. In his opinion, moreover, it was "not unsafe or inexpedient for the State Trust Company to continue business." The action he had taken met "every require-

[17] *New York Tribune,* January 14, 1900.

ment of public interests" so far as the company was concerned; if individuals merited more severe treatment the courts were open and public officials could be called upon to "take cognizance of illegal acts."[18]

The Kilburn-Andrews reports were never officially published, for after a conference with the banking superintendent on January 16 the governor announced that he had learned it was not "customary" to make public "confidential reports." Fear of a financial panic plagued Kilburn: only the month before the Produce Exchange Trust Company had created a sensation when it closed its doors, and the trust company field was known to have expanded dangerously. The Kling petition, furthermore, was definitely suspect of being a "raid" on State Trust Company stock and deposits, perhaps in the interest of The Trust Company of New York. "There has been a steady effort to get me to interfere in the stock war," Roosevelt informed C. R. Miller of the *New York Times* on February 5; "I have steadfastly declined to do it, unless there was a question of seeing justice done." Roosevelt's only action was to request a special investigation by the Clearing House Association, which on January 28 found State Trust to be in "first class condition."[19]

Officials of State Trust were hardly grateful. In their view

[18] New York *World*, March 12, 1900; *New York Tribune*, March 13, 1900. In some way the *World* also obtained a substantially accurate version of Andrews' report to Roosevelt, which it published on March 9, 1900, so it may be presumed that its information on Kilburn's report was authentic.

[19] New York *World*, January 17, 1900 (RS); *New York Tribune*, December 19, 1899; New York *World*, February 26, 1900; W. S. Johnston to Root, February 9, 1900, Root MSS.; Roosevelt to C. R. Miller, February 5, 1900, TR MSS.; *New York Tribune*, January 29, 1900. William H. Harbaugh (*Power and Responsibility: The Life and Times of Theodore Roosevelt* [New York, 1961], pp. 126–127) suspects that Roosevelt also may have wanted to protect Elihu Root from unfavorable publicity, but there is no evidence to this effect other than the New York *World's* assertions.

Roosevelt had been willing to imperil their firm's existence simply to get evidence to use against Lou Payn. Had the governor not lent credence to the charges by sending Andrews down, wrote President Johnston to Root, no newspaper would have dared to publish Kling's information. Even though the state government did not release the official reports, the publicity had been so unfortunate that to preserve deposits and stock values it would be necessary to merge with the smaller but quite respectable Morton Trust Company.[20]

The Kling faction, on the other hand, was dissatisfied that Roosevelt had gone no farther. They wanted the reports released and the attorney general directed to bring action to liquidate the company. For over three months, with the New York *World's* aid, they continued to press for state action. The merger with Morton Trust was merely an attempt to cover up past misdeeds, declared Kling's counsel, Charles P. Bacon, as he unsuccessfully opposed every legislative step toward final approval of the merger.[21]

Cutting a careful course between these opposing views, Roosevelt had attained a major object. He did not need to publish the information he had about the Payn loan, for Kling's counsel was telling anyone who would listen the same thing. On January 16 several New York City papers carried articles in which Bacon explained the relation between State Trust and American Surety: "It was probably easy for Mr. Payn to get this loan." The next day Bacon revealed that the $100,000 check which made up a part of

[20] Johnston to Root, February 9, 17, 20, 1900, Root MSS. See also letter from "H" in *New York Times,* January 18, 1900 (RS).

[21] *New York Times,* January 24, 1900 (RS); *New York Tribune,* January 24, 29, March 24, 1900; New York *World,* March 2, 3, 7, 1900; Bacon to Roosevelt, April 19, 1900, TR MSS. (LC). For defense of the State Trust directors, see P. C. Jessup, *Elihu Root,* 2 vols. (New York, 1938), I, 187–190; Mark Hirsch, *William C. Whitney: Modern Warwick* (New York, 1948), pp. 552–554.

Payn's collateral was drawn on the State Trust Company by the Metropolitan Street Railway and marked "Construction Account." And on January 18, as the New York *World* published a detailed list of the State Trust loans, Bacon pointed out that the value of Payn's collateral was actually slightly less than the $435,000 loan, instead of 15 percent greater as required by law.[22]

At the first publication of Kling's petition, Lou Payn denied that he was a "speculator in stocks" and called the loan "a strictly business affair." A fuller explanation was forthcoming several days later, as Payn granted Johnston permission to publish the letter of September 18, 1899, in which he had sought William C. Whitney's aid. At that time Payn had exhausted his funds in covering stocks which had fallen in value since their purchase on margin some months before; his wife was so ill that he could not leave her a day to save himself from bankruptcy; and in response to this appeal State Trust had taken over the Payn account from his stock broker, with Whitney in effect lending Payn $100,000 to make up the necessary collateral. The loan in no way involved the American Surety Company, contended Johnston, who later informed Root that Whitney's sympathy had gone out to Payn because his own wife had recently died. American Surety's President Lyman backed up Johnston's contention: at one time American Surety had been "quite largely interested" in State Trust, he stated, "but we have not been for many months . . . this company is absolutely independent and distinct from the trust company." [23]

But even if Payn had used personal rather than official influence

[22] *New York Tribune* and New York *World*, January 16, 1900; *New York Tribune*, January 17, 1900; *New York Times*, January 18, 1900 (RS). Kling had all this information prior to the Andrews investigation; see the statements of Andrews and Johnston, *New York Tribune*, January 18, 1900.

[23] *New York Tribune*, January 15, 16, 17, 1900; Johnston to Root, February 20, 1900, Root MSS.

to obtain the loan, a paper as impartial as the *Brooklyn Eagle* could ask embarrassing questions. It would have taken no less than $100,000 to buy these speculative stocks on margin, the *Eagle* estimated, yet the superintendent of insurance had been "a poor man" when he took office three years before: "Where did Payn get the money for the original margins?" In view of his official responsibilities, why was he speculating so heavily in Electric Storage Battery, Metropolitan Street Railway, and United States Express? Why did his appeal to Whitney meet with a generous response, and "why does the State Trust Company not call the loan, now that the margin of safety has disappeared?" [24]

The closest thing to a reply came from the *Troy Times*, which declared that Payn's privacy had been "ruthlessly torn open." Upstate Democratic papers already supporting Payn scoffed at the loan's seriousness, but the way in which Republican machine organs avoided any but the barest reference to the incident demonstrated just the opposite. G.O.P. leaders knew that sentiments similar to the *Eagle's* were widespread, and that the governor's power in the matter was greatly strengthened. On paper he still lacked the votes to confirm, but that could change now if he openly assaulted Payn's position. "When I go to war," Roosevelt remarked on January 15, "I try to arrange it so that all the shooting is not on one side." [25]

[24] *Brooklyn Eagle*, January 18, 1900 (RS). For the *Eagle's* earlier attitude on Payn, see November 25 and December 14, 1899 (RS).

[25] *Troy Times*, January 19, 1900; *Albany Argus*, January 18, 1900; *Rochester Union and Advertiser*, January 16, 19, 1900; *Albany Evening Journal*, January 15, 1900. Roosevelt to Lodge, January 22, 1900; to Slicer, January 15, 1900; both TR MSS. John A. McCall of the New York Life Insurance Company even feared that Roosevelt intended to launch a general attack on the industry, but as George W. Perkins soon discovered, the governor had no such intention. See Roosevelt, *Autobiography*, pp. 318–320; John A. Garraty, *Right-Hand Man: The Life of George W. Perkins* (New York, 1957), pp. 74–78. Roosevelt's autobiographical account of this particular incident, based largely upon a

More fearful than ever of a shooting war, Boss Platt resumed his effort to compose the dispute peaceably. On January 16 Odell and George W. Dunn arrived at Albany to go into a long conference with Payn. Within two days' time, Capitol newsmen were reporting some progress on compromise: Payn was willing to turn over the office to his chief deputy, while Roosevelt would name an acceptable candidate "as he had been trying to get it [the organization] to do for months." These maneuvers excited the New York *Evening Post*'s scorn, especially when it became known that on January 20 Roosevelt would "take his life in his hands" at another "bloody breakfast" with Platt ("a tyrannous boss") and Odell ("an unblushing spoilsman and corruptionist"). The governor's conduct "has been terribly lacking in the soldierly frankness and political courage that we should so like to see in him," asserted the *Post*, as it called on Roosevelt to forsake talks with Platt and carry the fight to the people.[26]

But as he explained to a friend afterward, Roosevelt went to the conference agreeable to an "honest compromise." He refused to compromise by appointing a man like Payn in his place, such as his deputy, "because I regard Payn as embodying the type of political corruptionist who looms up as of especially sinister significance in our American life." But if the machine leaders objected to Saxton, the governor was "perfectly willing to take any honest and efficient man" they would accept. "I . . . have offered to select any one of a *few men*," he added, "most of whom are straight organization republicans, who would probably not support me politically . . . if I got into a quarrel with Senator Platt; but who

Perkins to Roosevelt letter of April 8, 1913 (*ibid.*, p. 398n25), assigns too great an importance to the life-insurance limitation bill.

[26] *New York Tribune* and *New York Herald* (RS), January 18, 1900; New York *Evening Post*, January 19, 1900 (RS).

would administer the office in a perfectly clean and business-like manner." [27]

The elderly boss refused to commit himself to this offer, but before the conference on January 20 broke up he knew the governor's terms. Platt and Odell were to have until Tuesday, January 23, to accept one of the proffered names. If they failed to do so, then Roosevelt would take it that they stood with Payn and would send in his own personal selection to the senate.[28]

Judge Charles T. Saxton thoroughly approved this course. He graciously bowed out of the running when he learned that the machine objected to his candidacy. And in a letter two days later he suggested to the governor that Hendricks would be a good compromise nominee, for "Payn would as soon have him appointed as anybody." Roosevelt had not mentioned Hendricks on the 20th, without doubt because the Syracuse banker had already declined to serve, but he readily agreed with Saxton. "I do not know whether he would accept," the governor noted, "but I shall see about it at once." [29]

This was January 23, the last day Platt had to act. Roosevelt promptly got in touch with Hendricks, who made no immediate reply. At the same time the governor must have communicated with Odell regarding the Republican leader from Syracuse. According to Roosevelt, he met by prearrangement that evening with Odell at the Union League Club in New York City for a final conference. For half an hour they argued, as Odell contended that

[27] Roosevelt to Florence La Farge, January 22, 1900, TR MSS. The italicized words are too indistinct in the typewritten microfilm copy for absolute certainty.

[28] *New York Herald,* January 27, 1900 (RS); *New York Tribune,* January 23, 1900; New York *Sun,* January 21, 1900 (RS).

[29] Saxton to Roosevelt, January 20, 22, 1900; Roosevelt to Saxton, January 23, 1900; all TR MSS. (LC).

Platt would never yield and was certain to win the fight, bringing Roosevelt's career to a "lamentable smash-up." At last Roosevelt said that "nothing was to be gained by further talk" and rose to go. He had opened the door to leave when Odell stopped him: "Hold on! We accept. Send in . . . [Hendricks]. The Senator is very sorry, but he will make no further opposition!" [30]

The pith of this autobiographical account is without doubt accurate. Whether the conference occurred at the Union League Club (a not impossible feat), or in Newburgh, or even over the phone makes little actual difference. The fact remains that on Tuesday evening Odell notified Roosevelt and Hendricks that the senator was ready to support a successor to Payn. After an investigation of "business complications" Hendricks accepted by phone on Wednesday, January 24, the same day that Roosevelt agreed not to submit his name until the following Monday so that over the weekend Platt might have a final talk with Lou Payn. "We shall have 26 of the 27 republican votes," the governor assured the boss, "and my present information and belief is that the opposition will go absolutely to pieces, for the democrats are now satisfied that Payn is beaten, and they will of course drop him at once." [31]

Most New Yorkers did not know that agreement had been reached, but it was still an unfortunate moment for the Rev. Charles H. Parkhurst to wire the governor: "If you distinctly, uncompromisingly and promptly throw down the gauntlet to T. C. Platt the State will stand by you. 'Choose ye this day whom ye

[30] *New York Tribune*, January 24, 1900; Roosevelt, *Autobiography*, p. 317. Roosevelt mistakenly places the time of this meeting in an evening following a day conference with the senator.

[31] On Odell's whereabouts on the twenty-third, see *New York Times* and *New York Sun*, January 24, 1900, and *New York Press*, January 25, 1900 (all RS). Hendricks to Roosevelt, January 23, 1900, TR MSS. (LC); *New York Herald*, January 27, 1900 (RS); Roosevelt to Platt, January 24, 1900, TR MSS.

will serve.'" Published in the papers on January 25, for Roosevelt this message only confirmed his opinion that Parkhurst was a "professional impracticable." "If . . . I had yelled and blustered as Parkhurst and the similar dishonest lunatics desired," the governor wrote, "I would not have had ten votes." Moreover, "If I had not carried the big stick the Organization would not have gotten behind me." Parkhurst quoted Scripture, but it was the sage advice of the West African proverb that Roosevelt had been following: " 'Speak softly and carry a big stick; you will go far.' " [32]

Those who wanted to destroy boss rule were of course dissatisfied at the nomination and unanimous confirmation of Hendricks. The switch from Saxton to Hendricks was probably necessary, conceded the Rev. Thomas Slicer, but "Mr. Platt is too much deferred to, in appearance at least, for the moral quiet of the people who profoundly disbelieve in Mr. Platt's leadership." This disquietude affected the *New York Tribune,* which said the governor detracted from the dignity of his office when he went to New York to see Platt. It also affected an independent paper like the *Binghamton Herald,* which deplored the way the onetime Rough Rider "lamely surrenders" to the senator. In New York City the *Evening Post* and its companion the *Nation* criticized the governor's "lack of backbone"; Hendricks' "unsullied personal character, high business standing and ambitions to make a good record in public office" should make him a fine superintendent, but "good man as he is . . . the selection of Mr. Hendricks remains a signal triumph for the machine." [33]

It suited the Democratic party organs to agree. Unembarrassed

---

[32] Roosevelt to Lyman Abbott, January 13, 1900; to Low, January 25, 1900; to Henry L. Sprague, January 26, 1900; all TR MSS.

[33] Slicer to Roosevelt, January 27, 1900, TR MSS. (LC); *New York Tribune,* January 30, 1900; *Binghamton Herald,* January 27, 30, 1900; New York *Evening Post,* January 29, 1900; *Nation* 70:83 (February 1, 1900).

by its former defense of Lou Payn, the *Albany Argus* made fun of the "humbug" of a governor who claimed to have won when actually Platt had named the candidate and would see that he was confirmed. The boss had "dictated" Hendricks in retribution for Payn's aid to Black, charged the *Brooklyn Citizen,* but the public gained nothing because both the incumbent and his successor were "thorough-paced politicians." [34]

But most Republican and independent Democratic editors found Roosevelt's methods praiseworthy. The *Schenectady Daily Union* even called him a "political genius," while the *Utica Herald* and the *Albany Evening Journal* complimented "the tact displayed by the governor in accomplishing his purpose," and the *Brooklyn Times* termed his "the best method under the circumstances." The *Post's* contention that Roosevelt should have instituted war upon Platt brought emphatic denials from the *Brooklyn Eagle* and the *New York Times.* "This is not an issue that can be taken 'to the people,'" affirmed the *Times,* for Payn would have remained in office had that tactic been pursued. "To have compelled the machine to support the best man proposed because it was powerless to aid any poorer candidate is a triumph for the Governor and for the cause of clean politics." [35]

[34] *Albany Argus,* January 27, 1900; *Brooklyn Citizen,* January 30, 1900 (RS).

[35] *Schenectady Daily Union,* February 2, 1900 (RS); *Brooklyn Times,* January 30, 1900 (RS); *Utica Herald,* January 31, 1900; *Albany Evening Journal,* January 31, 1900; *New York Times* [n.d.], *Brooklyn Eagle,* January 30, 1900 (RS).

CHAPTER VI The Honest Broker

The brush with State Trust in the Payn dispute typified the experience of the governorship, for corporate interests were inextricably enmeshed in the processes of state government. On taking office Roosevelt had no special goal in legislation affecting corporations. What he did have was an attitude, an approach, a stance toward controversial issues of corporate privileges and regulation. His role, as he conceived it, was that of an honest broker among contending factions; his aim, a just yet acceptable compromise. That object accorded well with his character. In pursuing it, he would further clarify and develop his philosophy about government's relation to business.

These issues of corporate privilege and regulation had long been a fruitful source of controversy. Many requests for franchises had proved so outrageous that the public was automatically suspicious of the "grab" potentialities of any such bill: at first recognition a howl of protest arose. Measures designed to regulate or restrain business enterprise also had gained a bad repute. Too frequently such efforts were the work of blackmailing politicians, the "Black Horse Cavalry," striking to be bought off by the affected interests. To distinguish sincere attempts at state regulation was not always easy, even for a member of the legislature. At times, too, political motives were involved, making disinterested appraisal the more difficult.[1]

[1] See Roosevelt, *Autobiography*, pp. 77–84.

Political revenge alone inspired one regulatory bill introduced in 1899. Directly after the election, editorials advocating passage of a "pure beer" law appeared in numerous Republican party papers, and soon Platt issued a statement endorsing the move. It was at once charged that the Boss intended to retaliate against the brewers for the support they had given Van Wyck during the campaign. That was no doubt the machine's intent, but at a conference in January, Platt and Roosevelt agreed, reportedly at the insistence of the governor, that neither "pure beer" nor higher license proposals would be party measures. The only bill to get through the legislature to the executive chamber was Coggeshall's, which required that fermented liquors be made from pure hops. Despite Odell's importunity, Roosevelt vetoed it because the Public Health Law already contained a practically identical provision.[2]

Regulatory proposals for public utilities represented a complex of politics, "strikes," and reform. Several bills sponsored by Democrats to reduce the price of illuminating gas in New York City and Brooklyn were considered to be strikes, for a law of 1897 had adequately checked corporate abuse in this respect. Republican Assemblyman Delaney's cheaper gas bill for Syracuse had more legitimate backing, as did the reduction in telephone rates in Greater New York advocated by Democratic Senator Wagner. The *New York Tribune* agreed that the New York Telephone Company's rates were excessive but thought Wagner's flat rate of $50 per 1000 calls too radical a limit; it favored instead another proposal which would institute a three-man state board to investigate and enforce maximum rates in cities and towns but would

[2] *Utica Herald*, November 12, 1898; *Rochester Union and Advertiser*, November 18, 1898; New York *World*, November 11, 1898; New York *Evening Post* and *New York Tribune*, January 22, 1899; *Albany Evening Journal*, February 28, March 15, 1899; *Public Papers* (1899), pp. 125–126; Roosevelt to Coggeshall, May 27, 1899, TR MSS.

allow phone companies a 10 percent profit on actual investment.[3]

Neither gas nor telephone bills got by the legislature. The assembly committee on electricity, gas, and water supply bottled up cheaper gas proposals other than Delaney's, which passed the lower house only to have the senate fail to take action. Similarly the senate finance committee signed the death warrant of the proposed state telephone commission by striking out the appropriation and then having it referred to the committee on miscellaneous corporations, which was familiarly known as the "Committee on Miscellaneous Corpses." Adverse reports on both telephone bills subsequently appeared, and Republicans and Democrats in equal numbers joined to effect final defeat.[4]

With the legislature so obviously hostile to corporate regulation, it was not until the fight arose over the four trolley tracks on Amsterdam Avenue between 72nd and 125th Streets in New York City that the governor had an opportunity to participate. Residents of this area had entered no protest against these lines as long as horses drew the cars. Nor had they taken immediate alarm when first W. C. Whitney's Metropolitan Street Railway Company, which owned the two inside tracks, and then its rival the Third Avenue Company obtained permission to convert to electric trolleys. Only after the conversion was underway did the citizenry awake to the attendant dangers, particularly for the many children who had to cross Amsterdam Avenue for church, school, and play.[5]

---

[3] New York *Evening Post*, February 4, 16 and March 1, 1899; *Syracuse Journal*, April 26, 1899; *New York Tribune*, February 4, 1899.

[4] New York *Evening Post*, February 16 and April 25, 27, 1899; *New York Tribune*, March 3, 23, 1899; *Senate Journal* (1899), pp. 809–811. On the exorbitant rates of the New York Telephone Company, see *Inquiry into Telephone Service and Rates in New York City by the Merchants Association of New York* (June 1905), pp. 37–38.

[5] Harry J. Carman, *The Street Surface Railway Franchises*, Columbia University Studies in History, Economics and Public Law, vol. LXXXVIII, no. 1 (New York, 1919), ch. viii.

Initial protests to city officials accomplished nothing, nor would the two companies agree to joint use of but one set of tracks. So under the leadership of the Rev. John P. Peters of St. Michael's Protestant Episcopal Church at Amsterdam and 99th Street a Citizens' Committee formed to appeal to the state legislature. Several large property-owners along Amsterdam Avenue—including Columbia University and St. Luke's Hospital—retracted their consent to the conversion and joined the movement. Further support came from a number of prominent reformers and labor leaders, many of them attracted less by the immediate problems than by the larger issue of the People against the Corporations.[6]

The contending corporations each had its strength. Through Platt and its counsel, Ed Lauterbach, the Third Avenue Company enjoyed powerful support within the Republican organization. Metropolitan, on the other hand, relied chiefly upon Tammany Democrats, but of course, it contributed to G.O.P. campaigns and retained Elihu Root as its chief counsel. When the Rev. Mr. Peters implied that Root might presume upon the governor's friendship to advance Metropolitan's interests, Roosevelt replied that Root "is always careful to state to me, if he is retained on one side of any question that comes before me, that he shall not advise me as a friend." Still it was no disadvantage for this company controlling three-quarters of New York City's railways to have a legal adviser so respected by the governor.[7]

At Albany the Citizens' Committee found its path strewn with

[6] *The Political Nursery,* April 1899; New York *Evening Post,* November 15, 23, 1898; *New York Tribune,* February 2 and March 3, 22, 1899; New York *World,* March 6, 1899. The companies had obtained consents to the conversion from a majority of the frontage; see Roosevelt to Paul Dana, March 22, 1899, TR MSS.

[7] Mark Hirsch, *William C. Whitney: Modern Warwick* (New York, 1948), p. 455; Odell's testimony, *Barnes* v. *Roosevelt,* pp. 1835–36; Roosevelt to Peters, March 15, 31, 1899, TR MSS.

difficulties. As early as January a bill was introduced which would prohibit Third Avenue's conversion of the two outside tracks and would direct the courts to decide which company should use the remaining tracks. Roosevelt publicly approved of this solution, but the two companies did not. Guided by Root, Metropolitan proposed an amendment which in effect would drive its rival off Amsterdam Avenue. The Third Avenue Company countered with a change authorizing it, as compensation for any loss of its rights, to seek the use of the other's tracks. In late March a coalition of Republicans and Tammany Democrats put Metropolitan's version through the senate, but such was Third Avenue's influence with the G.O.P. that the assembly appeared unlikely to second that action. Thus the grave possibility arose that the legislature would not complete any move to forestall four electrified tracks.[8]

Assuring the four-track opponents that they would get some relief even if he had to call an extra session, Roosevelt continued to try as an honest broker to effect an equitable solution. In the "interests of justice" he had always maintained that the courts, not the legislature, should determine which company would remain on the Avenue. He had also endeavored vainly to get the two railways to settle their differences in conference. Now he bluntly informed the Republican leaders in the lower house that in his opinion they could not properly decide that the Third Avenue must be the trolley to relinquish its rights. His pronouncement had a telling effect, for the assembly committee on railroads at once requested a meeting with senate representatives to frame a compromise.[9]

The conference report subsequently approved unanimously by

[8] *New York Tribune,* March 10, 13, 1899.

[9] Roosevelt to Dana, March 22, 1899; to Peters, March 31, 1899; to Root, April 1, 1899; all TR MSS. *New York Tribune,* March 30, 31, 1899.

both houses substantially fulfilled the governor's specifications. The threat of four tracks was effectively removed, to the relief of the trainloads of citizens who had journeyed to Albany proclaiming "Life and Limb versus the Railroads." The courts, moreover, would have jurisdiction over the adjustment between the two companies. Certain of Root's amendments which Roosevelt had backed "heartily" were rejected "to my great chagrin," but the governor was relieved to affix his signature to the bill, closing a ticklish episode in political maneuvering.[10]

Privileges and regulation were but opposite faces of the same corporate coin, but since the legislative odds were against regulatory efforts, privilege most often turned up to trouble the governor. At times these bills conferred broad powers, such as those granted the General Carriage Company to initiate the cab business in New York, yet the majority of them were enacted with few if any questions raised. If no dissatisfaction was expressed during or after the legislative process, Roosevelt usually had no cause to suspect a measure's propriety. In consequence he relied heavily upon the vigilance of friends, press, and community, and his constant concern was with bills that aroused opposition.

When the controversy over a corporation grant involved an upstate community, Roosevelt as a rule took no part until the measure came to him for signature. He would then invite the interested parties to appear at the executive chamber; the arguments presented at these hearings, together with the opinions of state officials, formed the basis for his decisions. In this fashion he decided that the International Traction Company could run a street railway through the state reservation at Niagara Falls, but that the Mather

[10] Roosevelt to Platt, April 4, 1899; to Root, April 5, 1899; both TR MSS. Chapter 371, *Laws of New York* (1899). A year later Metropolitan leased the Third Avenue.

Power Bridge Company should not construct an experimental span over the Niagara River at Buffalo to test the commercial feasibility of waterwheel power. He also vetoed a bill to permit a Troy-Albany street railway line to build a new bridge across the Hudson at Troy.

This veto, administered primarily upon the advice of the superintendent of public works that the structure would interfere with canal traffic, found favor with the Troy press. But Roosevelt felt he owed a personal letter of explanation to Robert C. Pruyn, the president of the railway company and a powerful figure in business and Republican politics, at whose Adirondacks estate Roosevelt and his wife had just spent a delightful weekend. "To my very real regret I was unable to sign the bridge bill," Roosevelt asserted; he had heard nothing but protests against it from Troy, while Colonel Partridge would never approve the kind of bridge proposed or the location. "I am more sorry over it," the governor concluded, "than for any bill that has been before me this winter." [11]

Roosevelt's greatest concern was over corporation grants affecting New York City; when these aroused controversy he investigated at once. A measure of this type was the one designed to broaden the field of savings-bank investment still further by including among permissible securities the mortgage bonds of ten major railroads. Supposedly this bill was in the interest of savings banks, which had found it so difficult to maintain a 4 percent interest rate on deposits that the legislature had previously authorized them to invest in the municipal securities of out-of-state cities and the mortgage bonds of certain New York state railroads. But on March

[11] Of the four Troy papers, only the *Troy Observer,* March 12, 1899 (RS) favored the bridge bill. On Pruyn, see *Troy Times,* May 4, 29, 1899; Roosevelt to Pruyn, May 27, 1899, TR MSS.

23 the president of the Savings Bank Association of New York, J. Harsen Rhoades, was quoted as saying that it had been framed "chiefly at the insistence of the railway companies mentioned, for the purpose of enabling them to widen the field of investment of their bonds." Rhoades admitted that there would be "some advantage to us in widening the scope of our possible investments," but bankers feared the inclusion of "small and unimportant railways" such as the Fonda, Johnstown, and Gloversville, a thirty-mile line tacked onto the measure in the senate committee on banks; though backed by the New York Central, this amendment would set a poor precedent.[12]

The governor soon heard from his brother-in-law Douglas Robinson that in the City there was "great division of opinion" over this bill and "much talk as to some securities being let in which ought not to be let in." Roosevelt immediately asked the assembly majority leader to speak to Rhoades. At the same time he wrote Odell that "Merritt Trimble who is a big savings bank man should be seen and also the President of the Bowery Savings Bank." "We ought to get the leading representatives of the savings banks committed in favor of the bill," Roosevelt concluded; "Otherwise, if any disaster should occur it would redound greatly to our discredit."[13]

Roosevelt's fears dissipated before the assurance that Rhoades really approved the bill; the executive committee of the Savings Bank Association had prepared it originally, and the bank officials only feared more amendments that would force them to oppose it. Beyond the addition of the Fonda, Johnstown, and Gloversville

[12] Weldon Welfling, *Savings Banking in New York State* (Durham, N.C., 1939), pp. 24–27; Chapter 236, *Laws of New York* (1898); New York *World*, March 23, 1899; *Senate Journal* (1899), p. 835.
[13] Roosevelt to Odell, March 31, 1899, TR MSS.

no others occurred, so in the absence of further protests the governor signed the measure. Piecemeal enactment after this fashion was not the best policy, but savings-bank officials were slow to awake to that fact.[14]

The savings-bank bill paled into insignificance beside the corporate grants sponsored at the 1899 session by the Long Island Railroad Company, the rapid transit commissioners, and the Consolidated Gas Corporation. In varying degrees each of these three measures was suspect of being a "grab." Each involved financial interests of great magnitude. And each raised the question of franchise taxation, which was to bulk so large in Roosevelt's administration.

The Long Island desired to tunnel under the East River into Manhattan in order to expedite service and relieve Atlantic Avenue in Brooklyn of its railway congestion. But the company was unwilling to initiate this ambitious project unless there were legislative changes in the Greater New York Charter of 1897, which forbade municipal grants of franchises for a period longer than 25 years. In a bill introduced by Marshall of Brooklyn, it sought an unlimited franchise. Though many observers feared that the bill's wording might apply to subway rights as well as East River tunnels, the *New York Tribune* declared that the tunnel would be of such "incalculable benefit" as to be justifiable even on the Long Island Railroad's terms.

The rapid-transit commissioners sought a similar exemption in order that private capital might undertake the first underground railroad. The laws of 1891 and 1894 setting up the rapid-transit board had called for municipal construction, but the commissioners despaired of this method because the city was too close to its

[14] Roosevelt to Robinson, April 4, 1899, TR MSS.; Welfling, *Savings Banking*, p. 28.

maximum debt limit to raise the required funds. Hence they wished to be empowered to negotiate if necessary a contract with a private company. And since a corporation might well demand a perpetual franchise, the transit board wished to be relieved of the charter prohibition in this regard.[15]

Before the board's bill even appeared at Albany the senate minority leader revealed Tammany's opposition by submitting a counterproposal. Senator Grady thought private financing probably would be required, but he maintained that an exemption from the charter limit of fifty years should not be granted and was in fact not needed to attract a railroad company's investment. And Grady proposed that once the rapid-transit commissioners had disposed of the franchise, their existence should terminate and the city board of public improvements should assume the supervision of construction. To this came the immediate reply that Tammany only wanted to take control from the commissioners, who were men of a reform or business stamp. Advocates of municipal construction charged that Croker had purposely made that method impossible as long as he could not control it; he supported the private-capital method now solely out of a corrupt desire for jobs and graft.[16]

The "grab" possibilities were most obvious in a third bill, to "authorize the Astoria Light, Heat and Power Company of Queens County to supply gas and electricity conducted under and across the waters separating the boroughs of Queens, Manhattan and the Bronx in the city of New York." The New York *World* at once identified the originator as the Consolidated Gas Company, which it regarded as a part of the Standard Oil Trust because William Rockefeller and James Stillman of the National City Bank were

[15] *New York Tribune,* January 21, 22 and March 10, 11, 1899.
[16] *New York Tribune,* January 25 and February 16, 1899; New York *Evening Post,* February 16, 1899.

directors. The *World* further charged that under this bill Consolidated could tear up streets wherever and whenever it liked and could "condemn and seize any property in any part of those boroughs that may strike its fancy." [17]

To these and other accusations Consolidated replied through its counsel, Elihu Root, that it wanted to remove gas manufacture from its ten plants in Manhattan to the property recently purchased on Berrian's Island in Queens, because the city made things "most uncomfortable" at present with threats of new streets through and land condemnation of its properties. There was good precedent for the desired legislative grant, Root maintained, since Consolidated's chief rival, the New Amsterdam Company, already enjoyed this privilege through its ownership of the New York and East River Gas Company, which had acquired a tunnel franchise in 1892. This 1892 enactment was the model for the present bill, asserted Root, except that "we do not have any right to lay gas pipes in New York unless we first secure permission from the city authorities." [18]

Among the opponents of the Astoria project the most important, if the least noticeable, was the New Amsterdam Gas Company itself. This corporation organized in 1897 by Anthony N. Brady only did a quarter of the annual business of Consolidated Gas. But the directors of Consolidated were bent upon a monopoly, and New Amsterdam, together with Russell Sage's smaller Standard Gas Light, represented the only real competition. Anxious to eliminate a rival and acquire the valuable Ravenswood Tunnel under the East River, Consolidated had tried to buy Brady out. He had demanded too high a price. Thus the best explanation of

[17] New York *World,* February 4, 27, 1899. See Allan Nevins, *John D. Rockefeller,* 2 vols. (New York, 1940), II, 442; Frederick Lewis Collins, *Consolidated Gas Company of New York: A History* (New York, 1934).

[18] *New York Tribune,* February 24, 1899.

the Astoria bill was that Consolidated Gas was attempting to flank Brady's company through the legislature.[19]

Tammany supported Brady against Consolidated. Brady's political affiliation with Croker and Murphy before the 1898 convention had been close. Moreover, though Croker later maintained on the witness stand that he sold his New Amsterdam stock "at least ten days" before the Astoria bill came up to Albany, it is not unlikely that both he and his friends had a financial interest involved. So Croker made the bill a party measure: only one Tammany assemblyman dared to favor the proposal, and he was afterward asked to resign from the Hall.[20]

Among the bill's opponents were many citizens, however, who were solicitous of the city's best interest. They pointed out that the New York and East River Gas Company had agreed to pay three percent of its gross receipts to the city for this privilege, a part of the "model" which Root's draft had eliminated. And they became especially anxious as they observed what an industrious lobby was being promoted in Astoria's behalf at Albany. The City Club of New York's legislative committee put the measure on its undesirable list, and the *Troy Times,* reflecting perhaps a particular interest of the Payn-Black faction, took comfort that there was a watchful governor in the chair.[21]

By mid-March each of the three corporate-grant bills had been reported out of committee favorably and the governor was ready to act. "Will you please give me the answers to the enclosed criticism of the Astoria bill, marked with blue pencil?" he asked as he

[19] Collins, *Consolidated Gas,* pp. 316, 343; New York *World,* December 21, 1899.

[20] *Mazet Investigation,* pp. 546–547; *New York Tribune,* March 14, 15, 16, April 14, 1899.

[21] New York *Evening Post,* March 1, 1899; *New York Tribune,* March 17, 22, 25, 1899; *Troy Times,* March 9, 1899.

sent Elihu Root an editorial clipped from the *Troy Times*. "I don't want to be misled by any demagogic cry against capital on the one hand," added Roosevelt, "nor on the other do I want to sign a bill and find that I have either given away a franchise for which money should be paid to the public treasury or granted too extensive powers which could by any possibility be abused." At the same time he asked Douglas Robinson to help "find out about it—but *not* from men with stock in the rival gas companies!" [22]

Roosevelt's best source of advice on the Astoria proposal, and on the tunnel and rapid transit bills as well, was the able comptroller of the City of New York, Bird S. Coler. At a conference in March the comptroller made "certain suggestions" that, as Roosevelt informed the chairman of the senate committee on cities in a "horse-back judgment" afterward, "seemed to me to have some justification." Coler thought that the Long Island Railroad's bill "should be drawn so as not to estop us hereafter from taxing the receipts if they grow large." In the rapid-transit measure, Coler believed "there should be an arrangement for compensation to the city after earnings are shown," to which Roosevelt added that "my own belief is that it should be gross earnings, not net earnings." As for the Astoria bill, the comptroller maintained that though it was "to the interest of the city that the gas works . . . should be taken over to Queens," still the various privileges granted the company were great and should be taxed "in some intelligent way."

"All of this, I suppose is none of my business," remarked Roosevelt at the conclusion of this lengthy summary of Coler's views for the chairman of the committee on cities, Senator Stranahan, "for the bills are before the legislature body and not before me." In justification of his intervention, however, he thought that these bills "in their main purposes, subserve a useful public purpose,

[22] Roosevelt to Root, to Robinson, March 14, 1899, TR MSS.

and I only hope that they can be so drawn as to warrant my signing them should they come before me." [23]

At this point the governor was thinking primarily of a gross earnings tax on the particular franchises in each of these three bills. Odell, on the other hand, had suggested that "a general tax on franchises" be drawn which would cover other cases as well. Roosevelt was agreeable enough to Odell's plan, so long as there was "some understanding that we pass such a bill." "I know that Croker and our beloved opponents, both without and within our own party, are influenced by the basest motives in their opposition to these bills," Roosevelt wrote Odell on March 15, "and that they have schemes that really do invade the province of good government and work injury to the city." But, as Roosevelt put it, "I don't want us to be loaded with a bill that is a little bad, merely because they have a bill that is very bad." In particular, the governor desired to see the Astoria proposal properly amended, because when Mayor Van Wyck vetoed it "I want to be able to answer his veto message in such shape as to leave him not a leg to stand on." [24]

At his press conference on March 20 the governor dropped a broad hint that the Astoria bill should be amended so that the company would pay, as did the New York and East River Gas Company, a gross receipts tax to the city for its privilege. At this time the measure was still in senate committee, the assembly having passed it unamended five days before, by a vote of 103 to 41, with only two Republicans and most of the Tammany Democrats making up the opposition. On March 21 it appeared that the senate committee on miscellaneous corporations might heed Roosevelt's suggestion. However, when Senator Goodsell, Odell's man on that

[23] Roosevelt to Stranahan, March 15, 1899, TR MSS.
[24] Roosevelt to Platt, March 17; to Odell, March 15, 1899; both TR MSS.

committee, proposed the insertion of a three percent levy on Astoria's gross revenues, he was voted down five to one, Coggeshall, Wilcox, and Malby being the Republicans against, and Munzinger and "Dry-Dollar" Sullivan the Democrats. Obviously no amendment would be satisfactory to Tammany and the so-called "Tammany annex" with which Coggeshall, Wilcox, and Malby were often identified; what they wanted was the defeat of the measure.[25]

And defeat followed shortly after these same five men reported Consolidated Gas's bill adversely to the floor. The committee had found that the company would "really not pay any tax" under the three percent levy suggested by the governor, Senator Coggeshall maintained; the tax was simply "an attempt to bunco him." More than that, Coggeshall was "prepared to show that this is one of the worst bills ever introduced." Thereupon eleven Republicans joined the Democrats to kill the Astoria bill for that session.[26]

In the tunnel and rapid-transit bills, Odell's suggested "general tax on franchises" would satisfy that demand, but now a bid by Metropolitan Street Railway Company to the rapid-transit commissioners turned Roosevelt's attention to a further question: the length of lease. On March 28 Whitney's company offered to build the subway on condition of a lease in perpetuity and no greater payment to the city than five percent of the gross receipts after provision for a five percent deduction for construction costs and operating expenses. Not only were these hard bargaining terms, but within them, as Comptroller Coler said, were "half a dozen franchises." And Roosevelt had already been amply warned by Seth Low and others against a perpetual franchise for either the tunnel or the rapid-transit bills. On April 17 the governor announced that

[25] *New York Tribune,* March 16, 21, 22, 1899.
[26] *New York Tribune,* March 25, 1899; *Senate Journal* (1899), pp. 884–886.

he would only approve a lease of fifty years duration, whereupon the Metropolitan promptly withdrew its bid.[27]

Despite protests from the rapid-transit commissioners that anything less than a franchise in perpetuity would delay their project indefinitely, Roosevelt would only compromise to the extent that once the fifty-year lease was up, re-evaluations and renewals on a twenty-five-year basis could be arranged. This and another amendment designed to open competition to corporations other than the Metropolitan and Third Avenue companies were drafted under Roosevelt's direction and introduced in the senate. After a heated debate in which the minority leader called the governor a "Pooh Bah" who was dictating to the legislature, the upper chamber adopted the amendments by a vote of 37 to 7. Then the rapid-transit bill swept through both houses almost unanimously.[28]

The fate of the measure rested in the hands of Mayor Van Wyck, who after a hearing vetoed it without any explanation. It is most unlikely that he was influenced by the labor leaders and the Social Reform Club representative who had advocated a veto because they wanted municipal ownership. Rather, he probably believed that his previous approval of the tunnel bill—which after Roosevelt's ultimatum had also been amended to limit the franchise to a 50/25 year basis—would cover subways as well and would thus deprive the rapid-transit commissioners of supervisory power. But Roosevelt expressed doubt that the Long Island's tunnel bill

[27] *New York Tribune,* March 28 and April 1, 18, 1899; *Outlook* 61:8–9, 11 (April 15, 1899); New York *Evening Post,* April 27, 1899; Low to Roosevelt, March 21, 1899, Low MSS.; Roosevelt to Low, March 22, 1899, TR MSS.— "*just* what I wanted . . . simply invaluable to me." Roosevelt to F. W. Holls, April 12, 17, 1899; to Slicer, April 18, 1899; all TR MSS. In his defense of Metropolitan's bid, Hirsch (*William C. Whitney,* pp. 518–520) neglects to mention that Metropolitan would own valuable subway conduits free of tax.
[28] *New York Tribune,* April 19, 26, 1899.

would thus apply. The lesson he drew from the veto was that his resistance to a perpetual franchise was vindicated, for if Van Wyck could object to a "mild" fifty-year lease then the original proposal of the rapid-transit commissioners could not possibly have succeeded.[29]

In his handling of the rapid-transit bill the governor had hewed remarkably well to the "just middle" which he had assured William Howard Taft was his general aim. On the one hand there had been the labor and liberal reform elements that championed municipal ownership, on the other the big-business opinion, represented in such a paper as the *New York Times,* that regarded the commissioners' original bill as the best solution. Roosevelt had cut his own path between the two. In so doing he won high praise from Senator John Ford of New York City, who believed that the rapid-transit commissioners were prejudiced in the Metropolitan Street Railway's behalf, and who along with Seth Low had contributed most to Roosevelt's determination. The passage of the amendments which the governor had sponsored, Ford declared, was "the greatest victory of the people against political influence and corporate power that I have ever witnessed since I have been a member of the Legislature." [30]

Since the governor had taken a stand at variance with Elihu Root's on these bills, the rumor soon arose that he had "lost faith in Mr. Root as a political adviser." Roosevelt himself was worried about their relations, which were noticeably cooler than during the first two months of office, and after his intervention against the Metropolitan Street Railway Company in the Amsterdam Ave-

[29] New York *Evening Post,* May 11, 1899; *New York Tribune,* May 12, 13, 1899.

[30] Roosevelt to Taft, January 31, 1899, TR MSS.; *New York Tribune,* April 18, 26 and May 12, 1899; New York *Evening Post,* May 12, 1899; letter of April 25 to New York *World,* April 26, 1899.

nue affair he wrote Root a most conciliatory letter. At every place their paths crossed on these corporation measures, they seemed to be on opposite sides.[31]

Hence, it may have afforded Roosevelt some satisfaction that in the controversy which subsequently flared up over the state's sale of sixteen and one-half acres of underwater land to the Astoria Gas Company, he was able to side with the corporation. In October 1899 Consolidated Gas had applied to the state land commissioners for a grant of land immediately offshore the East River's Berrian's Island, where it was to erect the huge Astoria plant. At that time the land board had deferred action in order that it might investigate further Governor Roosevelt's suggestion that such property be leased rather than sold. However, in December the commissioners had approved the grant to the Astoria Company at the appraised price of $250 an acre: all that remained was for the governor to sign the letters patent.[32]

Although Roosevelt had no precedent for withholding approval, in New York the *World,* the *Journal,* and the *Herald* all exhorted him not to permit this "barefaced theft of public property"; they estimated the grant to be worth almost one thousand times the appraised value, and the *World* further reminded the governor of his suggestion in October that it was "questionable policy to alienate the land of the State." City Corporation Counsel Whalen also requested that action be deferred until the courts could dispose of legal objections he intended to raise; estimating the property to be worth $3,000,000, Whalen contended that the city bureau of docks and ferries, not the state land board, had jurisdiction over it.

[31] *New York Tribune,* March 25, 1899; New York *World,* March 24, 1899; Roosevelt to Root, April 1, 1899, TR MSS.

[32] *New York Tribune,* October 27, 1899. The commissioners were the lieutenant governor, speaker, secretary of state, comptroller, treasurer, attorney general, and state engineer.

And one of the state land commissioners even announced that he would ask the governor to have the land reappraised, since it was commonly asserted that the two Platt men who had made the original valuation had been prejudiced in behalf of the company.[33]

In his decision of December 26, 1899, the governor was sharply critical of the "extraordinary course" of the city corporation counsel "in writing me about this grant, although he has never communicated with me in reference to any previous grant, and in urging that I take action in reference to it such as I have never taken, and such as has never been suggested that I take, in reference to any other grant." Roosevelt strongly intimated that Whalen's activity was connected with the farflung war which New Amsterdam Gas had been waging with Consolidated Gas, and which was only to be resolved in 1900 through a merger of the Brady-Whitney-Ryan interests with the Rockefeller-Rogers group. For Whalen presumably took orders from Tammany, Tammany supported New Amsterdam, and as the governor said, "It is a matter of common notoriety that a rival gas company would have an immense pecuniary interest in securing a refusal of justice to the Astoria Gas Company."[34]

Roosevelt at the same time defended the land board's action as "entirely proper"; in fact, "any other action would have been a grave and flagrant wrong." The Astoria Gas Company had requested "nothing whatever which it has not been the immemorial custom of the State to grant in such cases." A review of comparable

[33] *New York Tribune,* October 27, November 27 and December 10, 12, 1899; New York *World,* December 9, 1899; *New York Herald,* December 10, 1899 (RS); *New York Journal,* December 8, 1899 (RS).

[34] On the battle of Brady and Rockefeller interests, see *New York Tribune,* May 2, 3, 4, 14 and November 24, 1899; R. R. Bowker, "The Piracy of Public Franchises," *Municipal Affairs* 5:886–899 (December 1901).

appraisals readily demonstrated that $250 an acre was "certainly a reasonable valuation from the standpoint of the public." There was not the slightest evidence that the City had ever considered doing anything with this land, whereas "it is greatly to the interest of the community to have the land improved . . . by the Astoria Company." Nor did the commissioners have the power to lease rather than to sell the property, Roosevelt asserted, and though he favored bestowing that power upon them where no improvement was contemplated, in other instances he did not consider it wise.[35]

"You hit right out so that the fellow that gets hit knows he's hit," wrote Frank H. Platt, who found the contrast with Governor Black's methods "exhilarating." Since the Boss's son had been counsel for the Astoria Company in this matter, his exuberance was understandable. Yet young Platt had found Roosevelt's decision to continue legal action to recover $1,000,000 in oleomargarine fines from Armour and Company in preference to an out-of-court settlement for $20,000 "equally admirable, even if it was not what I wanted." As the *Brooklyn Eagle* observed of the sale of land to Astoria Gas, the governor "makes out a good case for himself and for the company." Even the yellow press was stilled.[36]

In the long run, however, the most significant effect of the tunnel, rapid-transit, and Astoria Gas bills was that they directed Roosevelt's attention to the taxation of franchises as public policy. In his annual message in January 1899, the governor had declared that "No other question is of such permanent importance in the domestic

[35] Roosevelt to commissioners of the land office, December 26, 1899, in *Public Papers* (1899), pp. 212–219.

[36] F. H. Platt to Roosevelt, December 27, 1899, in TR MSS. (LC); *Brooklyn Eagle*, December 27, 1899 (RS). On the eventual failure of the suit against Armour, see *Rural New Yorker* 59:214 (March 24, 1900).

economy of our State as the question of taxation," yet he had come up with no specific proposal on this "exceedingly difficult subject." It was only as he puzzled over these grants of corporate privilege that he discerned a new and legitimate function of the state's power to tax. And this led him into a perilous struggle over the Ford franchise-tax bill.[37]

[37] *Public Papers* (1899), p. 7.

CHAPTER VII

The Ford Franchise-Tax Bill

It was on March 18, 1899, that Roosevelt first told reporters that he viewed "with favor the adoption of a system whereby corporations in this State shall be taxed on the public franchises which they control." He was not then thinking specifically of the measure which Senator John Ford of New York had introduced some two months before, and which ever since had remained in the committee on taxation and retrenchment. Nor did it appear likely, in the days immediately following, that he would do anything more at the 1899 session than support Platt's suggestion that a legislative commission investigate and report "to the next Legislature a proper scheme of taxation." It was only through a curious combination of circumstances that Roosevelt became committed to the Ford bill, so committed that he defied the organization in order to push it through. Then, in typical fashion, he retreated somewhat to enable Boss Platt to save face. More practical than any radical, yet more enlightened than most conservatives, he here demonstrated all the characteristics that would comprise "Roosevelt Republicanism."

When Roosevelt complained in his annual message in January that New York's tax system was "in utter confusion, full of injustices and of queer anomalies," he referred mainly to the old general-property levy, which as one authority declared "is beyond all doubt one of the worst taxes known in the civilized world." In theory this levy treated real estate and personal property uniformly throughout the state, but in practice local assessors had widely different standards. And because real estate was immovable and easily seen, it bore a greater tax burden than personalty, only three percent of which, it was estimated, was ever assessed. The state board of tax commissioners was powerless to remedy the faulty personal assessment, which in operation tended to favor urban areas and corporations at the expense of the farmer. Though the state board indirectly and partially corrected this disparity by increasing the real-estate valuations of the rich and populous counties such as New York, and decreasing those of the rural counties, this action merely increased the distrust between city and country.[1]

Commencing in 1880, the legislature had inaugurated a number of corporation taxes which supplemented the general property levy and thus helped to defray the increasing cost of governmental functions. Of necessity, however, the State of New York continued to rely heavily upon real estate and personalty taxes, the revenue from which in the fiscal year ending September 30, 1898, amounted to over $8,000,000 out of state receipts of $19,000,000. Barring the passage of an income-tax law such as Coggeshall (but few others) advocated, it appeared most unlikely that the state could relinquish these millions from the general property levy to local authorities. What was really needed at Albany was more money, and if this could be obtained through some improvement in the general tax system, so much the better.[2]

[1] *Public Papers* (1899), p. 7; E. R. A. Seligman, *Essays on Taxation*, 2 ed. (New York, 1897), pp. 4, 32, 36; Richard T. Ely, *Taxation in American States and Cities* (New York, 1888), pp. 176–187; *Report to the Legislature of New York by the Joint Committee on Taxation, January 15, 1900* (Albany, 1900), p. 5; H. A. E. Chandler, *The Equalization of the Tax Burden in the State of New York* (New York, 1916); Max West, "The Distribution of Property Taxes between City and Country," *Political Science Quarterly* 14:305–311 (June 1899); Harvey L. Lutz, *The State Tax Commission,* Harvard Economic Studies, XVII (Cambridge, 1918), 183–188.

[2] Frederick D. Bidwell, *Taxation in New York State* (Albany, 1918), pp.

Among those puzzling over this problem early in 1899 was Senator John Ford of New York City, who was inspired by Glasgow's example to find some way to tax franchises. In the Scottish city the taxation of municipal privileges provided all the revenues for local government. In New York, on the other hand, most of the valuable "monopolies" were "still in the possession of various corporations and with vested rights," Ford complained, "and therefore they are more beyond the control of the municipality than would be corporations with new franchises that might be granted." If only he could find a means to get at these old franchises "worth hundreds of millions," the great majority of property owners would benefit through increased valuations and possibly a reduced tax rate.[3]

Ford soon stumbled upon a peculiar feature of the New York tax law which, if amended, would serve his purpose. The "time-honored practice" of assessors had been to estimate the personalty of a corporation for the general-property tax by setting an "arbitrary valuation on the capital stock and deducting the value of the real estate." An 1891 decision of the court of appeals, however, held that not the capital stock but tangible assets were the proper basis for assessment. In effect this excluded intangible assets, principally franchises, from taxation as personalty. Nor could franchises be reached as real property, because the New York law under its definition did not so include them. To restore these corporate privileges "to the schedule of taxable property . . . where they were for more than forty years preceding 1891" became Ford's object.[4]

75–76; Seligman, *Essays*, pp. 152, 165, 170–171; *Manual for the Use of the Legislature of the State of New York, 1899* (Albany, 1899), pp. 664–665; *New York Tribune*, February 2, 1899; *Binghamton Herald*, February 7, 9, 1899; New York *Mail and Express*, February 6, 1899 (RS). In addition to the corporation taxes, inheritances bore a 5 percent tax, and a third of liquor license revenue went to the state.

[3] Ford quoted in New York *World*, January 17, 1899.

[4] John Ford, "Theodore Roosevelt's Feet of Clay," *Current History* 34:680

He might have framed an amendment to the tax law's famous Section 12 (Chapter 908, *Laws of 1896*), which set down the method of assessing the personalty of companies. Instead he chose to amend the legal definition of "real property" to include "the value of all franchises . . . to construct, maintain or operate" surface, underground or elevated railroads "in, under, above, upon, across, or through, any streets, highways, or public places . . . for conducting water, steam, heat, light, power, gas, oil, or other substances, or electricity for telegraphic, telephonic or other purposes." [5]

The reason for Ford's preference was plain. An amended Section 12 would still offer many loopholes in practice, whereas a corporation would find it difficult to evade a real estate assessment. And since New York law already treated wharfage rights as real property, Ford argued that it would be logical to extend this to other franchises. In late January he introduced his measure in the senate, which referred it for hearings to the committee on taxation and retrenchment. [6]

Over the next two months the New York *World,* the *New York Herald,* and in a less spectacular way the *New York Tribune* expressed approval of franchise taxation. At two hearings various New York City groups also supported the bill: the Central Federated Labor Union and District Assembly 49 of the Knights of

---

(August 1931); E. R. A. Seligman, "The Franchise Tax Law in New York," *Quarterly Journal of Economics* 13:446 (July 1899); Union Trust Company *v.* Coleman, 126 N.Y. 433; John DeWitt Warner, "The Ford Act: Taxation of Local Franchises," *Municipal Affairs* 3:279n (June 1899); *New York Tribune,* January 26, 1899.

[5] New York *World,* January 26, 1899. The word "across" was deleted in the version finally approved.

[6] Chandler, *Equalization of Tax Burden,* pp. 77–79; Seligman, "The Franchise Tax Law in New York," p. 448; John Ford, "The Taxation of Public Franchises," *North American Review* 168:730–734 (June 1899); *New York Tribune,* January 26, 1899; Warner, "The Ford Act: Taxation of Local Franchises," p. 276n.

Labor, the Real Estate Exchange and the West End Taxpayers Association, the Social Reform Club and the Association for the Public Control of Franchises. From corporation representatives, on the other hand, the committee heard protests, and north of the Bronx the Ford bill stirred no interest. Even in New York City the sentiment for tax reform did not coalesce around this one proposal: the *World* was campaigning chiefly against abuses of personalty assessment under the general property levy, while labor and reform elements found their attention deflected to the more immediate danger of the four trolley tracks on Amsterdam Avenue.[7]

The Ford measure might have continued to repose in committee had not the tunnel, rapid transit, and Astoria Gas bills coincidentally raised the question of "a general tax on franchises." Roosevelt was amenable to Odell's suggestion of this tax, as long as there was "some understanding that we pass such a bill"; that was why the governor remarked to reporters on March 18 that he favored "the adoption of a system whereby corporations in this State shall be taxed on the public franchises which they control." At the time Roosevelt was thinking of a tax on gross receipts rather than assessment as realty, yet his words appeared to give the Ford bill a boost. The taxation committee chairman at once repaired to the executive chambers, and on March 21 the senate received a favorable report on the Ford franchise-tax bill.[8]

His evident pleasure at the committee's quick response showed that as of March 21 Roosevelt contemplated the passage of a tax law at that legislative session. That did not mean that he favored Ford's method over any other; indeed, Roosevelt issued a warning that the method of local assessment under the Ford plan was dan-

[7] *New York Tribune,* February 17 and March 3, 1899; New York *Evening Post,* March 1, 1899.

[8] Roosevelt to Odell, March 5, 1899; to Platt, March 17, 1899; both TR MSS. *New York Tribune,* March 22, 23, 1899.

gerous because Tammany could "levy blackmail by discriminating in taxation for or against any particular corporation." What the governor did mean to indicate was that he favored some positive step toward franchise taxation that year.[9]

In his representations through Odell and then at a breakfast conference on March 24, however, Platt opposed this program. He decried the power which the Ford bill would put into the hands of Tammany. He further maintained that the problem of taxation had many facets and many possible solutions, all of which demanded careful investigation. He was willing to have a joint legislative committee "consider the whole question of taxation in order that a complete and intelligent law might be passed." But beyond that he would not go and, in particular, he wanted none of the franchise-tax bill, which he later described as "radical legislation . . . bound to strike the conservative business community . . . as an extreme concession to Bryanism." [10]

In view of Platt's opposition it did not seem to Roosevelt "as if any bill could be passed or agreed upon by the legislature" at that session. And in view of Platt's assurance (as Roosevelt afterwards put it) "that this Committee would be appointed and that a serious effort would be made to tax franchises," the governor agreed to support the organization proposal. Accordingly on March 27 he sent in a message recommending that a legislative commission investigate and report "to the next Legislature a proper scheme of taxation." The governor made it clear that he believed "a corporation which derives its powers from the State, should pay to the State a just percentage of its earnings as a return for the privileges it enjoys." He also gave the opinion—obviously in criticism of the

[9] *New York Tribune*, March 22, 1899; *New York Times*, March 21, 1899 (RS).
[10] Platt to Roosevelt, May 6, 1899, in *Barnes v. Roosevelt*, p. 2371.

Ford bill—that assessments on franchises should be determined by state rather than local authorities. But he concluded that the question of how these franchises should be taxed, whether as realty or on gross earnings or on some other basis, "can only be settled after careful examination of the whole subject." [11]

Conservative editors reacted favorably to this recommendation, the *New York Times* even declaring that the governor "brings hard common sense and a natural love of justice to the consideration of the subject and reaches a sound conclusion." But the papers that had endorsed the Ford bill expressed disagreement ranging from the mild rejoinder of the *Buffalo Express* to the blunt attack—"ROOSEVELT STOPS FRANCHISE TAX"—of the *New York Herald,* which at once attributed the move to Boss Platt's baneful influence. In a typical criticism the *New York Tribune* complained about the delay and called for immediate action before the corporations devised some means of evasion.[12]

Though Roosevelt preserved an official silence, these criticisms quickened his conscience. With some asperity he wrote the editor of *Leslie's Weekly* that it was "nonsense" to say he had interfered with the taxation of franchises; his message had provided "the one chance" to see that end achieved, and "the talk of the World, Herald, etc. is so utterly silly as not to be worthy one moment's serious consideration." More revealingly, he assured Paul Dana of the New York *Sun* that he was "inclined to think that Ford's bill is a good one" and he would "gladly" sign it if it came to him, "but

[11] Roosevelt to Platt, May 8, 1899; to Paul Dana, April 7, 1899; both TR MSS. *Public Papers* (1899), pp. 54–57.

[12] For favorable reactions, see *Troy Record, Troy Times, Watertown Times,* Rochester *Post Express, New York Times, Newburgh Daily Register* and *Albany Evening Journal,* March 28, 1899 (all RS). For criticisms, see New York *World,* March 28, 29 and April 2, 3, 1899; *Buffalo Express* and *New York Tribune,* March 29, 1899; *New York Herald,* March 28, 29, 1899 (all RS).

the men with whom I work in the legislature are not satisfied that the measure is right in its present shape." There is evidence that he confided also to the Albany correspondents that he would not oppose the Ford bill, but having submitted to the view that passage was unwise and improbable, Roosevelt made no further attempt to influence the senate's action.[13]

To his great astonishment, the senate on April 11 by a vote 33 to 11 approved the franchise-tax proposal. Various factors explained this unexpected development, but the fact that only two Republicans cast negative votes suggests that Platt's lieutenants, thinking it impolitic to kill the measure outright, preferred the indirect method of disagreement between the two houses and consequent inaction. Possibly they reasoned that since Tammany apparently favored the bill, an attempt to defeat it in the senate might well fail. Then, too, it was inadvisable to affront Ford and others supporting franchise taxation, at a time when the vote of every available Republican senator was needed to put across the state constabulary bill.[14]

The need for support for the state constabulary at least furnished Roosevelt with an explanation for his next move, a public announcement on April 14 that though the Ford bill was not in the best possible shape the assembly should pass it. The majority leader in the upper chamber, Senator Ellsworth, had suggested such a statement because "he thought we were being hurt by the impression that I had used my recommendation for the committee on taxation as a means of killing [the franchise-tax bill]," Roosevelt hastily informed Platt. "I told him I had kept silent because I understood our people in the Senate felt this to be the wisest course," the governor continued, "but that as they had joined in

[13] Roosevelt to John A. Sleicher, April 6, 1899; to Dana, April 7, 1899; both TR MSS. New York *World,* March 31, 1899; *New York Tribune,* April 15, 1899.

[14] *Senate Journal* (1899), p. 1336.

passing the bill I supposed the reason no longer obtained, and that I would gladly speak as he requested me to." Roosevelt then added that Ellsworth "thought it might have a favorable effect upon the other legislation pending, which was all the more necessary on account of the opposition to the State Constabulary." [15]

Had he been perfectly candid Roosevelt would have admitted that Ellsworth's request had furnished a convenient opportunity by which to ease his conscience over the Ford bill. The senate's action had reawakened the governor's interest in the whole problem. Immediately Roosevelt sought the aid of Seth Low, who referred him to Professor E. R. A. Seligman of Columbia University. On April 19 the governor sent Seligman a copy of the Ford franchise-tax bill.[16]

Meantime the Ford measure encountered expected difficulties in the assembly: it was tied up in committee as G.O.P. leaders promoted a rival bill, introduced by Rodenbeck of Monroe County, to amend Section 12 of the tax law to include specifically in the assessable personalty of a company "its franchises to construct, maintain, or operate any railroad or mains, pipes, tanks, conduits or wires." With some justification it was argued that this alternative proposal was superior because it applied to the right-of-way of steam railroads and thus would benefit rural counties, whereas the local taxes derived under Ford's plan would go almost exclusively to the cities. Yet, the proponents of the Rodenbeck proposal failed to mention that it would have little effect on steam railroads, because of their heavy bonded indebtedness, while the other interested corporations would certainly prefer this method to classification as real property. Nor could its advocates deny that to stifle the senate

[15] *New York Tribune,* April 15, 1899; Roosevelt to Platt, April 14, 1899, TR MSS.

[16] Roosevelt to Low, April 12, 14, 1899; to Seligman, April 19, 1899; to Platt, May 8, 1899; all TR MSS.

bill in favor of a substitute only eight days before the scheduled end of the legislative session would simply defeat a franchise tax of any kind.[17]

The governor had come to believe that the Republicans should recognize the principle of franchise taxation in some concrete fashion at this session. His own study of the problem had quieted the fears Platt had raised. Then, following his message of March 27, the "liberal" press had focused so much attention on the Ford bill that its defeat would confirm all the harsh things ever said about the Republican machine and its corrupt alliance with big business. And because of his own connection with the incident, it would expose Roosevelt increasingly to the criticism of the reform element.

Roosevelt was therefore pleased to find as the session entered its final week that Odell "agreed with me in the most unequivocal manner that some measure taxing franchises must be passed." At first Odell said he preferred the Ford bill, provided it was amended to give the taxing power to state authorities, but later that same afternoon he indicated that the Rodenbeck bill was more to his liking. To which Roosevelt replied "very well; that although I do not think it much of a measure, I would cordially back it if that was what the Organization wanted." [18]

But when the governor then asked the senate leaders to take up the Rodenbeck measure they "positively refused to do so and said that the Ford bill was what everyone wanted." Since Speaker Nixon and majority leader Allds in the assembly were just as determined to have the Rodenbeck version, the threat of legislative

---

[17] *New York Tribune,* April 13, 14, 15, 20, 1899; *Assembly Journal* (1899), pp. 2611, 3040; John Ford, "Taxation of Public Franchises," p. 732; Seligman, "The Franchise Tax Law in New York," pp. 448–449. As Seligman notes, bonded debt was deductible from the value of the capital stock for personal tax purposes under New York law.

[18] Roosevelt to Platt, May 8, 1899, TR MSS.

stalemate remained as serious as ever. The next day—Tuesday, April 25—Roosevelt formally requested Nixon and Presiding Officer Ellsworth to arrange a meeting that evening of several of the leading members of the two houses, to reach some agreement. He noted tactfully that his own preference was for the Ford bill: in his experience it was "always infinitely easier to tax realty and what is classed as realty than to tax personalty," Roosevelt asserted, and though he respected Assemblyman Kelsey's judgment that Ford's proposal would be unpopular in the rural areas, "Senators Higgins and Raines take very strongly the view that even for the country districts the Ford bill would be best, because it would amount to something and the Rodenbeck bill would amount to but little." Yet, the conferees failed to agree, and on Wednesday, April 26, the assembly committee on rules went through with its decision to report out the Rodenbeck instead of the Ford bill.[19]

By Thursday the sentiment for the Ford bill had attained such proportions that the assembly leaders had to retreat. That morning three assemblymen from New York City began the circulation of a petition to bring the measure out of the committee on rules. By noon they were said to have 112 signatures, or 12 more than the two-thirds majority required for such a move. At 2:15 P.M. a recess until 4:00 was called, and Nixon and Allds went down to the executive chamber to declare that "they could no longer withstand the pressure." They had "received orders not to pass" the franchise-tax bill but the situation was beyond control; they would have to report it to the floor, and they wanted the governor to share responsibility for this action. This Roosevelt agreed to do and the Ford bill was at last reported out of committee. A motion for unanimous consent to its immediate consideration was lost, however, when

[19] Roosevelt to Platt, May 8, 1899; to Nixon and Ellsworth, April 25, 1899; both TR MSS. *New York Tribune,* April 26, 27, 1899.

Kelly of Albany, representative of Anthony Brady's railway and utility interests, objected. Thus the Rodenbeck bill, which was on special order for the third reading, would still come up for prior consideration.[20]

To advance their measure the Ford bill managers turned to the governor. By now Roosevelt was convinced that the Rodenbeck bill would never get by the upper chamber. The senate leaders had assured him also "that if any amendment was made to the Ford bill . . . it meant simply its death." So when Assemblyman Fallows came in at 5:00 P.M. to say that "without an emergency message they could not pass the bill," the governor quickly dictated a message urging the lower chamber to pass the Ford bill at once. Had this message been read upon receipt, positive action might have resulted that evening. But in a desperate effort to follow machine dictates, the assembly leaders refused to have it read. "Exactly what became of it after it left my messenger's hands . . . I do not know; I believe it was torn up," Roosevelt later wrote Platt; "At any rate, the course was followed of refusing to entertain it." [21]

For several hours thereafter the assembly continued its deliberation on less consequential measures, the debate on which was finally broken off upon agreement of the majority and minority leaders that "no measure which should cause extended debate should be considered before tomorrow." Then, with Kelsey in the chair— Nixon had retired to the anteroom in a state of nervous collapse right after reporting the Ford bill—the Rodenbeck bill came up for action. To the consternation of Allds and Kelsey, Rodenbeck moved that the Ford bill be substituted for his own measure.

Immediately the chamber was in an uproar as Kelly of Albany

[20] *New York Tribune,* April 28, 1899; Roosevelt to Platt, May 8, 1899, TR MSS.; *New York Herald* (RS) and New York *World,* April 28, 1899.

[21] Roosevelt to Platt, May 8, 1899, TR MSS.

and two Kings County Democrats vociferously opposed, while several New York City men from both parties spoke for the motion. Allds collected his wits sufficiently to move a call of the house; as this proceeded, Nixon hurried in to hold a hasty conference at the speaker's desk. The upshot was that the Rodenbeck motion was laid aside until the next day, under the agreement that "political bills" that gave rise to debate would be so postponed, and amid cries for "yeas and nays" Kelsey summarily declared the adjournment.[22]

Any remaining doubt about the intent of the Republican leaders disappeared when Roosevelt discovered that his emergency message had not been read. At the same time he realized that if he continued to press the matter he would further endanger his political future. As he informed Platt afterwards, representatives of the affected corporations had admitted quite frankly that they intended to have no legislative recognition of franchise taxation, and they had "urged upon me that I personally could not afford to take this action for under no circumstances could I ever again be nominated for any public office, as no corporation would subscribe to a campaign fund if I was on the ticket." Having come thus far, however, and having been challenged so directly, Roosevelt saw "no alternative but to do what I could to secure the passage of the Ford bill without amendment—not that I altogether liked it, but that I thought it a great deal better than inaction." [23]

Accordingly a second message, much stronger in tone than the routine one of the previous afternoon, was prepared and sent directly to the assembly:

[22] *Assembly Journal* (1899), pp. 3573–77. The *Journal* is virtually useless for an understanding of what went on; for full accounts, see *New York Tribune* and *New York Herald* (RS), April 28, 1899.

[23] Roosevelt to Platt, May 8, 1899, TR MSS.

I learn that the emergency message which I sent last evening to the Assembly on behalf of the Franchise Tax Bill has not been read. I therefore send hereby another message upon the subject. I need not impress upon the Assembly the need of passing this bill at once. It has been passed by an overwhelming vote through the Senate. A large majority of the Assembly have signed a petition asking that it be put through. It establishes the principle that hereafter corporations holding franchises from the public shall pay their just share of the public burden. It is too late to try to amend or perfect the bill, even should such amendment or improvement be deemed desirable. It is one of the most important measures (I am tempted to say the most important measure) that has been before the Legislature this year. I cannot too strongly urge its immediate passage.[24]

This time the governor's communication was read (though the clerk did not include it in the *Journal!*) and the chance of further delay dissolved. Majority leader Allds tried to explain why the G.O.P. leaders had preferred the Rodenbeck bill, but he best indicated his attitude when just before casting his ballot against the Ford bill he termed it "revolutionary." As the seventy-sixth "aye" sounded a number of conservative members who had hesitated previously joined the majority, so by a vote of 109 to 35 the unamended Ford bill went to the governor.[25]

"Well, I suppose I have ended my political career today!" Roosevelt remarked ruefully to a jubilant assemblyman from New York City. "You're mistaken, Governor," came the quick reply, "this is only the beginning."[26]

Down in New York, the *Herald,* the *World* and the *Tribune* were most agreeably surprised that what the *Brooklyn Eagle* called this "epoch-making measure" had passed by such a "bold legislative

[24] *Public Papers* (1899), p. 89.
[25] *Assembly Journal* (1899), pp. 3585–86; New York *World* and *New York Tribune,* April 29, 1899.
[26] Reminiscence of Assemblyman Nathaniel Elsberg (RHP).

stroke." Among those who expressed approval to Roosevelt personally were Seth Low, tax reformer Thomas G. Shearman, Cornell's Benjamin Ide Wheeler, and the wealthy Gold Democrat, John D. Crimmins.[27]

From other sources, however, came rumblings of dissatisfaction. Russell Sage spoke for the affected corporations when he deplored the haste with which such a "radical" measure had been put through: the governor, he declared, had "taken a great responsibility upon himself" by his emergency message. Chauncey Depew viewed the discretion vested in local assessors as "something appalling," and Ed Lauterbach thought that pending the outcome of this "nebulous, uncertain" measure the Third Avenue line would hold up its bid for a rapid-transit contract. When the stock market fell off sharply on May 1 the *Commercial and Financial Chronicle* and the *Albany Evening Journal* at once observed an "EFFECT OF THE FORD BILL." [28]

Most conspicuous in their editorial criticism were the *New York Times* and the *Brooklyn Eagle*. The *Times* had thought the tax commission a sensible proposal, but "afterward he [Roosevelt] seemed to be carried off his feet by the flood of demagogy and ignorance that was pressing the Ford bill to enactment, and unwisely joined in the effort to pass it." The *Eagle* agreed: the governor's adjournment-morning message had been an "action of passion," and if this crude and hasty measure was signed it "would make New York State quotable with Kansas, Nebraska and Missouri

[27] *Brooklyn Eagle*, May 9, 1899 (RS); New York *World*, May 5, 1899 (RS); *New York Tribune*, April 29, 30 and May 2, 15, 19, 1899; Low to Roosevelt, April 29, 1899, Low MSS.; Roosevelt to John D. Crimmins, May 1, 1899, TR MSS.; New York *World*, May 6, 1899.

[28] *New York Tribune*, April 30, May 2, 1899; New York *Sun*, April 30, 1899 (RS); *Albany Evening Journal*, May 1, 1899 (RS); *Commercial and Financial Chronicle* 68:846 (May 6, 1899).

in the scale of communistic and social legislation, as a state for capital to shun, for investments to abandon and for enterprise and confidence to desert." Corporations were "as a rule blessings to the community," declared editor McKelway, they bore "even now more than their right share of taxation," and "the war of yellow politics and of yellow journalism on them is an infamous war." [29]

Though Roosevelt confided to C. Grant La Farge that he was feeling "rather despondent because I had, at the end, to go against the wishes of Senator Platt and the Organization leaders generally," he was in no mood to retreat. The corporation people were really at fault, he wrote Odell, because they "simply tried to do me at the last and not have any bill." He denied that the yellow journals had influenced his action: "I cannot afford to go against a thing merely because they champion it." Whatever the defects in the Ford bill, concluded the governor, "the system inaugurated is a right one, and I do not see how I possibly could refuse to sign it now." More positive assurance that the bill would be signed went to Senator John Ford, who was told that only one qualified man need appear at the hearing on May 11 to answer the corporation lawyers.[30]

Platt opened his own letter of criticism on May 6 by recalling that the "thing that did really bother me" at the time of the 1898 nomination was the report "from a good many sources that you were a little loose on the relations of capital and labor," and that "you entertained many altruistic ideas, all very well in their way, but which before they could safely be put into law needed very profound consideration." This last legislature had created a good opinion throughout the state, and that "very largely as a result of

[29] *New York Times,* May 5, 1899 (RS); *Brooklyn Eagle,* May 9, 1899 (RS).
[30] Roosevelt to C. Grant La Farge, May 1, 1899; to Odell, May 3, 1899; both TR MSS. Ford, "Theodore Roosevelt's Feet of Clay," pp. 682–683; New York *World,* May 6, 1899.

your personal influence in the legislative chambers," the Easy Boss conceded, but "at the last minute and to my very great surprise you did a thing which has caused the business community of New York to wonder how far the notions of Populism . . . have taken hold upon the Republican party of the State of New York."

In the hope that Roosevelt would show that "very rare and difficult quality of moral courage not to sign it after the part [he] took in its enactment," Platt then enlarged upon his previous objections to the Ford bill. Approval of this measure would not only expose franchise corporations to blackmail by Democratic assessors, he maintained, but would place Roosevelt "in the public mind in the Pingree and Mayor-Jones-of-Toledo class of statesmen" and would bring the Republicans "no single particle of strength" to counterbalance "the inevitable injuries it will inflict upon us." There had been "nothing behind this frantic Ford bill until you sprang forward as its champion except the clamor of two yellow newspapers," argued the senator, concluding with a lofty appeal as "one of the considerable body of Republicans who have come to see new reaches of Republican success under a leadership . . . which is as little to be misled as dismayed by sudden rushes of foolish clamor or factional bitterness." [31]

In a lengthy reply framed over the next twenty-four hours Roosevelt acknowledged that the "frankness, courtesy and delicacy" Platt had shown in his letter and "invariably . . . since my nomination" made it "more unpleasant than I can say to have to disagree." But disagree the governor did. Reviewing his actions step by step, Roosevelt asserted that he had not "gone off half-cocked in this matter," that he had "the most profound indifference to the clamor of the yellow papers," and that franchise taxation was "by no means a revolutionary measure." More important, he took a different view

[31] Platt to Roosevelt, May 6, 1899, in *Barnes v. Roosevelt*, pp. 2369–75.

of the bill's political effect. "I do not believe that it is wise or safe for us as a party to take refuge in mere negation and to say that there are no evils to be corrected," declared Roosevelt. Instead, he argued,

our attitude should be one of correcting the evils and thereby showing that, whereas the populists, socialists and others really do not correct the evils at all, or else only do so at the expense of producing others in agravated [sic] form, on the contrary we Republicans hold the just balance and set our faces as resolutely against improper corporate influence on the one hand as against demagogy and mob rule on the other.

The one point Roosevelt would concede was that the state rather than the local authorities should levy this tax. He thought that the Mazet committee's findings on the "utter corruption of Tammany in laying these taxes" could justify requesting the joint committee to prepare a proper tax bill promptly. He would then be "entirely willing" to call the legislature together, "it being always understood, of course, that this tax bill shall contain provisions under which these franchises will be taxed in reality and genuinely, and not nominally, so that they shall pay their full share of the public burdens." Though he could not accede to Platt's request that he not sign the Ford bill into law, the governor was amenable to its amendment in this fashion.[32]

At the hearing on May 11 a formidable array of corporation lawyers almost unanimously recommended that the governor recall the legislature "to consider the tax laws of the State, rather than to sign the Ford bill." This was a new thought to Roosevelt, who that same day talked with Odell about a Platt proposal to vest the assessment power in a state official and to substitute a tax on gross receipts. Only the first of these suggestions appealed to Roosevelt, who thought that it would correct "the serious defect in the bill." He

[32] Roosevelt to Platt, May 8, 1899, TR MSS.

also thought it might be well to change the effective date to "January first or thereabouts, so that the tax may be raised upon the whole State at the same time." To obtain these amendments, he wrote Platt on May 12, he would be willing to call the legislature into special session at once, provided that everyone clearly understood "that I will sign the present bill, if the proposed bill, containing the changes outlined above, fails to pass." [33]

Though Ford bill supporters expressed misgivings at the prospect of a special legislative session, the governor was not deterred. Anxious to relieve the dangerous strain on his relations with Platt, Roosevelt defended the prospective amendments as corrections of faults of the original bill and as reasonable adjustments to the protests of the corporations. To combat the *Times'* charge of demagogy, on the other hand, he asserted that the motives which inspired this taxation were righteous. In a speech on "The Uses and Abuses of Property" to the Independent Club of Buffalo he identified the struggle for franchise taxation with the struggle of all honest men to live up to the principles of the Decalogue and the Golden Rule in society.[34]

As for the *World's* contention that he should sign the Ford bill before trying for any amendments, Roosevelt sensed the peculiar control he exerted over the whole process. The unsigned bill was a veritable "big stick" by which he could influence the scope of the new measure: either the Republicans would restrict the changes to those he thought proper, or the Ford bill would become law. In the event the legislature tried to recall the bill from his hands, he would rely upon trusted senators "fighting for time while the word is sent to me, so that I may sign the bill." In the more likely event that

[33] *New York Tribune* and *New York Times* (RS), May 12, 1899. Roosevelt to Odell, May 11, 1899; to Platt, May 12, 1899; both TR MSS.
[34] Roosevelt to Lodge, May 27, 1899, TR MSS.; *Public Papers* (1899), pp. 317–318.

something unconstitutional was "surreptitiously introduced" into the altered version, he would have Judge William N. Cohen and E. R. A. Seligman on hand at Albany to point it out. He was prepared for every contingency.[35]

In the ten days before the legislature was to reconvene on May 22, the organization leaders stubbornly tried to get the governor to agree to a less rigorous measure. But except for a provision that any taxes already payable for public rights could be deducted from the franchise valuation, the governor made no further concessions. He rejected a gross-earnings tax because it would not produce as large a revenue and would discriminate in favor of the larger metropolitan companies with their relatively low operating costs as compared to income. He fought shy, too, of "seemingly innocent provisos which would have made the taxation a nullity." In the measure finally agreed upon, the only amendments incorporated were those approved by the governor.[36]

Hence the revision presented to the legislature at the Capitol on May 22 simply tacked several new administrative provisions onto the old Ford bill. The most important one provided that the state board of tax commissioners would fix valuation of the "special franchise"—a term adopted at the suggestion of E. R. A. Seligman. In addition, taxes paid to local authorities as a percentage of gross earnings or as a license fee would be deductible from the final assessment; the valuations of the state board would be subject to court review on a writ of certiorari; and the effective date was so

[35] Roosevelt to Higgins, to Slicer, May 17, 1899; to Raines, May 18, 1899; all TR MSS. *Public Papers* (1899), p. 321.

[36] New York *World*, May 15, 16, 1899; Odell to Roosevelt, May 17, 1899, TR MSS. (LC); Roosevelt to James R. Garfield, May 15, 1899, TR MSS.; *Brooklyn Eagle*, May 15, 1899 (RS); *New York Tribune*, May 16, 17, 20, 1899; Roosevelt to Lodge, May 27, 1899, TR MSS.; *Barnes v. Roosevelt*, p. 412; Ford, "Theodore Roosevelt's Feet of Clay," p. 683.

set that the first assessments would not occur until the next year.[37]

No change of consequence affected the text of this revised bill before its passage three days later. The dangers for which Roosevelt had prepared never materialized, and the Republican majorities held firm against Democratic opposition to the shift from local to state assessment. Clearly Platt had decided to make the best of a a bad situation. The aging boss would even contend afterwards that the governor had not forced franchise taxation through against the wishes of the organization, which had merely objected to the "carelessly drawn and thoughtlessly enacted" original bill and so had approved this "just and reasonable" substitute.[38]

Machine organs took Platt's statement at face value, but the proponents of franchise taxation were virtually at one in crediting the result to Roosevelt. "Shake, Governor, Shake!" crowed the *Oswego Times,* as the *Buffalo Express* called his courageous action "characteristic" and declared that "consistency marked every step in the Governor's course." In scoring this "great personal and political triumph" at the extra session Roosevelt had not surrendered to Platt, asserted the *New York Herald,* but had given "the finest exhibition of civic courage witnessed in this State in many a day." Pulitzer agreed that the governor had "not yielded an inch," and Whitelaw Reid's *Tribune* termed the new law "a great victory" for Roosevelt, who had been "the master of the situation at every stage of the proceedings." With a similar appreciation for "big stick" methods, the New York *Sun* recalled that when Cleveland came to Albany he regarded his task as "essentially executive," whereas "Governor Roosevelt has shown, more strikingly than in any other instance in recent years, that the office is likewise essentially legislative." [39]

[37] For Roosevelt's defense of these provisions, see *Public Papers* (1899), pp. 102–110.

[38] *New York Tribune,* May 25, 29, 1899.

[39] *Oswego Times* (RS), *Buffalo Express, New York Herald* (RS), New York

After such high praise the governor was shocked to find that the provision which the corporation lawyers hoped would invalidate the new statute was the very one which they had advocated at the hearing and the special session had adopted: the method of state rather than local assessment. Roosevelt had considered this point previously—the relevant case being the one in which the court of appeals had held unconstitutional an act empowering the governor to appoint tax assessment officials in New York City—and had decided that the transfer of function to state officials in the franchise tax would be as legal as it had been under the Raines excise tax law. He was nonetheless angered that the interested companies would attempt in this fashion to circumvent what he considered their just dues to society. "Just think of it!" the governor exploded in a speech at Rochester on June 9, "Of corporations striving to work the undoing of a law, seizing on the provision inserted for the protection of the corporations themselves."

I do not think it possible that the law can be declared unconstitutional on the grounds claimed, but I wish to emphasize the danger these men bring not only to the State, but to the corporations they represent. I say this as one who deprecates class and social hostility; the franchise tax has come to stay. [Applause] The corporations should make up their minds absolutely that if success attended the attempt to show the present law to be unconstitutional—a possibility I do not conceive—a more drastic law would be placed on the statute books.[40]

Four years later the court of appeals would hold that the franchise tax law was constitutional, but by then the franchise holders had found that they could restrict its effectiveness by claiming that

World, New York Tribune and New York Sun (RS), May 26, 1899. See also New York Press, New York Evening Post and Rochester Herald, May 26, 1899 (all RS).

[40] People v. Raymond, 37 N.Y. 428; New York Tribune, June 3, 6, 1899; Brooklyn Eagle, June 6, 7, 1899 (RS); Public Papers (1899), pp. 334–335. Mark Hirsch's treatment of this aspect of the franchise tax, in his William C. Whitney: Modern Warwick (New York, 1948), p. 513, is inadequate.

their assessment had not been "equalized" with that of other real property in the locality. Required by law to assess all real estate at its full market value, in practice no assessors did so, the standard varying considerably from one place to another. The only solution was to authorize the state board to equalize the "special franchise" assessments to the same percentage of full value as real property in the same district, but the framers of the franchise-tax bill had not adopted the principle because, as Seligman put it, "the law cannot recognize the existence of a practice which is in direct violation of its own mandate." By 1907, thus, approximately one-half the dollar value of the special franchise assessments made since 1899 were still in litigation. Not until 1911, when the legislature adopted the solution which Seligman and other experts had not considered feasible, did the number of contested cases lessen appreciably.[41]

Similar difficulties over full-value assessment would have arisen under the unamended bill. Had the original Ford bill ever gone into operation, moreover, other shortcomings would have turned up. The fears expressed as to Democratic maladministration were partisan but not without foundation. And where corporations held such extensive franchises as to be subject to several local taxing authorities, state assessment would be preferable because it would attain more uniform valuations. For Seligman, who might be termed a neutral yet informed observer, these considerations alone justified the shift to state control. For Roosevelt there was the added factor that through amendment he could enable Platt to "save face," and thus make their continued cooperation possible.[42]

Roosevelt's course throughout represented a series of practical

---

[41] Seligman, "The Franchise Tax Law in New York," p. 451; State Board of Tax Commissioners, *Report* (Albany, 1907), pp. 5, 6; Lutz, *The State Tax Commission*, pp. 198–200; Benjamin E. Hall, "Administrative Difficulties of the Special Franchise Tax Law," *State Conference on Taxation Addresses and Proceedings, 1911–12* (Albany, 1912), pp. 177–184.

[42] Seligman, "The Franchise Tax Law in New York," pp. 450–451.

adjustments to pressures from right and left. He had approached the question of franchise taxation as an "honest broker" with a few ideas gained through consideration of the rapid transit, tunnel, and Astoria Gas proposals. His view of the specific solution was not fixed; rather it shifted as he sought on the one hand to keep in with the machine and on the other to avoid offense to those "liberal" and independent elements that favored the Ford bill. Resolution of this conflict proved impossible before adjournment, so the governor at last threw his support firmly behind the Ford measure. Yet that radical action in turn bestowed on him the power to effect a kind of compromise, and that he did.

Roosevelt erected a rational framework of justification about this essentially pragmatic process. At its foundation was a basic belief: in return for the privileges they enjoyed from the state, corporations should assume their just share of public burdens. To the argument of principle he then added that of expediency: business interests should accept reasonable imposts in order the more effectively to counter drastic and unwise demands. And when corporation representatives challenged the state's authority as openly and boldly as they did on the day he sent up his first emergency message on the Ford bill, these "arrogant public and semi-public corporations" had to be put in their place: "in their own interests," Roosevelt wrote one reformer, "we must insist that they are the servants and not the masters of the people and that they must do their full share of bearing the burdens of the State." [43]

The next year was to supply further evidence, in the form of a crippling amendment to the mortgage-tax bill, that these arguments had not won over the corporations in New York. The joint legislative committee on taxation proposed in 1900 a 5 mill mortgage

[43] Syracuse *Post-Standard*, May 10, 1899 (RS); Roosevelt to Eli P. Miller, April 17, 1899, TR MSS.

tax to correct inequities in state assessment against real estate. This proposal would have affected many large business interests, and in particular those of J. Pierpont Morgan, who was engaged in the flotation of a $100,000,000 refunding 3½ percent mortgage bond issue for the New York Central Railroad. By the time the bill emerged from the senate committee on taxation and retrenchment, it had been amended to exempt individual and corporate mortgages bearing less than 4 percent interest. "Now this makes the bill to my mind a monstrosity," exclaimed Roosevelt. This bill was only defensible if it taxed "all, rich and poor alike," the governor asserted, as he told Platt and Odell that he "could not consent to it if it exempted the biggest corporations—the biggest financiers." On March 22 in the senate the Democrats and the city Republicans combined to kill the whole proposal.[44]

The move to put Roosevelt into the Vice-Presidency also was to demonstrate that his arguments had not won over the machine and the corporations in New York. Yet time was on Roosevelt's side, and even if the effort to shelve him had not backfired, he would have emerged as the new national leader. By championing the judicious acceptance of reasonable change he welded conservatism to reform; he provided a vehicle by which the party of property could move forward in an era of transition. The Ford franchise-tax bill was an early milestone along that path of enlightened conservatism. And so was the proposal he now advanced as the conservative answer to trusts.

[44] *Report to the Legislature of New York by the Joint Committee on Taxation, January 15, 1900* (Albany, 1900), pp. 6–18; E. R. A. Seligman, "Recent Discussion of Tax Reform," *Political Science Quarterly* 15:638–643 (December 1900); Roosevelt to Bishop, March 22, 1900, TR MSS.; *Senate Journal* (1900), p. 1127.

CHAPTER VIII The Conservative Answer to Trusts

Roosevelt's decision to devote a major portion of his annual message of 1900 to the trust problem reflected many of the attitudes that had influenced his stand on franchise taxation—the concern for public sentiment, the feeling that the criticism had some legitimate basis, the desire not to take refuge in mere negation but to find an affirmative position. But there were necessarily significant differences in his handling of the two issues. In the case of franchise taxation he had a specific bill and, ultimately, a fairly well-organized public opinion with which to work. The trust problem lacked this focus and definition, so that the governor had to assume a leading role in developing a feasible remedy and mobilizing support behind it. Eventually these differences would account in some part for the failure of the proposal he sponsored, yet his full participation in each phase of its development affords a more revealing insight into the methods of Roosevelt the politician-statesman.

The "rush toward industrial monopoly" had been the great economic fact of the last decade of the nineteenth century. From the Civil War to 1890 only twenty-six consolidations with an aggregate capitalization of half a billion dollars had been effected. By October of 1898, one yellow journal could list as then in existence or being formed one hundred fifty-six consolidations representing a total capital of two billion. The year 1898, with slightly over $900,000,-000 in new incorporations, set a record, yet in the first two months of 1899 that figure was well exceeded. In May the news that Andrew Carnegie was selling out portended the advent of a gigantic steel combine. Every week seemed to bring fresh developments in the reorganization of Big Business, until Washington Gladden, the reforming prophet of the Social Gospel, could say "It is a rather dull day which does not report to us some new trust with from one million to two hundred millions of dollars in 'securities.'" [1]

Public concern over the menace to free competition had resulted in a rash of antitrust legislation on both state and national levels. The effect of such efforts had been slight. Judicial interpretation had drawn the sting of the Sherman Act of 1890, and the states had found the going rough. When the state attorney-general attempted to initiate proceedings under the 1897 New York law prohibiting restraint of competition, for example, the courts had refused to issue an order because the immunity of witnesses had been insufficiently protected. To correct this shortcoming a new bill had been introduced under Tammany auspices and passed in 1899, but the very absence of opposition forecast its subsequent ineffectiveness. [2]

With giant corporations ever more strongly entrenched and antitrust action feeble, the only deterrent to a dangerous social situation such as had prevailed earlier in the 1890's was the general prosperity of the postwar period. Even so the seeming impasse aroused discussion and criticism. Captains of industry and their creations were sensational news in the yellow press, which treated

[1] Bryon W. Holt, "Trusts: The Rush Toward Industrial Monopoly," *Review of Reviews* 19:675–689 (June 1899); Luther Conant, Jr., "Industrial Combinations in the United States," American Statistical Society *Publications* 7:2–3, 19 (March 1901); New York *World*, Ocotber 25, 1898; New York *Evening Post*, March 7, 1899; *New York Tribune*, May 6, 9, 1899; Washington Gladden, "The Spread of Socialism," *Outlook* 62:117 (May 13, 1899).

[2] Ch. 716, *Laws of New York* (1893); Chs. 383, 384, *ibid.* (1897); Ch. 690, *ibid.* (1899); New York *World*, January 18, 1899.

trusts as powerful and unstoppable yet sinister and potentially oppressive. Socialistic groups sponsored mass meetings on the problem. Democratic politicians labelled their opponents the defenders of the plutocracy that throttled American life, while Republicans assumed the inevitability of industrial expansion and denounced the demagogues who inflamed the populace. "The outcry against corporations has become so deafening," observed the conservative New York *Evening Post* in August 1899, "as nearly to drown the voice of intelligent criticism." [3]

No prominent Republican politician was more sensitive to the dangers than Theodore Roosevelt. In April 1899 he had had a lengthy exposure to Brooks Adams' gloomy views. On his trip west in June for the Rough Rider reunion in Las Vegas, he had conversed with editors William Allen White and H. H. Kohlsaat and others about the trust problem. By early August he wrote Kohlsaat that he had become "exceedingly alarmed at the growth of popular unrest and popular distrust on this question." The agitation against trusts "is largely unreasonable and is fanned into activity by the Bryan type of demagogue, ably seconded by Gorman, Croker et al who want to change the issue from free silver," Roosevelt assured Lodge on August 10, 1899. "But when there is a good deal of misery and of injustice," he added, "even though it is mainly due to the faults of the individuals themselves, or to the mere operation of nature's laws, the quack who announces he has a cureall [sic] for it is a dangerous person." He was surprised at how many working men around New York who had supported McKinley in 1896 "are now sullenly grumbling that McKinley is under Hanna's dictation;

[3] *Review of Reviews* 20:398 (October 1899); New York *World*, March 10, 19, 1899, on Morgan's coal trust; *New York Tribune*, April 15, 1899; New York *Evening Post*, August 28, 1899.

that Bryan is the only man who can control the trusts; and that the trusts are crushing the life out of the small men." [4]

The Republicans needed "some consistent policy to advocate." For though the discontent was "largely aimless and baseless," there was "a very unpleasant side to this overrun trust development." If the responsible leaders of the party of property failed to advance a sensible remedy, then the "multitudes will follow the crank who advocates an absurd policy, but who does advocate something." It was the search for just such a remedy that occupied his attention, for that August Roosevelt had already decided to devote a major section of his annual message to trusts. [5]

Behind this search no doubt there lurked a personal motive. Upon his return from Las Vegas in late June he had admitted that he had no chance for the Presidential nomination in 1900 by issuing a statement endorsing McKinley. But if he would have to wait at least until 1904, and if "the hold I have for the moment on the voters" was as "entirely ephemeral" as Roosevelt thought it to be, then how best could he remain in contention and still have worthwhile interim work? McKinley's mid-July selection of Elihu Root to replace Alger as Secretary of War eliminated one position that had attractive possibilities. Lodge's suggestion of the Vice-Presidency did not appeal to Roosevelt; it would not mark him as McKinley's natural successor, and there would simply be too little to do, whether for his own content or for impressing the public at large. The more he thought of it, the more he favored standing

---

[4] Roosevelt to Lodge, April 27, 1899; to William Allen White, July 15, 1899; to Judge C. C. Kohlsaat, December 16, 1899; to H. H. Kohlsaat, August 7, 1899; to Lodge, August 10, 1899; all TR MSS. On the trip west, see H. H. Kohlsaat, *From McKinley to Harding* (New York, 1923), pp. 77–80.

[5] Roosevelt to H. H. Kohlsaat, August 7, 1899; to William Allen White, August 15, 1899; both TR MSS.

again for the governorship, for though fraught with difficulty it was a job worth doing. Despite his half-apologetic reference to his "parochial affairs," Roosevelt sensed that action taken in the state of New York upon a great domestic problem would have nation-wide significance. It was in part from that conviction that he set out to formulate a position and a program on the resurgent issue of trusts.[6]

Since any answer he devised had to be politically feasible, he first consulted Republican politicians and editors. H. H. Kohlsaat of the *Chicago Times-Herald* vouchsafed the advice that trusts were a "natural evolution of the times. They will work out their own ascending or destruction." William Allen White forwarded an address by a Kansas editor, Charles F. Scott, whose "sound, cool-headed sense" earned the governor's praise. At Plattsburgh, when he chanced to meet Attorney General Griggs, who had declared that the Federal Government was powerless to interfere with the corporate creations of the several states, the subject was unfailingly broached.[7]

What Roosevelt derived from his soundings was less plain. In a letter to Charles F. Scott on August 15, 1899, he admitted to being in a "great quandary," yet the same day to White he asserted "I am sure that the only ultimate successful plan with them is the exceedingly humdrum common-place and unexciting plan of demanding exactly the same good conduct from their formers as from every-body else." Exactly what he meant by "good conduct" he did not

[6] *New York Tribune*, June 30, 1899. Roosevelt to H. H. Kohlsaat, July 1, 1899; to Lodge, July 1, 21, August 28, 1899; all TR MSS.
[7] Roosevelt to Odell, August 7, 1899, TR MSS.; Kohlsaat to Roosevelt, August 9, 1899, TR MSS. (LC). Roosevelt to White, August 15, 1899; to Scott, September 9, 1899; to Platt, August 21, 1899; all TR MSS. For example, see Roosevelt to C. F. Manderson, Omaha, Nebraska, September 13, 1899, TR MSS., requesting a copy of Manderson's Bar Association speech on trusts.

elucidate, and perhaps he did not yet understand. Nor did his first major speech on trusts a month later provide a wholly reliable clue.

On September 23 an estimated 50,000 people at Akron heard Roosevelt open the Ohio campaign with a ringing declaration that on the two great issues of the day—trusts and imperialism—the Republicans had the right position. In the speeches of Bryan and other Democrats he had found "plenty of vague denunciation" but not "so much as an attempt to formulate a rational policy of relief." As for the remedies advanced by Democrats in Ohio, lower tariffs would not affect the beef, sugar, ice, or Standard Oil trusts, and silver at 16 to 1 would only bring disaster to the wage earner as well. Citing the franchise tax in New York as an example, he contended that the G.O.P. sought "to ameliorate and curb abuses and not to eliminate what may be useful." The Republicans would do their best to eliminate whatever "artificially lowers wages, or artificially increases prices, or puts it in the hands of one man, or one set of men, to become absolute in any branch of business." And in attacking these evils "we will find out how best and most wisely we can interfere before acting, and when we do act, our actions shall be effective." [8]

That was as far as most editors reported the speech, but at least two newspapers included an additional section in which the governor declared:

Our opponents say we have no plan for trusts. We have, and the plan is, as a first step, to try the effect of publicity, and then to supplement publicity by taxation, and then by licensing or whatever measure experience shows to be effective. The mere letting in of light will cure many evils, especially those of overcapitalization and the undue suppression of competition, and as for the evils that remain, when once we can see

[8] *New York Tribune,* September 24, 1899; Syracuse *Post-Standard,* September 26, 1899; *Akron Beacon Journal,* September 23, 1899 (all RS).

them clearly and distinctly, the remedy can readily be devised without entailing upon the innocent the awful misery that will surely follow any blind and ignorant attempt to smash parts of our modern industrial machinery, without taking the trouble to find out their relations to our industrial life itself.[9]

Though this section was not in the version he had given to the press in advance of delivery, and though one of the papers including it was the sometimes unreliable New York *World*, it is likely that Roosevelt did advance such a plan at Akron. Not only is the language Rooseveltian, but it is quite possible that the first time he aired the proposal he preferred to do so extemporaneously. And, of course, the major step suggested—publicity—was just the one which he was to put forward in his annual message.[10]

That Roosevelt should settle on the method of publicity was quite logical. Most of the other proposals then advanced involved federal action. And as was apparent at the Chicago Conference on Trusts, a pioneer gathering in September 1899 of interested parties from all over the nation, the requirement of greater publicity on corporate affairs was the only state action widely endorsed. Bourke Cockran of New York was probably its leading advocate at the conference, but university lecturer John Graham Brooks, ICC statistician Henry C. Adams, Congressman Francis G. Newlands of Nevada, civil-service-reformer William Dudley Foulke, and many other lesser figures all assigned it an important place at the state and/or federal level.[11]

[9] *New York Press* and New York *World*, September 24, 1899 (RS). The *World* had further remarks that no other paper included.

[10] Roosevelt to Frank Mack (Associated Press), to Charles Dick, September 13, 1899, TR MSS.

[11] Chicago Conference on Trusts, *Speeches, Debates, Resolutions . . . 13–16 September, 1899* (Chicago, 1900), pp. 50, 60, 39, 309, 582, 138–139, 220, 224. The most prominent New York delegates Roosevelt officially appointed to this conference were Cockran, Chauncey Depew, John G. Carlisle, Albert

Those who advocated publicity as the foremost remedy sought a middle way between two extremes. On the one hand they rejected the view of Bryan, Pingree, and others that the monopolistic corporation was wholly evil and hence to be annihilated. On the other they refused to follow George Gunton, F. B. Thurber, and those who maintained generally that the trust development was natural, inevitable, and healthy, attended almost completely by good results and thus to be fostered, not impeded. Rather they saw the drive toward business concentration as a mixture of good and evil; the benefits such as increased production and lower prices they would preserve, the abuses they would counteract through regulation. Publicity would afford the investor and stockholder greater protection against practices like overcapitalization and would show whether the advantages achieved through size were being equitably transmitted to the consumer in better and cheaper products. It would also provide a basis upon which to plan further regulative measures if needed.[12]

To advocate greater publicity had its risks for a Republican politician. The official line of the party leaders, as Kohlsaat had indicated, was to leave the trust problem alone. For Mark Hanna, Gunton had put "the whole question in a nutshell" when he had labelled the antitrust campaign a "war on corporations pure and simple" and had declared that "war on corporations without some

---

Shaw, George Gunton, F. B. Thurber, and Henry White. The criteria he used in his selection are not clear, but see Roosevelt to Samuel Gompers, August 7, 9, 1899; to R. M. Easley, July 24 and August 10, 1899; all TR MSS.

[12] Byran's views were represented at Chicago (Chicago Conference, *Speeches, Debates, Resolutions,* pp. 49–50, 113–114, 271–276, 331, 340, 366–370, 380) as were Gunton's (pp. 77–96, 124–136, 177–187, 276ff., 302–303, 617–618). On further regulation see especially Foulke (p. 582), and Newlands (p. 309), who was one of the few men at the conference to link publicity and taxation in the same way as did Roosevelt.

definite economic basis of discrimination . . . is simply a war on business success." [13]

Yet to propose, in the name of honesty, that companies make fuller confidential reports to stockholders and the government could hardly arouse vociferous objections, and even Governor Nash of Ohio came out in his 1900 message for increased publicity. The matter of degree was important: the radicalism of any proposal depended on the extent to which a corporation was forced to reveal its financial status. Until Roosevelt put his ideas into a specific bill, a judgment on his remedy was premature.[14]

By early December Roosevelt had the draft of the section of his message on taxation and trusts in good enough shape to invite E. R. A. Seligman and another leading thinker in the field, Cornell professor Jeremiah W. Jenks, to come to Albany to discuss it. At the suggestion principally of Jenks, who at the time was chief adviser to the Industrial Commission in its investigation of trusts, certain "corrections and emendations" were made. Then on December 7 copies were forwarded to a number of people for further criticism. One went to Yale President Arthur Twining Hadley, an authority in his own right, with whom Roosevelt had discussed monopolies the weekend of the Harvard-Yale game. Another copy was for Jenks, who would if possible obtain the comments also of New Jersey's corporation expert James B. Dill. Finally, the governor asked that Elihu Root, or if he lacked time then Griggs, should read it, for on "such a delicate matter as trusts I should be in some kind of relations with the National administration." [15]

[13] *New York Tribune,* October 23, 1899. Hanna was referring to Gunton's article, "Crusade Against Prosperity," *Gunton's Magazine* 17:169 (September 1899).

[14] See *Gunton's Magazine* 17:516 (December 1899); Jeremiah W. Jenks, "Publicity: A Remedy for the Evils of Trusts," *Review of Reviews* 21:445–446 (April 1900).

[15] Roosevelt had studied Hadley's "The Formation and Control of Trusts," *Scribner's* 26:604–610 (November 1899), where he had emphasized the need

The draft which Roosevelt circulated consisted of five sections—taxation, the franchise tax, the state and public utilities, modern industrial conditions, and trusts—which in his view were all related. The need for a broad revision of the tax system was evident, he began, but in the modern era the state had been compelled "to provide more or less complete remedies without waiting for a general scheme of reorganization." The resultant taxation of inheritances and of corporations had been justified, though "extreme caution" relative to such measures was necessary. "Our laws should be so drawn as to protect and encourage corporations which do their honest duty by the public," he asserted, "and to discriminate sharply against those organized in a spirit of mere greed, or for improper speculative purposes." In 1899 in New York, he added, "no corporate influence has been able to prevail against the interests of the public."

Turning to the future relations of the state with public utility companies, Roosevelt foresaw an enlarging sphere of the state's direct management or its "increasing and more rigorous control." No hard and fast rule could be applied, he maintained, but "when private ownership entails grave abuses, and where the work . . . can be performed with efficiency by the State or municipality . . . no theory or tradition should interfere with our making the change."

Under modern industrial conditions the contrast between the very rich and the very poor was "exceedingly distressing," particularly since "some of the wealth has been acquired by means which are utterly inconsistent with the highest rules of morality, and which yet under present laws cannot be interfered with." The evils

---

for greater responsibility of directors to their "trust"; Hadley apparently suggested Jenks to Roosevelt, too, though the governor had had dealings with Jenks in January. See Roosevelt to Jenks, January 27, 1899; to Hadley, November 9, December 7, 1899; all TR MSS.

of conspicuous wealth could not safely be ignored, yet "to strike at them in a spirit of ignorant revenge" might do "far more harm than is remedied." The answer rested only in "careful study of conditions" and in "action which while taken boldly and without hesitation is neither heedless nor reckless."

Such an attitude should guide the state in its consideration of the trust problem. There should be caution about radical changes "for fear the unseen effects may take the shape of widespread disaster." Yet there was no question but that abuses of "a very grave character" had existed and still did exist. "The chicanery and the dishonest, even though not technically illegal, methods through which some great fortunes have been made, are scandals to our civilization," declared the governor, likening the man who so enriched himself "to any predatory medieval nobleman." Any law that would punish such a man should be welcomed, and of course "such laws are even more needed in dealing with great corporations or trusts than with individuals."

Reviewing the chief abuses alleged to arise from trusts, Roosevelt concluded that "some of these evils could be partially remedied by a modification of our corporation laws." Publicity was "the first essential"—knowledge of what the stock represented, if anything, and of the manner in which the shares were disposed. "Care should be taken not to stifle enterprise or disclose any facts of a business that are essentially private," the governor cautioned, "but the State for the protection of the public should exercise the right to inspect, to examine thoroughly all the workings of great corporations just as is now done with banks." Where the public interest demanded it, the results of the examination should be published. "Then, if there are inordinate profits, competition or public sentiment will give the public the benefit in lowered prices; and if not, the power of taxation remains." [16]

[16] No copy of this draft remains, but all the quoted portions, except as noted

The Secretary of War must have been one of the few addressees to offer much constructive criticism, for in an effusive letter of thanks on December 15 Roosevelt said he would at once adopt both the changes Root suggested. "I see entirely the danger of carrying a suggestion to the community such as my phrase might carry," noted the governor, who thought that "for it I shall substitute some of the sentences you write in your letter." "Oh Lord! I wish there were more of you," Roosevelt confessed; "I think I have made a pretty good Governor, but . . . you would have made a better one, for in just such matters as trusts and the like you have the ideas to work out whereas I have to try to work out what I get from you and men like you." [17]

Actually Root had liked the trust section: the two criticisms he had made pertained to other matters. One was relatively minor, the alteration of a sentence to read: "But it is intended that property which derives its value from the grant of a privilege by the public, shall be taxed proportionately to the value of the privilege granted." The other and more substantial criticism was of Roosevelt's statement that "some of the wealth has been acquired by means which are utterly inconsistent with the highest rules of morality, and which yet under our present laws cannot be interfered with." Terming this a "dangerous suggestion," Root asserted that "It is not a function of law to enforce the rules of morality, and any attempt to do that would necessarily result in a statutory limitation on individual action and utter destruction of freedom, and be far more injurious than the evil which you are describing."

Ex-corporation lawyer Root then expanded upon this theme:

---

below, appear to have gone unchanged into the final message, *Public Papers* (1900), pp. 13–28.

[17] For acknowledgement of other suggestions see Roosevelt to State Senator N. N. Stranahan, December 11, 1899; to Hadley, December 12, 1899; both **TR MSS.**

There is altogether too general an impression that it is immoral to acquire wealth, and far too little appreciation of the fact that the vast preponderance of the grand fortunes which now exist in this country have been amassed, not by injuring any living being, but as an incident to the conferring of great benefits on the community.

The true question, Root contended, was whether in acquiring his wealth an individual had injured another, and if he had, then were the rights of the injured party insufficiently protected by law? "If they were, then that individual's rights ought to be protected by additional legislation," Root conceded, but "it is the protection of the individual against wrong to him that should be aimed at, and not any attempt to confine the acquisition of wealth by a statutory imposition of any general moral laws." [18]

Root's contention caused the governor to soften his reflections upon the immorality of certain wealth. He altered the offending sentence to read: "and some of the wealth has been acquired, or is used, in a manner for which there is no moral justification." He also strengthened the defense of capital acquisition, taking most of Root's position for his own. Indeed, much to Roosevelt's amusement, the only paragraph from his message which the *New York Times* subsequently quoted with approval was the defense of wealth he had cribbed from Root's letter. "That is an antidote for demagogy well compounded and put up in a compact package," observed the *Times*; "It ought to be freely applied to all socialists and to persons who ignorantly abet them in their crusade against what they call culpable wealth." [19]

[18] Root to Roosevelt, December 13, 1899, Root MSS.
[19] *Public Papers* (1900), pp. 20–21; *New York Times,* January 4, 1900 (RS); Roosevelt to Root, January 4, 1900, TR MSS. Roosevelt mistakenly identified the paper that did this as the *Brooklyn Eagle;* actually the *Eagle,* January 3, 1900 (RS), had marked "a union of sane conservatism with a fine humanitarian spirit in his observations."

Still Roosevelt preserved his protest. Where Root had maintained, for example, that the principal effect of the amassing of great fortunes had been to confer great benefits upon the community, Roosevelt said that "probably" such was the case, "whatever the conscious purpose of those amassing them may have been." In this section and elsewhere, moreover, he retained his basic condemnation of the morals and manners of the plutocracy. The "law of public opinion" might be the only possible check, yet he agreed with Lecky that " 'the colossal waste of the means of human happiness in the most selfish and most vulgar forms of social advertisement and competition . . . gives a force [and almost a justification] to [anarchical] passions which menace the whole future of our civilization.' " [20]

Reassured by Root's judgment that these sections were "full of sound sense," Roosevelt forwarded the entire message to Platt on December 19 with the request that he "make suggestions and criticisms with the utmost freedom." A week later Odell replied. The state chairman explained that his solicitude for Roosevelt's renomination had perhaps caused him to wield the blue pencil too freely, yet he had found many objectionable items, particularly in the major portion devoted to taxation and trusts.

Although he may have heeded several of Odell's comments on taxation, the governor rejected three out of four suggested changes in the section on trusts. He did eliminate a reference to oppression of minority stockholders, because Odell said they could always get a stock appraisal. But he did not yield before the further arguments that it would arouse criticism to include "the raising of prices above

[20] *Public Papers* (1900), p. 20. The bracketed words represent the portion of the Lecky original which Roosevelt, in an instructive fashion, omitted. Cf. William E. H. Lecky, *The Map of Life* (New York, 1899), pp. 65–66, a book to which Roosevelt had been referred by F. W. Holls (Holls to Lecky, January 29, 1900, Holls MSS., CUL).

fair competitive rates" among the chief abuses; that it would drive capital out of the state if the government inquired into payments for stock; and that it would be dangerous to declare that there was "no reason whatever for refusing to tax a corporation because by its own acts it has created a burden of charges under which it staggers."[21]

If Roosevelt had followed Odell's advice he would have discarded the remedy of publicity altogether. From his experience in the formation of these companies, Odell could see "no point where publicity would be of any value whatever"; quite the contrary, "it would only unnecessarily array against you a lot of people who are engaged in this kind of business." Roosevelt thus had ample warning that the party leaders would oppose the bill which Jeremiah Jenks was drafting for introduction at the next legislative session. And he must have realized that to put through that measure would require all the editorial support he could muster.

Press reaction to his message was encouraging. Republican editors thought he had handled the trust problem like a "statesman" and "while his conclusions may not please the radical they certainly will appeal to every thoughtful man as being just to all concerned." Among the metropolitan papers, which in general agreed that Roosevelt was in line with the best thought on the subject, a most complimentary verdict unexpectedly came from the *Brooklyn Eagle,* which asserted that no one "has put up more or better words on this 'problem' that may have presidencies in it." Even a Democratic organ such as the *Brooklyn Citizen* concluded that though "discursive" and "vague" the sections on taxation and trusts were "readable and indicative of thought at least on matters of large public importance." [22]

---

[21] Cf. Odell to Roosevelt, December 26, 1899, TR MSS. (LC) with *Public Papers* (1900), pp. 26–28.

[22] *Brooklyn Times* [n.d.] (RS); *Albany Evening Journal, Ithaca Daily*

To translate thought into action, Jenks designed a complete Business Companies Act "intended not to repeal the present law, but to provide an alternative law under which corporations that wished to do so might organize and act; others might act under the present law." To entice corporations into organizing under the new measure, as well as to meet the competition of New Jersey and Delaware in this field, the proposed statute offered greater privileges. But companies desiring these privileges would in turn have to submit to more stringent requirements. Jenks hoped, in short, to gain consent to greater publicity in return for liberalization or modernization of the New York law on incorporation.[23]

The privileges afforded under the Jenks bill were similar to those by which New Jersey and Delaware had attracted companies. The incorporation tax was reduced from one-eighth of one percent on the amount of capital stock to one-fifteenth of one percent. Changes in the capital structure through the issue of preferred stock were made somewhat easier. Stockholder liability was limited strictly to the face value of their shares, and the judgment of directors about the value of property offered for stock was accepted as conclusive. The responsibility of the directors for the corporation debt was alleviated. And the form of charters was liberalized so that highly integrated industries could include their manifold operations under one certificate.[24]

Unlike competing states, however, New York required businesses

Journal and *Ogdensburg Journal* (RS), January 3, 1900; New York *Mail and Express,* January 4, 1900 (RS); New York *World* (RS) and *New York Tribune,* January 4, 1900; New York *Evening Post* and *Brooklyn Eagle* (RS), January 3, 1900; *Brooklyn Citizen,* January 4, 1900 (RS).

[23] The best explanation of this bill is found in Appendix D of Jeremiah W. Jenks, *The Trust Problem* (New York, 1900), pp. 244–279.

[24] On the Delaware statute passed in March 1899 see J. E. Smith, "Delaware Corporation Law," *Moody's Manual of Industrial and Miscellaneous Securities, 1900* (New York, 1900), pp. 1059–78. See also Jenks in *The Trust Problem,* pp. 251n, 264, and "Publicity: A Remedy for the Evils of Trusts," p. 448.

organizing under the Jenks proposal to reveal much more about their structure and finance. Stock and transfer books open to every stockholder were to be kept at a registered office in the state. Prospectuses for any stock or bond issue would be strictly regulated. A balance sheet was to be supplied to every stockholder in advance of the annual meeting, and to the state government in the annual report. This report would contain much more information than that required under the existing law. It would also be verified by one or more auditors, who were to be other than directors, chosen by ballot at the annual meeting, and empowered to inspect the detailed "private balance sheet" used by the company officials. In a number of ways, moreover, the directors would be rendered more responsible to the stockholders.[25]

Though companies could still incorporate under the present law —a feature of the proposal calculated to enhance the possibility of favorable legislative action—Jenks was confident that the scheme would have a good effect. Corporations with nothing to hide would be glad to come under the new act's provisions, he reasoned, because their securities would thus become more attractive investments. The speculative promotion, on the other hand, would be discriminated against, to the benefit of the public and the investors. And there was always the consideration, added Professor Jenks, that the information gathered "might lead as time went on to regulation more definite and more rigorous." [26]

The very duality of the Jenks bill nevertheless weakened the support behind it. Antitrust spokesmen tended to oppose the liberalizing features and to regard the compensatory regulations

[25] Jenks, *The Trust Problem*, pp. 253–256, 257–259, 263–264, 277–278. The only information currently required in the annual report was the amount of capital stock and the proportion issued; the amount of the company's assets; and the amount of the debts.

[26] *Ibid.*, p. 226.

as insufficient. At the same time businessmen thought the increased supervision would nullify the effort to attract capital to New York; one man even maintained that the total effect would be to drive companies out of the state, while another thought that the "full reports" required would interfere with legitimate private business. The volume of these latter protests could be gauged by the care Jenks afterwards took to combat such fears. Certainly Roosevelt appreciated the difficulty, for he urged Jenks to do an article for the *Review of Reviews* to build up popular sentiment behind their "practical measure."[27]

Prior to the bill's introduction the governor invited several leading members of both houses to discuss it with Jenks, Francis Lynde Stetson, and Victor Morawetz. He also took it up with Platt at a conference in March, and the senate committee on judiciary subsequently reported it favorably. But on March 28 Jenks disconsolately informed Roosevelt that Odell had decided against action that year. Election-year politics accounted only in part for that decision. The basic objection of the party leaders became clear a year later, when with Odell as governor the corporation law was liberalized in many ways without any attendant increase in publicity. Indeed, if anything the directors were given a freer rein than they had previously possessed.[28]

In terms of actual achievement, then, the Roosevelt program for

[27] New York *World*, February 19, 1900; *Buffalo Enquirer* and New York *Sun*, February 20, 1900 (RS). Roosevelt to Willis A. Barnes, February 15, 1900; to Arthur W. Soper, February 28, 1900; to Jenks, February 27, 1900; all TR MSS.

[28] Roosevelt to Jenks, February 9, 1900, TR MSS.; New York *Sun*, March 11, 1900 (RS); *Senate Journal* (1900), p. 1051 (March 20, 1900); *New York Tribune*, April 18, 24, 1901. The legislature also pigeonholed three bills introduced by a Roosevelt supporter, Assemblyman Alfred W. Cooley of Westchester, designed to extract fuller information from New York companies incorporated under the existing law. *Assembly Journal* (1900), pp. 534–535; *New York Tribune*, February 10, 1900.

trusts was a failure. Its value was rather in the definition it gave his own thought. For the plan he had enunciated as governor remained "the first essential" as President. The "only sure remedy" he told Congress in December 1901, was "knowledge of the facts—publicity." And after a hard struggle Roosevelt obtained in 1903 an instrument for his purpose—the Commerce Department's Bureau of Corporations, the historical forerunner of the Federal Trade Commission.[29]

Transfer to the national scene, of course, brought some change in Roosevelt's outlook. Efforts to cope with trusts on the state level he then termed inadequate, even as had some critics of his annual message of 1900. Regulation of interstate commerce and of railroad rate discrimination came to occupy his attention. And he discovered new possibilities in the Sherman Antitrust Law. Yet his basic attitude toward large corporations remained substantially the same thereafter. His pronounced caution over disturbance to the "delicate" economic order might diminish, his assertion of the sovereignty of the government might swell in volume. Still he continued to hold that the trend toward consolidation was irrevocable; that the line should be drawn against the evil effects and not the movement itself; that what was needed was supervision and regulation by the government to curb abuses, not aimless destruction of combination whether good or bad. The degree to which he would have the government interfere to obtain the desired end was what changed, not the end itself. That kept steady from 1899 onward.

[29] Hermann Hagedorn, ed., *The Works of Theodore Roosevelt*, 20 vols., National Edition (New York, 1926), XV, 91; Henry F. Pringle, *Theodore Roosevelt: A Biography* (New York, 1931), pp. 340–342.

CHAPTER IX

The Erie Canal

Pertinent though they were to the needs of the day, the Ford franchise tax and the Jenks bill were hardly the measures New Yorkers had in mind when they elected the Rough Rider governor. Above all else they expected action on the Erie Canal. The selection of Colonel Partridge as the new superintendent of public works was little more than a good start. The present operation of the department, the prosecution of Aldridge and Adams for past misdeeds, the future program of canal improvement—all these demanded Roosevelt's attention. Since each was the subject of sharp controversy, the rocks and shoals were only too apparent. Whatever Roosevelt did, he would encounter criticism.

To restore operations to an efficient basis Partridge first needed a new deputy superintendent, "a man of backbone who realizes that the knife must be mercilessly used." The independent press was gratified when the legislature quickly approved the governor's selection of Elon H. Hooker, a talented young civil engineer recommended by Congressman-elect James M. E. O'Grady of Rochester. Roosevelt and Partridge then reviewed the records of the three assistant superintendents. The Aldridge appointee in charge of the western division, a brother-in-law of ex-Governor Levi P. Morton, was found incompetent and was removed. The evidence on the middle division head, Republican State Committeeman Thomas Wheeler of Utica, was more conflicting: Partridge said he was "a good man and ought to be kept," but Roosevelt had heard "that he is the worst man in the whole canal, and *must* be turned out!" Unable to uncover the true facts, Roosevelt at length acceded to Partridge's view that this powerful Platt lieutenant was efficient.[1]

Though critical of the failure to remove Wheeler, the anti-machine papers had to admit that Roosevelt and Partridge made performance rather than politics their general guide. When Partridge discovered that the district attorney of Herkimer County had neglected to act on evidence that a section superintendent had falsified payrolls, the governor directed that the prosecution be carried forward "without fear or favor." Again, when the assembly-man from Wayne County warned that the superintendent there ought not to be reappointed because he had "run his office in aid of the toughest politicians," his advice was followed despite strong machine protests. In fact, once the department was in better order, Partridge and the governor agreed to fill vacancies wherever possible by promotion from the civil service ranks rather than by political appointment.[2]

By the time he had been in office a year, Roosevelt could point with pride to the public works department record. Not only had Partridge demanded the "highest standard of integrity," but in the eight months ending October 1, 1899, despite an increase in water-way traffic, the department had effected a twenty-five percent saving over the expenses of the previous year. It would be too much to say that politics had ceased to be of influence under the new

[1] Roosevelt to James M. E. O'Grady, January 17, 1899, TR MSS.; *New York Tribune,* February 2, 1899; Roosevelt to William F. Wharton, January 21, 1899, TR MSS.; *Buffalo Courier,* February 25, 1899; *Albany Argus,* February 2, 1899. Roosevelt to Partridge, January 23, 1899; to F. S. Fincke, January 23, 24, 1899; all TR MSS.

[2] *Public Papers* (1899), p. 46; *New York Tribune,* March 8, 9, 1899; Roosevelt to Partridge, January 19, 1899, TR MSS.; *New York Tribune,* April 8 and September 2, 7, 1899.

administration, yet the New York *Evening Post* held up Partridge as a model by which to judge other state officials.[3]

The second phase of the canal problem—the prosecution of Aldridge and Adams—demanded an even greater effort to eliminate suspicion of partisanship. When Roosevelt took office he might have accepted Judge Countryman's earlier finding that the canal mismanagement justified the initiation of criminal proceedings, but influenced possibly by Attorney General Hancock's disagreement with that opinion, he chose to conduct his own inquiry. "I would like to appoint a counsel to represent me in this canal business," the governor notified Odell early in January 1899, "and in view of the possibility and even probability of failure, I want a strong man, one who is not identified in any way with my interests, so that there shall be no possible question as to our having made every effort to get a conviction, so far as the effort can honestly and properly be made." After several refusals from lawyers who "like to talk reform but . . . don't want to give one hour's work or five cents worth of time," Austen G. Fox and Cleveland's former District Attorney for New York Wallace Macfarlane finally accepted the delicate assignment.[4]

In July 1899 these two Democrats of high standing submitted their finding that the state did not have a case warranting criminal prosecutions, because there was insufficient legal evidence of fraud, conspiracy, or collusion. They admitted that on some of the work

[3] *Public Papers* (1900), pp. 11–12; *New York Tribune,* March 20, 1899; New York *Evening Post,* February 18, 1899.

[4] *New York Tribune,* December 1, 1898; Roosevelt to Odell, January [4], 1899, TR MSS.; *Public Papers* (1899), pp. 37–38; Roosevelt to Franklin D. Locke, January 9, 1899, TR MSS.; *New York Tribune,* January 11, 1899; New York *Evening Post,* January 12, 1899. Roosevelt to Bill Sewall, January 18, 1899; to Platt, January 12, 1899; both TR MSS.

preliminary to contracts of the winter of 1896–1897 they might have made out "a prima facie case of 'wilful neglect' or 'omission' to take steps necessary 'to ascertain with all practicable accuracy' the quantity of work to be done," but the statute of limitations prevented any such prosecution. As for the reclassification of "earth" as "rock" by the engineers, which the Black canal investigating commission had criticized most severely, the Fox-Macfarlane report declared that Aldridge and Adams had acted within the Acts of 1895 and 1896. The principal fault was in the 1896 law which had changed the basis of contracting from the gross sum principle to the estimated quantity system and had thus vested these officials with "unduly great" discretionary powers which they had "abused." [5]

On the Republican side the partisan press at once claimed that Aldridge was "vindicated," on the Democratic, that this investigation had just been a "whitewash" of the deeds of the "canal thieves." But most New York editors were resigned to much the same philosophical acceptance of the result as was Roosevelt. To the deputy from the attorney general's office who had assisted in the probe, Roosevelt confided that he was "of course sorry we cannot either give a clean bill of health, or else have the offenders put in jail," but the case was comparable to that of an inefficient bank president who could be removed but not indicted.

[I believe that] *Perhaps* Aldridge should have been removed and Adams impeached last summer, but there is no use in [expressing such a belief] *talking about it,* for they are now both out of office. This is *not* for quotation. Thank Heaven, their successors are men of a very [different] *high* standard of public duty.[6]

[5] New York *Evening Post,* July 20, 1899.

[6] For Republican views, Rochester *Democrat and Chronicle* and *Schenectady Union,* July 20, 1899; Rochester *Post Express,* July 19, 1899; *Troy Times,* July 21, 1899 (all except last RS). For Democratic, *Brooklyn Citizen, New*

Up to this time Roosevelt's sincerity had gone unquestioned, but in a press interview on July 21, 1899, Judge Countryman put the matter in a different light. He had been willing to take over sole charge of the prosecutions in December, the judge declared, but without assurance of unimpeded support from the new administration he had refused to have anything further to do with the case. Could he have acted before the statute of limitations covered any "wilful neglect" in the early contracts? Countryman replied in the affirmative. At once some Democratic editors seized on this as evidence that Roosevelt had employed the "special counsel trick" simply in a "filibustering attempt" to protect Aldridge and Adams.[7]

That they had needed such protection could also be inferred from the attitude of Comptroller William Morgan, who picked this occasion to serve the first of several notices that he would refuse to settle payment of a completed canal contract which Black's investigating commission had found to be "improper." The specific contracts at issue were again those of the 1896–1897 period which fell within the statute of limitations. So the Comptroller's action lent itself to the use of those who accused the governor of playing politics with prosecution of the offenders.[8]

Roosevelt still might have ignored complaints about his handling of the canal investigation had not the *New York Tribune* adverted to the subject in an anti-Platt editorial the day after Morgan's announcement. The people had retained the Republican party in

---

York Journal, Utica Observer and New York *World,* July 20, 1899 (RS). Other: *Brooklyn Eagle,* July 20, 1899; *New York Tribune,* Syracuse *Post-Standard, Newburgh Daily News* and New York *Evening Post,* July 21, 1899 (all except last RS). Roosevelt to Benjamin J. Shove, July 19, 1899, TR MSS., the italicized words following brackets indicating Roosevelt's textual changes.

[7] New York *World,* July 22, 1899; *Brooklyn Citizen,* July 27, 1899 (RS).

[8] *New York Tribune,* July 27 and September 11, 1899; Comptroller, *Annual Report, 1899,* p. lxii.

control the November before, the *Tribune* recalled, "on the explicit and reiterated promise of its candidate for Governor and other accredited spokesmen that the canal frauds should be punished."

There was, to be sure, an "if possible" attached, but in view of facts which appeared to be indisputable, and of the candidate's reputation for capacity and moral courage, little attention was paid to that condition. Yet now the people are confronted with the frank confession that, aside from the Controller's spirited refusal to pay certain comparatively small claims, nothing can be done at present, or presumably at any time, to redress their wrongs or punish their unfaithful servants.

Platt was the man "primarily and chiefly responsible for this miserable affront and default," the editorial concluded, but the danger was that the taxpayers would blame the political party "that was made to appear in the light of sustaining Mr. Platt and may now be brought under suspicion of at least excusing Mr. Aldridge."[9]

On August 1 Roosevelt called the attention of Fox and Macfarlane to this "particularly dishonest editorial" and suggested that they publish a reply. "Of course," remarked the governor, "it comes because Whitelaw Reid having failed to extort some position for himself from the republican administration wants to get even with all the republicans." Roosevelt nevertheless thought that "the part attacking me for your work may possibly do some mischief." In his estimate, "a good cut at these slanders at the very beginning might be of avail."

Whitelaw Reid's importunity for high office and Platt's adamant opposition thereto were well-known within the party, the latest clash having come six months before when McKinley chose Joseph H. Choate over Reid as Ambassador to the Court of St. James. But however sound Roosevelt's analysis of Reid's motive, to some extent the *Tribune* was reflecting the dissatisfaction then being

[9] *New York Tribune,* July 28, 1899.

expressed over the delay which had worked to the advantage of the accused officials.[10]

Though Roosevelt's investigators did not make the suggested reply, and though Whitelaw Reid did not touch on the canal issue again, the *Tribune's* criticism continued to rankle in the governor's breast. Thus when on August 30 a member of his audience at the Hornellsville fair in the anti-canal county of Steuben interrupted his speech on the need for honesty in public life with the remark "How about the canals, governor?" Roosevelt interpreted it as another slight at the Fox-Macfarlane inquiry. "That is asked as though you are not quite sober," he shot back as he launched a spirited defense of his action in appointing "two of the best democratic lawyers I could get" to "probe that matter to the bottom." "They had the time, they had the money, they had the aid of the best counsel in the State," the governor wound up, "and they found that the charges made by you and your type were infamous lies and slanders, and so declared." [11]

The applause that followed this "bugle blast" reechoed in many Republican papers. Elsewhere, however, it was maintained that Roosevelt had gone too far in his denunciation. "Infamous Lies and Slander, Eh?" gloated the *Brooklyn Citizen* editor as he dipped his caustic pen, while the New York *World* summed up the Hornellsville reply as "an intemperate statement at variance with the facts." The *Brooklyn Eagle* saw evidence here of Roosevelt's "limitations": the Fox-Macfarlane report had shown that the canal officials "had done wrong, but that it was according to law," so the governor had "failed to distinguish between moral wrong and legal wrong."

[10] William R. Thayer, *The Life and Letters of John Hay*, 2 vols. (Boston, 1915), II, 183–197; Platt, *Autobiography*, pp. 260–261.

[11] *New York Journal*, August 31, 1899 (RS). The *Watertown Times* of the same date had a slightly different version.

Godkin's organ agreed, as the *New York Tribune* added that the questioner should have had "an accurate answer or none." [12]

Roosevelt had a stock answer to those who inquired about the Hornellsville incident.

> The man was drunk. He was simply trying to make a disturbance as he showed by all his subsequent actions. He started to interrupt me when I made my explanation. He was not asking in good faith . . . He was trying to break up my speech . . . He had probably been put up to it, for the sake of deceiving exactly such good citizens as yourself. Any man who knows anything about the canals and can question my conduct in having the best democratic lawyers I could choose decide upon the charges and then abiding by the result of their decision, cannot be considered as acting in good faith.[13]

Two days after this outburst at Hornellsville, on September 1 at the Jefferson County fair at Watertown, Roosevelt devoted most of his speech to the canal management past and present. The first question that had faced him in January, he declared, was "whether the contractors had done their work in certain cases with such slovenliness or with such indifference to the contract as to warrant our refusing to pay them"; he had concluded that "in certain instances at least this was true," and Comptroller Morgan had taken appropriate action. Then there had been "the question as to whether or not any State officials . . . had been guilty of any criminal misconduct"; after taking the "somewhat unusual course" of appointing two Democrats to probe the matter he had found that

[12]For favorable comments, *Watertown Times,* August 30, 1899; *Lockport Daily Journal,* August 31, 1899; Syracuse *Post-Standard* and *Poughkeepsie Evening Star,* September 1, 1899 (all RS). Also Rochester *Democrat and Chronicle,* September 1, 1899; *Syracuse Herald,* August 31, 1899. For criticism, *Brooklyn Citizen, Utica Observer* and *Brooklyn Eagle,* August 31, 1899 (RS); New York *Evening Post,* August 31, 1899; New York *World* and *New York Tribune,* September 1, 1899.

[13] Roosevelt to Theodore McGarrah, September 4, 1899, TR MSS.

the charge of criminal misconduct "fell to the ground." But finally there had been the question whether "the canals had been so handled in point of economy and efficiency as to leave no room for a change for the better"; the canal management had not been what it ought to have been, Roosevelt admitted, so he had picked Partridge as superintendent of public works and, with Bond as state engineer, both departments were now in excellent shape.[14]

The *Brooklyn Times* came close to the mark with its observation that at Watertown "Governor Roosevelt showed to considerably better advantage . . . than he did in his unpremeditated discussion . . . at Hornellsville." Yet his critics remained dissatisfied. Roosevelt had "modified his language without greatly modifying his statement," concluded the New York *World*, which continued to maintain that Countryman should have been told to go ahead with the prosecutions. The *New York Tribune* thought the governor still misinterpreted the Fox-Macfarlane report, and the New York *Evening Post* pointed out that the whole charge of criminal misconduct had not fallen to the ground, but only the opportunity for prosecution.[15]

The closest Roosevelt ever came to coping with this criticism was in a letter to Grant La Farge on September 18, shortly after the comptroller had held up payments on two more 1896 contracts. "This beating of tom-toms by the Comptroller amounts to absolutely nothing and is largely carried on at the expense of innocent contractors, who will get their money of course, but will have to wait for it," wrote the governor. He then added: "The statute of limitations really did not enter into the case as a factor at all, for

[14] *New York Tribune,* September 2, 1899.
[15] *Brooklyn Times* (RS) and New York *Evening Post,* September 2, 1899; New York *World,* September 3, 1899 (RS); *New York Tribune,* September 4, 1899.

the matters which it barred were exactly like those it admitted." If by this he meant that a case for "wilful neglect" or "omission" in the estimates on the early contracts could *not* be made, he was denying the contention of his critics. But he was also going beyond Fox and Macfarlane, who had thought such a case at least possible. It is significant that Roosevelt never expressed this opinion publicly.

The most likely explanation of Roosevelt's attitude is that he realized that the decision to ignore Countryman's opinion and to pursue a fresh investigation had influenced the final result. At the time the decision was made, in all probability he had acted in good faith, influenced primarily by the advice of Black's attorney general that Countryman's view was unsound. On the whole that advice had been good, for in important respects Fox and Macfarlane had gone against the judge's finding. Yet once the report was made, the fact remained that quicker action might have resulted in prosecutions. That circumstance was unpleasant. And Roosevelt, ever sensitive to any imputation that he had gone back on a campaign promise, had first to ignore it and then to explain it away to his own satisfaction.

Neither Roosevelt nor his critics operated in a vacuum devoid of politics. The Democratic press attacked the investigation's disinterestedness, while the Republican organs exaggerated the "vindication" of Aldridge. Because he bore responsibility for the probe and more especially because he shared his party's concern over the coming November's election, Roosevelt inevitably moved closer to the machine viewpoint. Not being under a similar compulsion, the more independent editors could hew closer to the balanced view, yet they in turn tended because of their anti-Plattism to exaggerate Aldridge's culpability and Roosevelt's expediency.

Thus, as the fall elections approached, the New York *Evening Post* grew increasingly critical until by October it was harping on the Hornellsville outburst, which it now viewed as the "price" which the governor had had to pay for "harmony" with Aldridge, and was conveniently ignoring the Watertown speech. In fact, nothing Roosevelt did pleased the *Post*: he purveyed Sunday School platitudes at the county fairs, cut a "sorry figure" when he had to back down from a request that the G.A.R. be first in line in the Dewey parade, condoned by silence McKinley's affront to the civil service, should take a lesson from his own speeches and distrust "tricky" men like Platt. Not even a Thanksgiving Day proclamation was immune; the "slap-dash Governer" in "wretched taste" had written a "silly proclamation" which gave "very much the impression of firing a revolver in the middle of a prayer, or of making the responses with three cheers and a tiger." [16]

So unusual was this reaction, and so derogatory did it become, that the canal investigation alone hardly accounted for it. This harder line arose out of the *Post's* fanatical opposition to boss rule at home and an expansionist policy abroad. Godkin's organ wanted to destroy Platt, not compromise with him. It wanted to retreat from imperialism, not defend it as Roosevelt did so vociferously on the stump that fall. When he quit the *Post* for the New York *Commercial Advertiser* the following January, Joe Bishop confided that he did so partly because the recent editorial orders had been to "break down" the governor at every opportunity. That word delighted Roosevelt, who had been complaining that the "Evening Post of course lies deliberately, simply because Godkin, Bishop, Garrison and the rest of the crowd have grown accustomed to use deliberate lying and slander as their ordinary weapons." And it confirmed the marked shift in the *Post's* editorial attitude after Hornellsville.[17]

[16] New York *Evening Post*, September 22, 23, 25, 30 and October 2, 5, 21, 23, 31, 1899.
[17] Roosevelt to Bishop, January 29, 1900; to Lucius B. Swift, February 13, 1900; to John H. Finley of *Harper's Weekly*, November 13, 1899; to John

Amid these repercussions of the Fox-Macfarlane investigation the governor turned with a feeling of relief to the final phase of the canal problem, the future improvement program. This aspect was equally controversial, as Roosevelt indicated when at Platt's suggestion he named a special board to sift possible solutions and come up with a comprehensive plan for the 1900 legislature. Only here the division of opinion did not fall between the reformers and the machine, exposing Roosevelt to the most damaging cross-fire. Rather it cut a wide swath through New York State, sundering normal political alignments and leaving the commercial interests opposed to the railroads, the urban areas (particularly Buffalo and New York City) to the upstate rural communities. Whatever the state determined to do about the completion of the nine-foot deepening project, no New Yorker would be unaffected by the decision.

Boss Platt obviously saw political advantage in delaying that decision, yet the appointment of a special committee found favor with diverse factions. A pro-canal paper such as the *Buffalo Express* would have preferred immediate action upon the Black canal investigating commission's recommendation that $15,000,000 additional be appropriated to complete the nine-foot 1895 project, yet the *Express* concluded that "the Governor has clearly acted from conscientious motives." At the same time the foes of the water-ways welcomed the opportunity to promote their case for abandon-ment or for sale to the federal government for a ship canal. Be-tween these extreme positions were those who sought an adequate solution to the controversial problem and therefore shared the governor's expressed desire for "the opinion of a body of experts,

C. Rose, November 10, 1899; all TR MSS. Oswald Garrison Villard, *Fighting Years: Memoirs of a Liberal Editor* (New York, 1939), pp. 128–129.

who shall include in their number not merely high-class engineers, but men of business, and especially men who have made a study of the problems of transportation." [18]

In his selection of this "body of experts" Roosevelt made some effort not to favor the pro-canal forces. Ex-Mayor George E. Green of Binghamton, for one, could be classed as an anti-canal man. The committee chairman, Francis Vinton Greene of New York City, was not noted for his preferences one way or the other, though the asphalt firm with which he was associated had performed contract work on the nine-million-dollar improvement. And before choosing John Scatcherd of Buffalo the governor was careful to ascertain that he had no stake in the elevating business, for "in the non-canal counties there is a great suspicion of any canal report from men who have an interest in Buffalo grain elevators." [19]

But as a leading lumber merchant Scatcherd could have as much interest in the Erie's future as did Buffalo's George H. Raymond, operator of several grain-transfer towers and an admitted canal exponent. And the two men whom Francis Vinton Greene recommended to complete the five-man committee were obviously partisan: Frank S. Witherbee was the owner of large iron mines at Port Henry on Lake Champlain, while Major T. W. Symons was a United States Army engineer best known for his advocacy of a 1500-ton barge canal over the Erie route. For one reason or another,

[18] *Buffalo Express,* March 9, 11, 1899; *Rochester Union and Advertiser,* March 13, 24, 1899; Roosevelt to F. V. Greene, March 8, 1899, printed in Canals Committee, *Report,* p. 235; *Daily Saratogian,* March 10, 1899 (RS); *Utica Herald,* March 11, 1899; Rochester *Post Express,* March 21, 1899 (RS); *Utica Observer,* March 14, 1899 (RS).

[19] Greene to Roosevelt, February 11, 1899, Greene MSS., NYPL; Roosevelt to Scatcherd, February 20, 1899, TR MSS. Actually the dominant elevator interests at Buffalo were controlled by the railroads; see Commerce Commission, *Report,* pp. 115–117, 836, 989–1023, 1171, 1192, 1355.

Scatcherd, Witherbee and Symons qualified as experts, but on balance they gave the Greene committee a pro-canal aspect.[20]

Knowing the scrutiny to which their views would be subjected for trace of bias, Greene and his colleagues made an exhaustive survey of the various alternatives. The editor of *Engineering News* particularly impressed them with his contention that the railroads would soon be able to reduce costs from the current 2½ mills to 1 mill per ton mile for wheat, but since "practical railway managers" did not sustain this argument the committee held to the belief that "water transportation is inherently cheaper than rail transportation." To keep the waterways competitive would nevertheless require further enlargement and more modern methods. This expense was justified, the board finally concluded, for otherwise Canada would capture much of the Great Lakes export grain trade, the prospective development of the iron and steel industry in Western New York would suffer, and the reputed value of the Erie Canal as a natural regulator of rail rates would surely disappear.[21]

Roosevelt's investigators accorded short shrift to proposals that canal management be turned over to the national government or that a ship passage be constructed. The former alternative had only a few advocates in the southern part of the state and had earned the unanimous censure of the Chamber of Commerce of New York. As for the deep waterway program, the committeemen found "certain insuperable difficulties in the way of such a canal ever

[20] Noble E. Whitford, *History of the Barge Canal of New York State,* Supplement to the Annual Report of the State Engineer and Surveyor for the Year Ended June 30, 1921 (Albany, 1922), p. 39; Thomas W. Symons, "The United States Government and the New York State Canals," Buffalo Historical Society *Publications* 13:126–129 (1909).

[21] Canals Committee, *Report,* pp. 47–54, 244–246, 251–252, 262, 271–274, 292–527. See also F. V. Greene, "The Inception of the Barge Canal Project," Buffalo Historical Society *Publications* 13:109–120 (1909).

being a success, no matter by whom constructed." The use of a single type of vessel on ocean, canal, and lake would simply not be economical compared to the system then in use or to one in which 1000-ton barges made it possible to break bulk only at New York. The tremendous cost of construction, moreover, put it clearly into the federal domain, "even though, as is probable, the result of such an examination shall be the abandonment of the project."[22]

If not these, then what did Greene and his colleagues recommend? Certainly their easiest course would have been to favor the appropriation of $15,000,000 to complete the 1895 project, since that would have been politically expedient and would have dovetailed with the final report of the commission which since early 1898 had been considering the causes of the decline of New York commerce. The findings of this body, made public at the same time as the Greene committee's, represented a strong indictment of the discrimination practiced by the trunk-line railroads against the Port of New York. For the system of differentials that diverted export trade to Boston, Philadelphia, and Baltimore the commissioners had no direct remedy, but they called on the state government to strengthen the Erie Canal as a regulatory force. Better terminal facilities, the repeal of the $50,000 capitalization limit on canal transportation companies, a reduction of one-half cent a bushel in the legal elevating charge—these and other measures should be taken. Above all the Commerce Commission recommended that New York carry through the 1895 project, which if finished as Engineer Adams had suggested would admit two 400-ton boats in a single lockage for west-east traffic.[23]

But the Greene committee came out for a bolder solution. Taking

[22] Canals Committee, *Report,* pp. 15–22.
[23] Commerce Commission, *Report,* pp. 39–72, 87–91, 94–95, 106–107, 114–115, 118–131. Under the original 1895 plan, a single lockage would take two boats of only 320 tons each.

initial expenditure and the resultant freight rate as its main guides, the committee concluded that it was "unwise to spend large sums of money in a mere betterment of the existing canal," that what was required was "a radical change, both in size and management." Accordingly the members unanimously recommended that the state spend close to $60,000,000 to build a 1000-ton barge canal. Such a canal would compete successfully with the St. Lawrence canals and with the railroads. It would permit transport rates comparable to those of a ship canal. It would be, in short, "a complete and permanent solution of the canal problem." [24]

Realizing that this tremendous expenditure would encounter the heaviest opposition, the Greene committee recommended further measures to make it more attractive. To overcome the hesitancy of citizens discouraged by past mismanagement, the legislature should take specific steps to place canal construction and operation upon a nonpolitical, business basis. And to counter hostile sentiment in the areas not served by the waterways, the legislature should provide that the river and canal counties alone would bear the cost of the improvement. The committee did not think such a step would be unconstitutional. Nor would it work a hardship on the affected regions, for these already possessed 90 percent of the state's assessed valuation and should be willing to assume the extra 10 percent of the cost in return for benefits received.[25]

On January 25, 1900, Roosevelt submitted the reports of the Commerce Commission and the Committee on Canals to the legislature. With all the suggestions of the former body he agreed except on one vital point—the enlargement of the Erie Canal. There he declared himself convinced by the "irrefutable" argument of

[24] Canals Committee, *Report*, p. 30. In addition, the committee recommended completion of the 1895 project on the Oswego and Champlain Canals, bringing the total estimated cost to $61,536,788.

[25] *Ibid.*, pp. 36–44, 34–35.

Greene and his colleagues for the 1000-ton barge canal. The expenditure called for was indeed great, Roosevelt asserted, but this bold project was the only solution adequate to New York's commercial needs.[26]

The pro-canal reports and the governor's endorsement cheered the commercial groups of the state, but most editors outside of New York City and Buffalo opposed or expressed disappointment with the 1000-ton barge canal proposal. Delegates to the New York State Farmers' Congress manifested their opposition by adopting a resolution introduced by that outspoken champion of the railroads, editor John I. Platt of the *Poughkeepsie Eagle*, that the state should only keep the canals in repair pending sale to the federal government for a ship canal. This rural attitude found many adherents in upstate cities bordering the Erie. As they saw it a ship passage might help their business interests, whereas the recommended project would accommodate chiefly through freight and so would profit only Buffalo and New York City. "In the proposed transaction," the *Utica Herald* gloomily remarked, "the interior of New York state occupies the position Manhattan boro [*sic*] would occupy in an enterprise that sought to connect Jersey City and Brooklyn by tunnel." [27]

"We shall soon have to decide about the canal business," Roosevelt wrote Platt at the end of January, to which the Easy Boss replied that he was "very much at a loss to decide what is wise and politic." The senator agreed that the improvement would be "good business and for the material welfare of the great State of New

[26] *Public Papers* (1900), pp. 69–82.
[27] *Albany Evening Journal,* January 27, 1900; *Utica Press,* February 27, 1900; *Utica Herald,* January 26, 1900 (RS); also Rochester *Post Express,* January 27, 1900 (RS); *Syracuse Herald,* February 9, 1900. According to Whitford, *History of Barge Canal,* p. 125, Editor Platt admitted in 1903 that the New York Central was paying his expenses.

York," yet the farmers were "so sensitive on the subject of taxation that we are in grave danger of wasting away our narrow margin of majority." When wisdom and expediency balanced out so closely, the politician found refuge in delay. "Perhaps it would be best to defer decided action on the Canal question until another year," concluded Platt. "By that time the Presidential election will be out of the way and the selection of a new legislature will have occurred, both of which results may relieve us from much embarrassment."[28]

In the weeks following, Roosevelt discovered that other influential citizens were hesitant about implementing the Greene committee's proposal. On February 20 Odell indicated that the organization definitely desired to postpone action until after the fall elections. That same evening the governor found canal advocates John D. Kernan, George H. Raymond, and Assemblyman Hill of Buffalo equally reluctant; in their opinion a proper bill could not be ready before March 10, a date so late as to render favorable consideration unlikely before adjournment. In Buffalo for his Washington's Birthday speech Roosevelt learned further from editor George E. Matthews of the independent Republican *Express* that pro-canal men in that area wanted first to have a thorough survey of possible routes and costs. By the time the governor returned to Albany he was ready to adopt this view.[29]

"It is evident that there will be no chance of passing the referendum resolution at this session," Roosevelt informed Francis Vinton Greene on February 26, yet "to be idle in the matter would be

[28] Platt to Roosevelt, February 3, 1900, in *Barnes* v. *Roosevelt,* pp. 2473–74.
[29] For Roosevelt's early plans for the bill, see Roosevelt to Frank S. Gardner, February 8, 1900; to F. V. Greene, February 10, 14, 1900; all TR MSS. See also New York *World,* February 21, 1900; *New York Tribune,* February 22, 1900; Roosevelt to George E. Matthews, to Greene, February 26, 1900, TR MSS.

little short of criminal." The effort to frame a suitable bill should continue; at the same time the legislature should put through an appropriation "for permitting a survey by the best engineers, but under the State Engineer and Surveyor, to determine exactly what route the canal shall take." The governor would do his best to persuade the organization leaders to support this plan, but even if they didn't, "I shall strive for this anyway, for it seems to me I am on safe grounds in taking this position."

Actually the proposal for a more detailed survey had much to commend it. The route which the Greene committee had mapped out represented a radical departure in canal building, since almost a third of the existent structure was to be superseded through the canalization of rivers. At some places the committee had not settled on a final course, at others it had suggested changes which would have an important bearing on individual towns and cities. Granted that it was wise neither to abandon the barge-canal project nor to attempt to rush it through at the 1900 session, a survey bill offered a sensible compromise. Indeed only by such a halfway step could the canal advocates hope to secure the necessary support of Senator Platt.[30]

Although Platt did not commit himself publicly until a month later, he must have consented to the introduction early in March of a bill appropriating $200,000 for the use of the state engineer in a complete 1000-ton barge-canal survey. If he thought the measure would go through without his active intervention, he was to be disappointed. Its opponents believed a survey would virtually commit the state to a later vote on the whole project, so they fought it in just as determined a fashion. Their chance of defeating it was particularly good in the senate, where they had a narrow but

[30] See Henry Wayland Hill, *Waterways and Construction in New York State,* Buffalo Historical Society Publications, XII (Buffalo, 1908), 250.

firm majority in the committee on finance. If this majority resisted all party and public pressures, passage appeared impossible.[31]

The pro-canal forces fired their opening salvo on March 10 at the Waldorf Astoria, where 500 diners representative of sixteen different commercial organizations heard Roosevelt warn against "fretful impatience" that would throw over the whole project just because the barge canal was not immediately secured. In words particularly aimed at Speaker Nixon, majority leader Allds and other leading legislators who had been invited to the affair at his suggestion, the governor argued that "careful preparation" was needed: the survey bill was an essential step in what he liked to call "this stupendous undertaking." At the same time, "thorough and ardent missionary work" was required to convince New Yorkers that the canals were not obsolete and would be run on a "strictly business basis." [32]

The arguments which Roosevelt and other speakers employed that evening were soon resounding at Albany. The New York Board of Trade and Transportation was particularly active in the lobby. So was the Buffalo Merchants' Exchange, in the person of George H. Raymond. As the session's end approached, letters and memorials rained into the legislative chambers.[33]

Still it took a bold parliamentary maneuver by the majority leader, Ellsworth of Niagara County, to extract the survey bill from committee. The anti-canal majority on the finance committee had been successfully resisting every pressure to release the measure, but two days before adjournment Ellsworth took the "most unusual" and indeed "very unkind and improper" step of having the committee's clerk report it out without notification to any of the

[31] *Albany Evening Journal,* March 7, 1900; *Buffalo Express,* April 4, 1900. See Hill, *Waterways,* p. 256.

[32] *New York Tribune,* March 11, 1900; *Brooklyn Eagle,* March 12, 1900 (RS); Roosevelt to Gustav V. Schwab, February 10, 1900, TR MSS.

[33] Hill, *Waterways,* p. 255.

members! A motion from the committee on rules to make it the pending order of business was then adopted by a vote of 31 to 16, all but one of the opposing votes coming from a Republican. The next day, with Lieutenant Governor Woodruff in the chair supporting Ellsworth on every ruling, the $200,000 appropriation passed the third reading in the senate 29 to 17.[34]

The floor manager of the survey bill in the assembly knew the committee on rules opposed it; in a quick canvass he found he lacked the two-thirds majority to compel its report. Here was the point for Senator Platt to exert his influence, and that he did. Shortly before noon on the last day of the session, the rules committee finally gave in. After a heated debate in which one outspoken opponent declared that the governor's attitude meant the "death knell" of Republicanism in New York, a bipartisan majority sent the measure to the executive by a vote of 97 to 47.[35]

Of course Platt had assumed a share of the responsibility for this affront to the anti-canal Republicans in upstate communities, but as Roosevelt reported to Lodge, "I am in office and I am the man with whom they will feel discontented." To the secretary of the New York Board of Trade and Transportation, Frank S. Gardner, with whom he had cooperated so closely throughout, the governor communicated his hope that the commercial interests "will see to it that something is done to offset the losses our action may possibly cause in certain sections." The Democrats thought the G.O.P. leaders had made "a fatal mistake," concluded Roosevelt, "and I trust that the commercial interests will undeceive them." [36]

Opponents of the 1000-ton barge canal did not surrender easily.

[34] *Senate Journal* (1900), pp. 1744–46, 1786–87; New York *Evening Post* and *Albany Evening Journal,* April 5, 1900.
[35] Hill, *Waterways,* pp. 256–357; *Albany Evening Journal* and *Buffalo Express,* April 6, 1900.
[36] Roosevelt to Lodge, April 9, 1900; to Gardner, April 6, 1900; both TR MSS.

The next year Odell laid aside the survey report of the state engineer and came out in favor of a less expensive improvement plan which the Greene committee had considered but discarded. Such an attempt at compromise satisfied no one and therefore failed. Not until 1903 did the barge-canal advocates convert Odell to their cause. Then in a memorable contest first the legislature and then the populace approved a referendum resolution identical in most respects to that advanced by the Greene committee three years before.[37]

Completed with a rush during World War I, and utilized since mainly for gasoline transport, this expensive project may not have fulfilled the hopes once held for it. It is more significant that men here called on government to intervene drastically in the economy in order to promote the public welfare. As several scholarly studies have demonstrated, the canal-building of the first half of the nineteenth century had been mercantilistic in character; the retreat of the state from such enterprises had marked the shift from mercantilism to laissez-faire liberalism. New York alone had clung to her artificial waterways, first because of their profitability and then because of their value as a regulator of railroad freight rates. Had the canal advocates been more farsighted in 1900 they might have realized that the effective entry of the federal government into the regulatory field would soon supersede the Erie's function. But given the immediate means at their disposal their solution had much logic behind it.[38]

[37] The 1903 referendum called for greater improvements and would cost over $100,000,000. Because of its dubious constitutionality the plan to assess only the river and canal counties was dropped. See Whitford, *History of Barge Canal*, chs. iv–vi.

[38] Cf. Louis Hartz, *Economic Policy and Democratic Thought: Pennsylvania 1776–1860* (Cambridge, Mass., 1948); Oscar and Mary F. Handlin, *Commonwealth; A Study of the Role of Government in the American Economy: Massachusetts 1774–1861* (Cambridge, Mass., 1948). See also John D. Kernan,

Roosevelt shared their attitude to such an extent that he forsook political expediency in the matter. His similarity of view sprang in part from his New York City background. It also owed much to his Hamiltonian belief in the positive functions of the state. Though he had reservations about the extent to which government should interfere in society, the boundaries he set were amenable to change once the wisdom and justice of further collective action were evident. The dynamic possibilities of this doctrine became more apparent when as President he was freed of the limitations placed upon the individual states by the federal Constitution. But in his stand on the barge canal proposal was a harbinger of the position he would later assume toward government regulation of the railroads.

"The Function of New York's Barge Canals in Controlling Freight Rates," Buffalo Historical Society *Publications* 13:135–156 (1909).

CHAPTER X The Needs of Labor

No economic group concerned Roosevelt more than labor. As governor he would support bills to extend the protection of the labor law and to improve its enforcement. He would devote much attention to the day-to-day administration of that law by subordinate officials. Any legitimate effort to improve the lot of the workingman could enlist his aid; he would only draw the line at extralegal actions that endangered the peace and property of the community. And in the rare instance when he intervened in a strike, he at least sought to remedy the cause of the dispute.

Of course Roosevelt did not minimize the dangers of state intervention in the "delicate and complicated" machinery of business. As he stated in his first annual message, "no amount of legislation . . . can supply the lack of individual initiative" and great care should be exercised that "the good to be achieved is undoubted" and will not be "counteracted by harm." But then he added that "the development in extent and variety of industries has necessitated legislation in the interest of labor," from which "much good has resulted." Direct action by the government was "not necessarily against the interests of capital"; "on the contrary, if wisely devised it is for the benefit of both laborers and employers." It was to the formulation of just such a program that he had turned as one of his first postelection tasks.[1]

For advice in this field the governor initially brought together

[1] *Public Papers* (1899), pp. 9–10.

three prominent trade unionists—Henry Weissman of the Bakers Union, Henry White of the United Garment Workers, and William Derflinger of the Typographical Union—for a conference with his friend Jacob A. Riis, social worker James B. Reynolds of the University Settlement, and George Gunton, director of the Institute of Social Economics and editor of *Gunton's Magazine*. When Quigg learned of the projected meeting he warned that Weissman "was in general disfavor with the very people [whom he] claimed to represent" and that "Gunton's publications issued from a scab office and have done so for a number of years to the great scandal of all regularly constituted labor people." If Roosevelt heeded these criticisms it was not obvious at the time. An acquaintance from police commissioner days, Weissman was not conspicuously consulted thereafter, but Gunton continued to enjoy the governor's confidence.[2]

It is indeed significant that Roosevelt valued Gunton's opinion on labor matters but not on trusts. Gunton considered the growth of big business not only inevitable but almost wholly good—a view quite compatible with the contention of some that Standard Oil subsidized his publications. But at the same time this publicist advocated "big labor" to match "big business." Protegé of Ira Steward, a prominent leader in the eight-hour movement in the 1890's, Gunton had developed Steward's philosophy in *Wealth and Progress* (1887) and *Principles of Social Economics* (1891). Aside from Quigg's critical observation, few questioned Gunton's concern for the development of union organization and labor interests generally.[3]

[2] Quigg to Roosevelt, November 19, 1898, Quigg MSS.; Roosevelt, *Autobiography*, p. 221.
[3] Daniel C. Weary, "George Gunton: Advocate for Labor, Defender of Trusts, Social Darwinian," unpub. thesis (Harvard College, 1949).

The men whom Roosevelt called together on November 22 were familiar with the strides made in New York since 1883, when the establishment of the state bureau of labor statistics had "marked the real beginning of labor legislation in this State." At the same time they recognized that much of this advance was more illusory than real, since enforcement was weak. It was their considered opinion that labor's major requirement of the moment was not more laws, but better enforcement of the existing statutes. In his annual message the governor incorporated their several recommendations to this end.[4]

In the first place he proposed that "the enforcement of the entire body of legislation relating to labor be placed under the Board of Factory Inspectors"; and for this purpose that the number of inspectors be increased from thirty-six to fifty and the governor empowered to appoint additional unsalaried deputies. The bill subsequently introduced and passed fell short of this request, for no provision was made for unsalaried deputies and the associated dry-goods merchants successfully opposed the transfer of the enforcement of the Mercantile Act (which had extended to stores the same hour and age restrictions upon minors in industry, except during the Christmas rush season) from the boards of health to the factory inspector. On the other hand certain provisions, notably a regulation that children under sixteen were not to operate dangerous machinery, and an extension to *all* women of the ten-hour

[4] Adna F. Weber, *Labor Legislation in New York* (Albany, 1904), pp. 3, 10–11, 17; Fred R. Fairchild, *The Factory Legislation of the State of New York,* American Economic Association Publications, vol. VI, no. 4 (New York, 1906), p. 10; Clara M. Beyer, *History of Labor Legislation for Women in Three States,* U.S. Department of Labor Bulletin of the Woman's Bureau, no. 66 (Washington, 1929), pp. 69–70; Elizabeth P. Baker, *Protective Labor Legislation,* Columbia University Studies in History, Economics and Public Law, vol. CXVI, no. 2 (New York, 1925), pp. 41–42.

law for minors, were positive steps for which Roosevelt had not asked.[5]

The governor's second recommendation concerned regulation of the "sweatshop system, which is practically the conversion of the poorest class of living apartments into unwholesome, pest-creating, and crime-breeding workshops." The main difficulty under the 1897 law, which permitted members of the "immediate family" to use a room or apartment in a dwelling house or tenement for purposes of manufacture, was that the factory inspector found it virtually impossible to distinguish the illegal sweatshop. Roosevelt proposed a new system, modelled upon that of Massachusetts, whereby all such quarters would be licensed by the inspector to insure that "the common demands of sanitation, domestic decency and wholesome industrial methods" were observed.[6]

Though not as stringent as he desired, the bill which both houses finally approved was, in Roosevelt's view, an "enormous stride in advance." It tightened the qualifications for licensed manufacture, permitted the factory inspector to enter all shops to assure their "clean and sanitary condition," and required that contractors keep a register of subcontractors so that the whole "task system" could be supervised more readily. With this new authority, and with an augmented inspection force, the governor had high hopes for better regulation of the sweatshop evil.[7]

[5] Chapter 192, *Laws of New York* (1899). On the bill's shortcomings, see Baker, *Protective Labor Legislation*, pp. 309–310, 151.

[6] Industrial Commission, *Report*, 19 vols. (Washington, 1899–1902), VI, 27–28, 185–186; Mabel H. Willett, *The Employment of Women in the Clothing Trade*, Columbia University Studies in History, Economics and Public Law, vol. XVI, no. 2 (New York, 1902), pp. 152–153; *Public Papers* (1899), pp. 13–14.

[7] *Public Papers* (1899), pp. 65–66. Gunton had suggested several amendments which Roosevelt approved but which did not get in: Roosevelt to Costello, March 13, 14, 1899; to Gunton, January 5, 1900; all TR MSS.

A final recommendation was that "the law requiring an eight-hour day and a prevailing rate of wages for State employees" should be entrusted to some enforcing authority. Ostensibly the law enlarging the factory inspector's office covered this requirement, but the Workingmen's Federation really desired a complete prohibition of overtime for "laborers, workmen or mechanics" on government work "except in cases of extraordinary emergency caused by fire, flood, or danger to life or property." Roosevelt had not contemplated such a drastic step, and while the legislature was considering it he privately questioned the wisdom of including locktenders and certain building employees within its scope. When the measure came before him for action he nevertheless accepted it (with these reservations) as pursuant to his proposal that the eight-hour law "be so amended as to make it effective." "The permission to work overtime for additional compensation has resulted in such widespread evasion and nullification of the purposes of the law," he concluded, "that it is wise to take it away in most cases." [8]

Roosevelt also came to endorse a bill to set a ten-hour day (and seventy-hour week) for drug clerks, who reportedly worked from "fourteen to sixteen hours daily" and often "slept on cots in the back of the store." In response to protests from druggists and clerks he agreed to a hearing before acting on the bill, however, and afterwards he confessed he was "very much puzzled." Some employees had indeed favored the measure—as had Riis, Reynolds, and Seth Low—but there had been a "larger number of protests also from drug clerks who insist . . . it . . . would knock out their day off." The smaller druggists with but one clerk had contended that it would be an "absolute ruin," and that "in their occupation the hours of the drug clerk have to be long for the same reason that doctors

[8] *Public Papers* (1899), p. 14; Roosevelt to Henry White, February 15, 1899, TR MSS.; *Public Papers* (1899), pp. 94–95.

[*sic*] hours are long." Admittedly the labor unions favored the bill, but Roosevelt thought that simply meant "that they go for anything that calls for shorter hours"; he had been "by no means impressed" by the union representatives at the hearing.[9]

Roosevelt was genuinely perplexed. He had not been prejudiced in advance against the secretary of the Druggists' League for Shorter Hours, Tammanyite Edward Thimme, but this official hardly advanced his cause by charging afterwards that the conduct of the hearing had been "manifestly unfair" and by appealing to the people to force the governor's hand. Roosevelt asked Jake Riis to conduct a quick poll of pharmacies in New York City, in an effort to discover the true situation. When Riis reported back that smaller druggists generally were opposed and that sentiment did exist among the clerks against elimination of their every-other-Sunday holidays, the governor decided to withhold his approval until the following year, at which time another bill that better met these objections was finally enacted.[10]

Far more important in their ramifications were the employer's liability measures which the Workingmen's Federation of New York sponsored to obtain a better legal remedy in case of injury than the common law, as narrowly interpreted by the United States courts, then allowed the employee. The governor had no chance to take an official stand on these proposals in 1899, for railroad

[9] Roosevelt to Riis, April 12, 1899, TR MSS.; Howard L. Hurwitz, *Theodore Roosevelt and Labor in New York State, 1880–1900*, Columbia University Studies in History, Economics and Public Law, no. 500 (New York, 1943), p. 230, citing Edward Thimme, "Drug Trade Slavery," *American Federationist* 5:241–242 (February 1899); Roosevelt to Riis, May 11, 1899, TR MSS.

[10] Hurwitz (*Theodore Roosevelt and Labor*, pp. 230ff.) not only is unsympathetic to Roosevelt in this incident, but through an error in dates gives the false impression that the governor was prejudiced prior to the hearing. On Thimme's activities, see *New York Tribune*, May 13, 1899. See also Roosevelt to Riis, May 17, 1899, TR MSS.; *Public Papers* (1899), p. 127.

opposition obstructed passage of one bill based on the thorough-going English act of 1897 and another modelled on the less drastic Massachusetts law. Unofficially, however, he favored legislation of this type. And despite Odell's objection, Roosevelt came out in his annual message of 1900 for increased protection for workers in dangerous occupations. That advocacy marked Roosevelt as a man who understood labor's needs, but in terms of actual accomplishment it meant little, for the employer's liability bill also failed at that session.[11]

The refusal of the assembly committee on rules to discharge the milder bill based on the Massachusetts statute of 1887 (under which the employee would still have to prove that he had been "exercising due care" at the time of the injury) was an instructive lesson in the politics of labor legislation. The narrowly divided senate had been no obstacle, for Democrats were wont to favor proposals in labor's interest. The real opposition came from the Republican leaders. They stopped the employer's liability bill, and they would have given Roosevelt trouble with other labor measures that affected important business interests adversely. Increased factory inspection, improved regulation of the sweatshop, and enforcement of high standards on public works were good measures which laboring men approved. But these also were conservative efforts at reform, which in good part explained their unopposed success.

The situation that confronted Roosevelt as he turned to the administration of the labor law was more complex and more dis-

[11] Adna F. Weber, "Employer's Liability and Accident Insurance," *Political Science Quarterly* 17:256–283 (June 1902); Industrial Commission, *Report,* VII, 815, 305; *New York Tribune,* April 28, 1899; Sarah S. Whittlesey, *Massachusetts Labor Legislation,* Ann. Am. Acad., Supplement (January 1901), pp. 30–31, 134–135; Roosevelt to James Roosevelt, April 17, 1899, TR MSS.; Odell to Roosevelt, December 26, 1899, TR MSS. (LC); *Public Papers* (1900), p. 31.

couraging. Anxious though they were to have good enforcement, social reformers and independent editors often disagreed on appointments and policies. So did the leaders of organized labor, who were divided racially and religiously as well as politically. And Republican politicians were chiefly concerned not with efficient performance, but with the placement of loyal party men in a state job. Roosevelt could least afford to ignore the organization's wishes, yet he could not disregard contrary interests, either, particularly when they challenged the record of the state's agencies. Out of this recurrent conflict evolved the course Roosevelt followed in his labor policy.

His first major appointment revealed something of the difficulties. The election of James T. McDonough as secretary of state had opened up his old post of commissioner of labor statistics. Of the various Republicans suggested as successors Roosevelt was inclined to favor ex-Assemblyman John Williams of Utica, an official in the carpenters' union. As for John McMackin of New York City, deputy in the department since 1896 and personal choice of McDonough to succeed, the governor asserted that the "labor men object very strongly to him, and tell ugly stories about his connection with the Coogan campaign." Merchant George Coogan's lavish expenditures as Labor party candidate in the New York mayoralty campaign of 1888 had been the scandal of the labor world. But Platt had so committed himself to McDonough that Roosevelt reluctantly agreed to name McMackin.[12]

The ensuing protests in New York City labor circles seemed to

[12] Roosevelt to Platt, January 12, 16, 1899, TR MSS.; *Barnes* v. *Roosevelt*, pp. 740–741; Samuel Gompers, *Seventy Years of Life and Labor: An Autobiography*, 2 vols. (New York, 1925), I, 323; Hurwitz, *Theodore Roosevelt and Labor*, pp. 209–211. The interpretation of this episode here presented differs somewhat from Hurwitz's. By treating "organized labor" as an entity, Hurwitz fails to discriminate the political and religious complications of the labor world. He also errs in details; thus William Martin is not just a "casual correspondent" but a leader in the Knights of Labor (*ibid.*, p. 211n122).

confirm the governor's fear that this would "not be a wise appointment." McMackin, it was charged, had not worked at his painter's trade since 1885 and had not been endorsed by a single trade union or Knights of Labor Assembly in the city: he was simply a Republican politician who had managed the notorious Coogan campaign.[13]

But behind these protests lurked other motives. When the Allied Printing Trades Council called the appointment "an insult to organized labor" it did not add that an ex-president of the typographical union, C. J. Dumar, had also been a candidate for the position. Nor did the Democratic papers airing the charges mention the fact that most metropolitan union men were not Republicans. Among many Irish Catholic labor leaders, the dislike for the nominee went back to the 1886–1887 period when McMackin, then prominent in the United Labor party, had stood by Father Edward McGlynn in his famous controversy with Archbishop Corrigan. Many of McGlynn's following, McMackin among them, had subsequently gone over to become "'the John the Baptists' of Republicanism in New York labor circles." Hence it was no coincidence that one of the strongest recommendations for McMackin came from the Rev. Sylvester Malone of St. Peter's and St. Paul's in Brooklyn, a Republican, a University regent, and a foremost defender of McGlynn within the church.[14]

Actually Roosevelt never had cause to regret his acceptance of

[13] New York Journal, January 18, 1899; New York World, January 19, 20, 1899; New York Telegram (Tammany), January 18, 1899 (all RS).

[14] New York Journal, January 18, 1899 (RS); Frederick J. Zwierlein, "The Catholic Church in New York State," in A. C. Flick, ed., History of the State of New York, 10 vols. (New York, 1933–1937), V, 193–196; Henry George, Jr., The Life of Henry George (London, 1900), pp. 505–506; Gompers, Autobiography, I, 314, 320, 322; Roosevelt to Malone, January 26, 1899, TR MSS.; Sylvester L. Malone, ed., Memorial of the Golden Jubilee of Rev. Sylvester Malone (Brooklyn, 1895), pp. 61–63, 71–73.

McMackin, who proved an efficient administrator and in 1901 was appointed New York's first labor commissioner by Governor Odell. But it was far easier to perform satisfactorily in a fact-finding body such as the bureau of labor statistics than it was in the office charged with enforcement of the labor law. The work of the factory inspector's agency was the true measure of the Roosevelt administration's attention to workingmen's interests.

Charges against the assistant factory inspector (whose duties encompassed the Greater New York area) were already on file when Roosevelt entered office, so principally on Quigg's recommendation he interviewed and approved a replacement at the expiration of the incumbent's term in April 1899. Chief Inspector Daniel O'Leary's term would be up then, too, but as Roosevelt wrote Platt on February 10, "O'Leary is seemingly doing pretty well, and I understand you want him reappointed." Nor did the governor alter his view when protests arose over O'Leary's alleged failure to prosecute the laws against sweatshops, for upon investigation Jake Riis reported that the office was doing as well as could be expected with its inadequate force. Roosevelt had no sooner accepted this finding and dismissed the charges brought by the United Brotherhood of Tailors, however, than he discovered "poor O'Leary" had written some "dreadful" letters to his assistant in New York City with reference to political work required of the deputies in the last election. He at last determined to supplant O'Leary with John Williams of Utica, the man McMackin had beaten out for the commissionership.[15]

[15] Roosevelt to Quigg, February 6, 1899; to Platt, February 10, 1899; to O'Leary, March 9, 1899; to M. M. Dawson, to Gunton, March 13, 1899; all TR MSS. Riis to Roosevelt, March 21, 1899, Riis MSS.; Roosevelt to Gunton, March 31, 1899, TR MSS. Also New York *World*, February 24, 25 and March 2, 5, 15, 1899; *New York Tribune*, April 2, 3, 4, 1899. Hurwitz intimates (*Theodore Roosevelt and Labor*, p. 205) that Roosevelt took the easy way

Roosevelt hoped that Williams' appointment and the new laws effective in September 1899 would improve this agency's work. On May 3 he held another labor conference which reviewed methods of enforcement and the tests for applicants for deputy inspectorships. The governor also directed Williams to consult with Riis and with Mrs. Florence Kelley, formerly chief factory inspector in Illinois under Governor Altgeld and presently secretary to the newly organized National Consumers' League. This body sought to abolish rather than simply to regulate tenement manufacture, yet Mrs. Kelley was eager to cooperate with state officials. So, too, was social worker James B. Reynolds, with whom Williams was admonished to work closely.[16]

After four months' operation under the new law Roosevelt could report that "4,942 licenses have been granted and 918 refused," but such figures did not satisfy the reformers, who found particular fault with ex-State Inspector O'Leary's work. O'Leary had not languished long without a job, for Williams had taken him on in August as head of the licensing bureau in the New York City area. Several times thereafter Reynolds had complained to the governor about O'Leary's uncooperative conduct, until Roosevelt notified Williams in mid-November that "I shall tolerate no refusal to enforce the provisions of the law and no failure on the part of any of my subordinates to show proper courtesy to individual citizens, especially those disinterestedly anxious to help in the work of the Department." Yet in December Mrs. Kelley among others came

out of an embarrassing situation, but the governor's attitude was as much that of the civil-service reformer as the expedient politician.

[16] *New York Tribune,* May 3, 1899; Bureau of Labor Statistics, *Bulletin* (June 1899), pp. 29–33; Roosevelt to Williams, June 2, 1899, TR MSS.; Maud Nathan, *The Story of an Epoch-Making Movement* (New York, 1926), pp. 55–56, 67–69; Consumers' League of the City of New York, *Report for the Year Ending December, 1899,* pp. 13–16; Roosevelt to Williams, October 7, 1899, TR MSS.

forward at a protest meeting in New York City to attack O'Leary's office and to recommend that a list of 200 unfit shops recently licensed be sent to the governor. Though irritated that she had not approached him first with these grievances, Roosevelt conceded the need for a fresh investigation into "any matter where abuses are charged now to exist." [17]

The special inquiry which Jacob Riis accordingly undertook in December 1899 confirmed the criticisms of the reform element. O'Leary had indeed been derelict in his duty. More than that, Riis found that Williams had done as well but no better than previous chiefs; the trouble was that the office had never fulfilled its opportunities, had "never risen above the political organization." A good state factory inspector, averred Riis, would have held frequent conferences to see that his deputies understood their responsibilities: Williams had not done that, and the governor would not be justified in requesting additional inspectors until more efficient use of the present force had been attained. [18]

These faults were more easily marked than remedied. The governor thought it "was perfectly evident that O'Leary will have to go" and so informed Williams. But Factory Inspector Williams refused to consider his deputy guilty as charged. In that decision he had the support of the Republican organization, for Odell warned Roosevelt on January 7 to exercise care "in any action taken with O'Leary, Factory Inspector, as he has been a pretty good friend of ours." And Williams' view corresponded to that of

[17] *Public Papers* (1900), p. 30; Roosevelt to Williams, November 16, 1899, TR MSS.; *New York Tribune*, December 10, 1899; *Glen Falls Republican*, December 15, 1899 (RS); Roosevelt to Reynolds, December 13, 1899, TR MSS. Roosevelt had advised the Civil Service Reform Association not to protest the appointment because with the exception of the political letters O'Leary had rendered excellent service: Roosevelt to McAneny, August 7, 1899, TR MSS.

[18] Riis to Roosevelt, January 15, 1900, TR MSS. (LC).

an investigating committee of the Workingmen's State Federation, which declared that the factory inspectors had done a fine job particularly in New York City. Much as he distrusted such findings, Roosevelt was stymied; the only way to get at O'Leary was to remove Williams, and that was impossible except by "practically impeachment proceedings before the Senate." [19]

Legislative opposition further checked remedial efforts. In his annual message he had repeated his request, ignored the previous year, for the power to appoint unsalaried deputies. Following another detailed complaint from Mrs. Kelley in early February 1900, Roosevelt instructed Reynolds to prepare a suitable bill and begin agitation for its passage. "I am not entirely satisfied that the best results are being obtained from that department," Roosevelt wrote the chairmen of the finance committees, "and I can be dead sure that they will be obtained if I am given permission to appoint unpaid volunteer factory inspectors." A measure to that effect was introduced on February 15; a month later it still rested in committee. Though a strong appeal by the governor resulted in a favorable report to the senate "with some amendments," the measure eventually progressed no further than the committee of the whole. [20]

These developments did not quench Roosevelt's determination. In late May he and Riis made a dramatic foray into the tenement district of the lower East Side. They found conditions there improved from the year before, but the governor suggested a number of changes to Inspector Williams. And since Mrs. Kelley always

[19] Roosevelt to Williams, to Riis, December 30, 1899; to McAneny, February 16, 1900; all TR MSS. *New York Tribune*, January 15, 1900; Roosevelt to Josephine Shaw Lowell, February 20, 1900, TR MSS. For Williams' defense against "sometimes misguided" philanthropists see Factory Inspector, *Annual Report, 1899*, pp. 43–44, 52–53.

[20] *Public Papers* (1900), p. 30. Roosevelt to Williams, February 8, 1900; to Reynolds, February 9, 15, 1900; to Higgins, to Allds, February 9, 1900; to Brackett, March 17, 1900; all TR MSS. *Senate Journal* (1900), p. 1051.

held up Massachusetts as a model for factory inspection, Roosevelt had his officials make a personal investigation of that state's system. As a result, some of the Bay State's methods were introduced in New York.[21]

Criticism of the enforcement of the antisweatshop law nevertheless continued, and inevitably so. The real object of the National Consumers' League and the garment worker unions was the prohibition of tenement manufacture; since that appeared unconstitutional under the court's decision in the Jacobs case, they accepted state regulation only as an expedient, and always in the hope that it would lead to the progressive elimination of industrial homework. They were dissatisfied with the progress which Riis observed toward abatement of the worst conditions. They were unappreciative of the "herculean task" which confronted even the earnest factory inspector. They were therefore partial judges of the Roosevelt administration's policies.[22]

The governor would have pleased the National Consumers' League if he had tried to appoint Mrs. Florence Kelley in O'Leary's place originally, but Roosevelt had regarded that as an impossible move politically. She was not a New Yorker, he had pointed out to Jacob Riis, and "to all the people who do not know (and they include practically everyone) the fact that she was appointed by Altgeld is a most tremendous handicap." Certainly her experience as Illinois' chief factory inspector had fitted her for the position, but in the public's view she would always be associated with the

[21] Roosevelt to Riis, May 2, 1900, TR MSS.; Jacob A. Riis, *Theodore Roosevelt The Citizen* (New York, 1904), pp. 216–220; Hurwitz, *Theodore Roosevelt and Labor*, p. 98; *New York Times*, June 1, 1900 (RS); Roosevelt to Williams, June 4, 1900, TR MSS.; Consumers' League for the City of New York, *Report, 1900*, pp. 18–19.

[22] National Consumers' League, *Second Annual Report, year ending March 6, 1901*, p. 8; Factory Inspector, *Annual Report, 1900*, pp. 16–17, 29–30, 34–37.

governor who had pardoned anarchists and sympathized with Pullman strikers. "Any recommendation she makes against the interests of the employers," Roosevelt had concluded, "would be at once met by the cry that 'this is Altgeldism.'"[23]

The frustrating difficulties in enforcing the labor law were confined largely to the antisweatshop provisions. When the governor received reports of other violations, notably of the eight-hour day and the prevailing rate of wages on public works, he customarily referred them to the factory inspector. Seldom did that agency's disposition of such cases require Roosevelt's attention, for the social reformers had far less experience and interest in these matters than in tenement manufacture. Thus it was usually under the acute and unfavorable conditions of a strike that the governor here became actively concerned.[24]

Conciliation of industrial disputes was the task of a three-man board of mediation, a state agency which had been under editorial fire as a "useless" and "expensive" body. Roosevelt, who recognized that the board "really amounts to nothing at all now," planned to devote "particular attention" to its work and if possible to improve its standing. In making appointments to the three places early in his term he nevertheless found that politics, geography, and willingness to serve all hampered his selection. As a result the new board, though perhaps the better for the replacement of an antilabor Democratic editor by a court reporter who was the brother-in-law of ex-United States Senator Murphy, left much to be desired from the standpoint of experience in industrial disputes.[25]

[23] Roosevelt to Riis, January 23, 1899, TR MSS. Both Riis and Maud Nathan (*The Story of an Epoch-Making Movement,* pp. 55–56, 68) had suggested Mrs. Kelley. For Roosevelt's later reaction to this suggestion, see Roosevelt to Josephine Shaw Lowell, February 20, 1900, TR MSS.
[24] See, for example, Roosevelt to Williams, July 26, 1899, TR MSS.
[25] *Utica Herald,* February 20, 1899; *New York Tribune,* February 18, 1899;

The first major controversy into which the state mediators stepped was at the Buffalo docks, where 2,000 unskilled workers who shoveled grain out of ships refused to report for work at the beginning of the new season. The men directed their protest principally at William J. Conners, publisher of the *Buffalo Courier/Enquirer*, Democratic politician and holder of the contract with the Lake Carriers' Association for the transfer of grain from ship to elevator. The year before he had paid shovelers the going rate of $1.85 per 1000 bushels, enabling them to earn $400 or $500 a season, but now he proposed to pay 25 cents per hour of actual work, a move which the men claimed would drastically reduce their total pay. The shovelers, recently organized as an A. F. of L. local, demanded replacement of the contractor middleman by direct agreements with the elevators. They also disliked being hired and paid in a saloon, but the abolition of the Conners contract was their main objective.[26]

On his part Conners maintained that he could not abrogate his contract, on which he had put up a $100,000 bond, without being sued for heavy damages. The man behind the new union, claimed the Buffalo publisher, was a Republican politician, Rowland Blennerhasset Mahany, who though popular among Polish Catholics had failed in his bid for reelection to Congress in 1898 and now with the help of the *Catholic Union and Times* was fomenting trouble as a means of revenge. Conners maintained that 25 cents

Auburn Bulletin and Rochester *Post Express,* April 4, 1899; Rochester *Democrat and Chronicle,* May 12, 1899 (all RS except *Tribune*). Roosevelt to John R. Commons, January 9, 1899; to H. H. Vreeland (Pres., Metropolitan Street Railway), January 23, 1899; to Seth Low, January 23, 31, 1899; to Charles S. Fairchild, February 20, 1899; all TR MSS.

[26] *Buffalo Express,* May 5, 1899; Mediation Board, *Annual Report, 1899,* pp. 147–148; *Utica Herald,* May 25, 1899; Hurwitz, *Theodore Roosevelt and Labor,* p. 244.

an hour would mean $2.50 a day, the highest wage in the state for unskilled labor. He also claimed that he intended to abolish the connection between his boss scoopers and the saloons. Stout support for Conners came from a former state mediator, William Purcell, whose *Rochester Union and Advertiser* asserted that the only question at issue in this "bootless controversy" was the inviolability of contracts.[27]

Though technically no strike or lockout had occurred, Roosevelt directed the mediation board to proceed to the scene and advised Major General Charles F. Roe to ready the militia in the area in case of an emergency. When labor representatives carried their protest against this decision to the executive chamber, the governor told them that "the militia would not be called out unless the local authorities stated that they needed them; but that the minute this condition was found to exist, they would be called out." Several killings and fights did occur at the docks, but no riot or widespread disorder ensued. Sympathy with many of the men's objectives was so widespread and respect for their good conduct so high, that Buffalo's Democratic mayor was under no public pressure to call in state troops.[28]

Through the first two weeks of May, as shipping piled up in Buffalo's harbor and grain at Chicago was diverted to an all-rail route east, the state mediators negotiated without success. On May 14 the shovelers' union finally agreed not to insist on the abrogation of the contract as long as all supervision was taken from Conners and entrusted to a superintendent appointed by

[27] *Buffalo Courier,* February 26, March 13 and May 3, 4, 1899; *Rochester Union and Advertiser,* May 11, 1899. Boss scoopers were usually Irish, as were the new union leaders, but package-freight handlers were mostly Polish Catholics.

[28] Roosevelt to Platt, May 8, 1899, TR MSS.; *Buffalo Courier,* May 4, 1899; *Buffalo Express,* May 7, 15, 20, 1899; *New York Tribune,* May 21, 1899.

Bishop Quigley of the Buffalo Diocese. No sooner had the men returned to work, however, than they went out once again, complaining that Conners' "scabs" were still on the job. With the freight handlers, the ore handlers, and many of the skilled elevator men also out on strike, the situation in the port was worse than ever.[29]

In Buffalo on May 15, 1899, for a speech at the Independent Club, Roosevelt went over the new difficulty with the labor member of the state board and concluded that a public investigation was demanded. Open hearings accordingly began two days later. Of the three mediators, William H. H. Webster of the Brotherhood of Locomotive Firemen manifested the most sympathy for the strikers, but even he bristled when union officer Hennessey charged that the board was "a tool in the hands of corporations" and that Webster had tried to get the governor to call out the militia. If anything the testimony but further strained relations between the disputants, so after the second day the governor's representatives were not disposed to resume their inquiry.[30]

Shortly thereafter settlement was reached: the strikers dropped their renewed insistence upon contract abrogation, while Conners not only restored the old pay scale but granted the union's demand for a majority voice in the hiring of shovelers and bosses. The *Buffalo Express* conjectured that some big Chicago operator had induced Conners to make these concessions; certainly the state board had not done so. Yet as the mediators later reported, this dispute was "most difficult of adjustment on account of the personal and political elements which were involved in it." Inconclusive though their efforts had been, they had at least silenced those who in the initial stages of the strike had criticized their ineffectiveness.

[29] Mediation Board, *Annual Report, 1899*, pp. 156–157.
[30] *Buffalo Express*, May 16–19, 1899; Roosevelt to Slicer, May 16, 1899, TR MSS.; Mediation Board, *Annual Report, 1899*, p. 157.

In the end the governor could declare that they had labored tactfully and well.[31]

The Buffalo strike had been unrelated to enforcement of the labor law, but in Greater New York in July 1899 there arose a dispute involving the ten-hour day for street railway employees. The center of dissatisfaction was in Brooklyn among streetcar men on the old Nassau lines, who before the absorption of this system by the Brooklyn Rapid Transit Company (BRT) in January had been paid by the hour, counting delays as well as running time, but now were paid by the day and required to make so many trips that completion within ten working hours was impossible. Their demand was for a ten-hour day at twenty cents an hour. And it was quickly taken up by workers elsewhere in the BRT system and in the Metropolitan Street Railway Company in Manhattan, for the Knights of Labor were then engaged in a drive to organize streetcar employees throughout Greater New York.[32]

The affected companies at once indicated that they would resist. Metropolitan's president H. H. Vreeland maintained that 2,897 of the company's 3,149 employees had signed a statement that they were satisfied with their hours and pay; he rejected the suggestion of the state board of mediation and arbitration that he at least give an audience to the grievance committee of the newly formed union. And though BRT president Rossiter did agree to talk with union representatives, afterwards he declared that "labor agitators"

[31] *Buffalo Express,* May 23, 1899; *Utica Herald,* May 25, 1899; *New York Tribune,* May 24, 1899; Mediation Board, *Annual Report, 1899,* p. 23; *New York Tribune,* May 26, 1899, cited in Hurwitz, *Theodore Roosevelt and Labor,* p. 246. For initial criticism of the board, see Rochester *Post Express,* May 6, 1899; *Auburn Bulletin,* May 10, 1899; Rochester *Democrat and Chronicle,* May 12, 1899; *Rochester Union and Advertiser,* May 8, 1899.

[32] *New York Tribune,* January 13 and April 14, 1899; New York *World,* July 3, 1899; "Municipal Rapid Transit: A Gripman's View," *Outlook* 61:398–403 (February 18, 1899); New York *World,* June 25, 1899.

were stirring up Nassau division men and that no justifiable complaints existed.[33]

President Rossiter further charged that Albert Johnson, ex-president of the Nassau system, and his brother Tom L. Johnson of "single tax" fame were actively abetting strike sentiment in order to depress Brooklyn Rapid Transit stock. In reply Albert Johnson admitted that he had donated five hundred dollars to the railway employees' fund but only because legitimate grievances existed. Amid charge and countercharge the Knights of Labor District Assembly called a strike for July 16. Both Rossiter and Vreeland rejected the state board's last-minute offer to mediate the dispute —a rejection that angered the board since the men had agreed to arbitration. The strike was on.[34]

The cause of the 1,500 striking streetcar workers evoked little sympathy in the press or among churchmen. It was commonly believed that a stock-jobbing operation on Wall Street had much to do with the BRT's troubles, and the papers were glad to see that Chief Devery promptly dispatched 1,400 extra police across the East River. Roosevelt instructed Roe and Andrews to have the local militia ready, but the situation never got out of hand. Service on the BRT was irregular the first three days, with traffic on the Nassau line at a standstill, but before a week had passed, normal daytime operations had resumed throughout the Greater City.[35]

Controversy over the merits of the union's action nevertheless continued. The *New York Tribune* argued that the union leaders

[33] *New York Tribune*, June 30 and July 1, 4, 9, 11, 18, 1899; Mediation Board, *Annual Report, 1899*, pp. 279–281.
[34] *New York Tribune*, July 17, 1899; Mediation Board, *Annual Report, 1899*, pp. 17, 278, 280.
[35] *Public Opinion* 27:105 (July 27, 1899); New York *World*, July 17, 19, 1899; *New York Tribune*, July 17, 23, 1899; Roosevelt to Major General Roe, to Adjutant General Andrews, July 17, 1899, TR MSS.

should have sought a legal remedy instead of calling an "extremely foolish strike." In seeming agreement Tammanyite Samuel Prince, an official in New York City's Central Federated Union, stated that District Attorney Asa Bird Gardiner had promised to indict the company if complainants would only file affidavits. But the Knights' Grand Master Workman John N. Parsons, a moderate who had resisted the strike call himself, at once replied. Gardiner would not act on any labor protest, Parsons declared, nor had Tammany hesitated to send in the police to aid BRT. Labor could no more depend on the city than on the state government for the protection of its rights, concluded the Knights' spokesman, hence the only recourse was a separate party in Greater New York devoted to the workingman's interest.[36]

At Roosevelt's direction the state factory inspector did institute an investigation of the complaints against the BRT, the mediation board having reported that there appeared to be no violation of the ten-hour law in Manhattan. The fault, Inspector Williams found, was with the ten-hour law itself, which contained permissive features that made evasion easy. In his next report to the legislature, Williams recommended an amendment absolutely prohibiting work in excess of ten hours on the street railways.[37]

Anxious initially that some peaceful settlement to the dispute be found, Roosevelt had been equally willing once trouble began to supply the state's military force if needed to preserve order. In this attitude he differed not a whit from Tammany; indeed, Chief Devery had announced during the strike that if there was violence the police would show no mercy. The Socialist-Laborite candidate for governor in 1898 might have taken a different view, but Demo-

---

[36] *New York Tribune*, July 22, 23, 1899.
[37] Roosevelt to Williams, July 25, 1899, TR MSS.; Factory Inspector, *Annual Report, 1899*, pp. 18–20.

crats and Republicans generally were at one with Roosevelt on the matter of strikes.[38]

Thus, when the sheriff of Westchester County notified Major General Roe in April 1900 that 750 laborers had seized the half-finished Cornell Dam at Croton Reservoir, Roe and Roosevelt quickly responded to his request that two militia companies be sent in to assist the sheriff's deputies. By Monday, April 16, just two days later, Roe had over four hundred guardsmen at the scene, and the governor advised him that

> I am glad you ordered out plenty of troops. I need not say that I trust you have a discreet and firm man in charge. No disorder must be permitted and the rioters must not be allowed for a moment to gain the upper hand. On the other hand, discretion is of course just as much needed as firmness, and I earnestly hope that a collision can be avoided.

That evening one soldier was killed on picket duty around the dam, so Roe took steps to double his forces. This, the only time during Roosevelt's governorship that troops were employed on strike duty, was an impressive display.[39]

At the time the militia was called in, 200 of the 700 men employed on the project had been on strike for over two weeks. These strikers were Italians, the bulk of them aliens, recruited by *padrones* to perform common labor at $1.25 or hand drilling at $1.30 per day. They were demanding that these "starvation wages" be raised to $1.50 and $1.75 respectively. And to enforce their demand they were determined to stop all work on the dam. Better paid workmen

[38] Roosevelt to Delehanty, July 18, 1899; to Webster, July 19, 1899; both TR MSS. Hurwitz, *Theodore Roosevelt and Labor*, p. 242; *New York Tribune*, July 20, 1899.

[39] *Albany Evening Journal*, April 14, 1900; *New York Tribune*, April 16, 17, 1900. The initial report of the seizure was exaggerated, but it formed the basis for Roe's action. Similarly, the source of the shot was never identified, but it was widely assumed a striker was responsible.

stayed off the job through sympathy or fear of reprisal, and the carloads of stone ceased to issue from the quarry. When the contractor attempted to bring wagonloads of cement over the four-mile route from the Hudson River, a horde of Italians blocked the way and frightened the drivers.

On appeal from the employer—and not at Roosevelt's order—the sheriff had brought up over 100 deputies, but even they were cowed by the demonstration that greeted them. Armed mostly with stones and clubs, the Italians had just enough knives and guns to make the lawmen wary. No doubt the importunity of the contractor weighed heavily with the sheriff when he called for the state's assistance, yet Westchester County was reportedly "in a state of alarm over the lawlessness of roving bands of Italian strikers." As the *Albany Evening Journal* saw it, there was "no question that the presence of troops here cannot have anything but a salutary effect and will be the means of preventing bloodshed." [40]

Since the presence of the national guard emboldened the contractor to plan for the resumption of operations, the fear of an eventual clash spurred efforts at amicable settlement. State mediator Delehanty was there to confer with the employers, as was an official from the Italian consulate in New York City. The latter proposed an increase of 12½ instead of 25 cents a day for the 120 lowest paid workers, but the contractor turned down this compromise, arguing that $1.25 was the prevailing rate elsewhere and that any concession would bring demands all along the line that would run the total cost well over the nominal fifteen dollars a day. He would only agree to boost the wages of hand drillers to $1.50 a day, and shortly thereafter these men returned to work satisfied.[41]

[40] *New York Tribune*, April 14, 15, 16, 1900; Hurwitz, *Theodore Roosevelt and Labor*, p. 250; *Albany Evening Journal*, April 16, 1900.
[41] *New York Tribune*, April 15, 18, 19, 1900.

On April 18, four days after the militia had been called out, 200 men responded to the first whistle sounded at the site in over two weeks. Threats of violence were thought to have kept down the number of those willing to return, so warrants were issued and served on 26 of the "ringleaders." The arrival of new alien laborers and the reports that jobs on the New York subway construction were not as plentiful as had been imagined also weakened the determination of the strikers. By April 26 a full force of 700 workers was on hand, the recalcitrants had lost their places to new employees, and the guard's duty was over.[42]

Roosevelt assumed that organized labor would object to his approval of strike duty for the national guard, yet no vociferous protests were made and the New York City Central Federated Union postponed consideration of a resolution of censure pending further investigation. The Italian workers concerned were "a peculiarly friendless class," for politicians did not have to cater to their votes and the unions resented their competition. Unwilling to organize these unskilled aliens, the state labor bodies wished to restrict immigration and to limit employment on public works to American citizens. Had the Croton strike occurred within the bounds of Greater New York, furthermore, the city police would have broken it up as promptly as they did a similar dispute at the Jerome Park Reservoir in May 1899. If Tammany could act so summarily, Roosevelt had little to fear, especially when his political supporters thoroughly approved his action.[43]

The governor nevertheless desired to get at the roots of the workers' discontent. On April 17 he asked the board of mediation

[42] *New York Tribune*, April 19, 20, 26, 1900.
[43] Roosevelt to Lodge, April 17, 1900, TR MSS.; *New York Tribune*, April 23, 1900; *Nation* 70:311 (April 26, 1900); *New York Tribune*, May 10, 11, 1899. Hurwitz (*Theodore Roosevelt and Labor*, p. 254) exaggerates the labor protests in this incident.

and arbitration for "the most thorough investigation" of the Croton situation "as to the amount of wages paid to the Italian laborers, whether they are lower than those paid ordinarily, etc. etc." Two days later he impatiently asked mediator Francis B. Delehanty: "Have you not made sufficient inquiry into the Croton Dam strike to report to me what the facts are?" Roosevelt was particularly concerned to know whether there had been any violation of the law requiring an eight-hour day on public works; had such a violation occurred, he was prepared to take steps to enforce the statute.[44]

Undoubtedly there was a violation, but presumably the contractors maintained that the eight-hour law abridged the constitutional guarantee of "freedom of contract." This was a contention frequently advanced at the time; of the 117 complaints on eight-hour violations sustained by the state factory inspector in 1900, compliances were obtained in only 48 cases, while 61 others were "referred" to proper authorities, the referral in many cases representing legal protests by contractors. In 1901 the state courts decided in favor of the contractors' argument; it took a constitutional amendment in 1906 before the court of appeals upheld the eight-hour law. Thus Roosevelt had to admit that "we are powerless to make the contractors give larger wages, though I myself personally think the wages are too low." [45]

Elsewhere the state board enjoyed greater success. "The number of controversies amicably adjusted directly and indirectly through

[44] See Hurwitz, *Theodore Roosevelt and Labor,* pp. 253–254.

[45] Factory Inspector, *Annual Report, 1900,* pp. 16–17; Mediation Board, *Annual Report, 1899,* pp. 177–180; New York State Department of Labor, *Bulletin* 10:406–414 (December 1908); Roosevelt to Jane E. Robbins, April 20, 1900, TR MSS. The official report of the mediators (Mediation Board, *Annual Report, 1900,* p. 165) makes no mention of the eight-hour law; Roosevelt probably got his facts directly from Delehanty. Cf. Hurwitz, p. 254.

its influence," Roosevelt reported at the end of 1899, "has been greater than that during any year since its creation." Of the 547 strikes or lockouts that occurred in 1900, 225 received the mediators' attention and 46 were settled at least partly through their influence. The next year an economy move was to cut short the board's independent existence, but conciliation of industrial disputes had proved its usefulness and remained an integral function of the new department of labor.[46]

All told, Roosevelt had achieved much of what he set out to accomplish in the labor division. Observers at the time did not single out for special mention these efforts to improve the lot of the workingman. Rather they related his policies here to his general attempt to improve state administration and to deal justly with all elements in the economy. His true position was that of a mediator in labor's struggle to attain its legitimate needs. It was a position that he would continue to assume as President, in such a case as the great anthracite strike of 1902. It was a position that befitted an exponent of the neutral state, as he sought to promote the welfare of society generally.

[46] *Public Papers* (1900), p. 29; Mediation Board, *Annual Report, 1900,* *passim.*

CHAPTER XI Housing, Education, Conservation

Promotion of the people's welfare has been an age-old function of government; men have differed not so much over the objective, as over the means by which to attain it. Many New Yorkers of the late 1890's believed that a strict limitation upon state intervention would best serve the public interest. But on issue after issue affecting the economy Theodore Roosevelt advocated a larger and more effective role for the political authorities. This was his attitude as he turned to such social questions as tenement housing, education, and conservation.

Sentiment for tenement-housing reform arose in good part out of a more general concern over vice and corruption. This concern prompted Josephine Shaw Lowell to seek Roosevelt's support for a bill extending the Vagrancy Law "to provide for the punishment of men who profit by the commission of immoral acts by women." The same concern led F. Norton Goddard and other reform Republicans in New York City to advocate further restrictions upon the "numbers" racket and prize fighting. And this concern also produced a new investigative commission and eventually a most influential revision of the tenement housing act.[1]

---

[1] On the extension of the Vagrancy Law see Roosevelt to J. S. Lowell, December 4, 6, 1899, TR MSS.; *Public Papers* (1900), p. 41; Roosevelt to Elsberg, February 8 and March 17, 1900, TR MSS.; Chapter 281, *Laws of New York* (1900).

Roosevelt's endorsement of the Vagrancy Law extension favored by Josephine Shaw Lowell may have contributed something to its unopposed passage, but his support of Goddard's bill restricting the numbers or "policy" game held less promise. Much as Roosevelt admired this fellow Harvardman ('82) for his reform work on New York's East Side, where Goddard resided by preference and engaged actively in Republican politics, the anti-policy bill was not an organization measure. What was more, it was strongly opposed by Senator Grady and other representatives from Tammany Hall, which was often accused of being allied with the gamblers. And to Tammany's aid, unexpectedly, came that famous though often misguided crusader, the secretary of the Society for the Suppression of Vice, Anthony J. Comstock, who feared that the provision making possession of a policy slip a misdemeanor was too radical to be effective. In its stead Comstock wished proof that the policy-slip holders were "knowingly" in possession "with intent to use them unlawfully." [2]

Although Goddard obtained Comstock's consent not to press this enfeebling amendment, and though the governor along with a number of important legislators attended a Union League Club dinner designed to send the bill off to a good start, the omens were unfavorable. When the measure came up in the senate in March 1900, the minority leader proposed insertion of the word "knowingly" on the grounds that Comstock himself favored this alteration. Ten Republicans joined with twenty Democrats to carry the amendment, whereupon the crafty Grady proceeded to weaken the bill still further, until its promoters gave up in disgust. It was to take another year of agitation, sparked by Bishop Potter's ringing denun-

[2] On Goddard, see the Sunday Supplement of the *New York Tribune,* September 24, 1899. See also *Mazet Investigation,* pp. 1617ff.; New York *Evening Post,* March 9, 1900; Heywood Broun and Margaret Leech, *Anthony Comstock: Roundsman of the Lord* (New York, 1927), pp. 202–209.

ciation of conditions in the "Tenderloin," before the legislature passed an anti-policy bill that met Goddard's specifications. In December 1901 the Society for the Prevention of Crime finally got evidence to break up the syndicate and send "policy king" Al Adams to prison.[3]

Even more objectionable to the righteous elements of the community was the betting associated with the professional prize fight, which one clergyman called "a beastly, lowdown, degrading sight from beginning to end." In New York State the promotion of boxing matches to which admissions fees were charged was supposedly illegal, but a proviso in section 418 of the penal code permitted "sparring exhibitions" with gloves of not less than 5 ounces in weight, conducted by an athletic association owning or leasing the entire building in which the affair occurred. Ostensibly designed to encourage the manly art of self-defense, this proviso had in fact become a vehicle for prize fights between highly touted professionals at various athletic clubs in Buffalo, Syracuse, and New York, the gate receipts being termed "dues" paid by members and their guests. Had they been zealous in their duties, local officials could have interfered with these bouts, but particularly in New York City the police and the district attorney made a farce of the law's observance, threatening to "crack down" only when promoters without the right political connections attempted to stage a contest.[4]

[3] *New York Tribune,* January 21, March 3, 5, 8, 29, 30 and April 7, 1900; *Senate Journal* (1900), pp. 1168–70, 1346–47; *New York Tribune,* March 8, 15 and April 24, 1901; Society for the Prevention of Crime, *Report* (New York, 1903), pp. 5–7. On the policy game, see W. F. Howe and A. H. Hummel, *In Danger: or, Life in New York* (New York, 1888), pp. 204–209.

[4] For clergymen's views, see *New York Journal,* December 19, 1899 (RS); New York *World,* February 6, 1900; *New York Tribune,* February 8, 1900. Among newspapers opposing prize fighting were the *New York Tribune,* New

Thus, when the Coney Island Athletic Club signed Jim Jeffries and world's heavyweight champion Bob Fitzsimmons for a title match in June 1899, Police Chief Devery announced that he would be on hand to see that there was "no slugging or heavy hitting, nothing but a clean-cut lawful sparring exhibition for points." Newsmen took this to mean that State Senator Tim "Dry Dollar" Sullivan did not take kindly to fights staged outside his own clubs in Manhattan, but if so some arrangement must have been worked out, for the affair went off as scheduled with over 9,000 spectators and receipts of $100,000. After eleven punishing rounds in which "Fighting Bob" was several times floored, Jeffries administered the first knockout ever scored against the doughty Australian. Devery sat through it all and never lifted a finger to enforce his threat that "the first heavy blow will mark the end of the contest." [5]

As agitation mounted to repeal the proviso permitting sparring exhibitions, the governor found himself in an embarrassing position. Few might know that he occasionally exercised in the executive mansion's gymnasium with "Professor" Mike Donovan, ex-middleweight champion of America and boxing master of the New York Athletic Club, but it was a matter of public record that as police commissioner he had attended and had refused to interfere with a Broadway Athletic Club "exhibition" in which Peter Maher knocked out Joe Choynski in six rounds. It was the contention of the New York *Evening Post*, moreover, that the governor should have intervened through the district attorney or the sheriff in November 1899 to stop Jeffries' defense of his crown against Tom Sharkey in

York *World, Rochester Union and Advertiser, Buffalo Courier, Buffalo Express, Lyons Republican, Steuben Courier* and *Utica Herald.*

[5] *New York Tribune,* June 6, 8, 10, 1899; Alexander Johnston, *Ten- And Out! The Complete Story of the Prize Ring in America* (Garden City, 1927), 1927), pp. 137–143.

a 25-round decision match at Coney Island. The *Utica Herald* and the *New York Tribune* disagreed, but the "strenuous governor" was clearly on the spot.[6]

In his annual message of 1900 Roosevelt artfully blended principle with expediency as he came out for repeal of the penal code's proviso. Boxing, he argued, was really a "fine sport"; it was to be encouraged, as was "every exercise that tends to develop bodily vigor, daring, endurance, resolution and self-command." But the fact that boxing was so commendable did not justify prize fighting, "any more than the fact that a cross country run or a ride on a wheel is healthy justifies such a demoralizing exhibition as a six days race." When any sport was carried on mainly as a business it was "in danger of losing much that is valuable, and of acquiring some exceedingly undesirable characteristics." This was just what had happened to prize fighting, which had not only come to have a "very demoralizing and brutalizing effect" but had attracted "unlimited gambling and betting." Such would be the case as long as New York police authorities interpreted the law as they presently did. However proper the proviso had been "in its intent and as originally construed and administered," concluded the governor, "the gross abuses in its present administration, make its existence on the statute books of the Empire State an offense against decency."[7]

Since the fight game was principally a Democratic preserve, and repeal sentiment particularly strong in the upstate area, the Republican organization had every reason to endorse the governor's stand; the only question was whether the G.O.P. majority in the

[6] Michael J. Donovan, *The Roosevelt That I Know* (New York, 1909), p. 6; *Rochester Union and Advertiser,* January 3, 5, 1900; *New York Tribune,* November 18, 1896; New York *Evening Post,* November 4, 1899; *New York Tribune,* November 18, 1899; *Utica Herald,* November 21, 1899.

[7] *Public Papers* (1900), pp. 39–40.

senate would follow Platt's instructions. Tammany first tried to lure votes with a cleverly conceived amendment to regulate rather than ban prize fighting and earmark five percent of the gate receipts for the agricultural societies. When that failed, the Democrats attempted to postpone the repeal date to February 1901—in the hope that the next legislature might be in their control. To the dismay of Big Tim Sullivan, however, the "Tammany annex" Republicans did not succumb to the blandishments of the boxing interests; by a one-vote margin the repeal bill squeaked through unamended.[8] The moral pressure which pushed through the repeal bill was strong enough to keep prize fighting out of New York for ten years thereafter.

Tammany's domination of the building-codes commission set up under the charter of the Greater City of New York lent particular urgency to the movement for tenement-housing reform. Back in 1894 a state commission headed by Richard Watson Gilder had remedied some of the more glaring evils affecting metropolitan construction, but many of its proposals had failed of adoption or had been abused in practice. The commission of builders and politicians set up in 1898 by Tammany to frame a new code was deaf to reform appeals, yet efforts to supplant this body with an expert group appointed by the governor came to naught in the 1899 legislature. It was only as the Mazet investigation supplied fresh evidence of the need for reform that the distinguished tenement house committee of the Charity Organization Society renewed its agitation for state intervention.[9]

[8] *New York Tribune*, February 14, 16 and March 2, 1900; *Assembly Journal* (1900), pp. 495, 660; *Senate Journal* (1900), pp. 1336–37; F. C. Iglehart, *Theodore Roosevelt: The Man as I Knew Him* (New York, 1919), pp. 138–140.

[9] Lawrence Veiller, "Tenement House Reform in New York City, 1834–1900," in Robert W. deForest and Lawrence Veiller, eds., *The Tenement*

The society's propaganda drive culminated in the opening of the impressive Tenement House Exhibition at Sherry's in February 1900. Before a notable gathering of civic and philanthropic leaders Roosevelt called for state-initiated action. "We must have intelligent legislation to penalize the doings of those who cannot be reached by the motives of humanity," declared the governor. "They must be forbidden to build places for the propagation of crime and degradation," he added, and this matter was "rather one for statutory regulation than one to be left to local regulations." [10]

The direct outcome of the two-week exhibition was the introduction at Albany of the tenement-house committee's bill to appropriate $15,000 for the use of a new commission appointed by the governor to investigate conditions and report a remedial program the next year. To this measure, which he appropriately dubbed "my ewe lamb," Roosevelt devoted fatherly attention. He obtained the organization's approval, prompted the majority leaders in the assembly to push it along, and insured its final success with a special message to the legislature:

It is probable that there is not, and has not been, before your body a measure of more real importance to the welfare of those who are least able to protect themselves and whom we should especially guard from

---

House Problem, 2 vols. (New York, 1903), I, 105–107; Veiller to Riis, May 22, 1900, Riis MSS.; Roy Lubove, "Lawrence Veiller and the New York State Tenement House Commission of 1900," *Mississippi Valley Historical Review* 47:666–671 (March 1961); "Report of the Tenement House Committee," in the Charity Organization Society of the City of New York, *Seventeenth Annual Report* (1899), pp. 41–48; *New York Tribune*, March 8, 1899; *Mazet Investigation*, pp. 3448–60, 4456–59.

[10] *New York Sun, February* [?], 1900 (RS). Among the members of the society's tenement-house committee were F. W. Holls, Robert W. deForest, R. W. Gilder, E. R. L. Gould, Felix Adler, I. N. Phelps Stokes, Jacob Riis, George B. Post, Ernest Flagg, and Lawrence Veiller. In his recent study of the committee's agitation, Roy Lubove ("Lawrence Veiller and the New York State Tenement House Commission of 1900," pp. 666–671) stresses the contribution of Lawrence Veiller, who became the commission's secretary.

the effects of their own helplessness and from the rapacity of those who would prey upon them . . . The tenement house in its worst shape is a festering sore in the civilization of our great cities. We cannot be excused if we fail to cut out this ulcer; and our failure will be terribly avenged, for by its presence it inevitably poisons the whole body politic and social.[11]

Reduced to a $10,000 appropriation and extended to Buffalo as well as New York, the bill received the governor's signature the same day as its passage. Roosevelt would not be around to put through the subsequent recommendations, which as adopted in 1901 constituted the "chief working model for most of the tenement-house legislation in America since that date." To that end he contributed something, though, in his selection of the commission's members. Since Platt here had little interest, Roosevelt was free to give the reformers what they wanted. He met their every expectation with the group of fifteen headed by Robert W. deForest, I. N. Phelps Stokes, James B. Reynolds, Paul D. Cravath, and Alfred T. White.[12]

The interest Roosevelt took in the people's welfare was equally manifest in measures affecting education. In the Empire State as elsewhere the primary responsiblity for schooling rested with local authorities, but the state was still vested with important functions. Changes in school administrative structure required legislative approval. The legislature could establish conditions of teachers' employment. And through the department of public instruction and the regents of the University of the State of New York, the state

[11] Charity Organization Society of the City of New York, *Eighteenth Annual Report, 1900,* pp. 39–44; Roosevelt to Allds, March 23, 1900, TR MSS.; *New York Tribune,* March 24, 1900; Roosevelt to Nixon, April 3, 1900, TR MSS.; *Public Papers* (1900), pp. 99–100.

[12] James Ford, et al., *Slums and Housing with Special Reference to New York City: History, Condition, Policy,* 2 vols. (Cambridge, Mass., 1936), I, 217.

exercised supervision over not only public schools but also academies, universities, museums, and libraries.

The removal of politics from school administration had been a problem for municipalities in the 1890's, the direction of reform being toward smaller, more responsible boards of education. In 1892 Albany and Troy had adopted seven-man boards appointed by the mayor, and five years later Binghamton had substituted this system for the unsatisfactory one of popular elections by wards. At that same session in 1897 Syracuse had secured a charter amendment reducing its board to seven men elected on a city-wide instead of a ward basis. Therefore, of the second-class cities (Albany, Troy, Syracuse, Rochester), only Rochester's cumbersome twenty-man commission was left to be reformed. Changes there followed Boss Aldridge's setback by the good-government forces in 1897: the next year the comprehensive Dow Law divorced the board of education absolutely from the city administration, and in 1899 Roosevelt signed another measure setting up a new five-man board to be chosen at large that fall.[13]

The danger that "reform" could mask a political objective was only too apparent in the Troy school bill of 1900, which would have supplanted the Collar City's seven-man board with a single commissioner appointed by the mayor. Although ex-Governor Black, State Senator Horace White, and other Republican leaders defended this step, the secretary of the board of regents convincingly argued that under the present system the mayor would soon be able to change the board's complexion and that no city in the country

[13] Rutherford Hayner, *Troy and Rensselaer County, New York: A History,* 3 vols. (New York, 1925), I, 288; Board of Public Instruction of the City of Albany, *Annual Report, 1892,* pp. 16–18; *Binghamton Herald,* February 13, 1899; *Syracuse Herald,* September 21, 1898; Franklin H. Chase, *Syracuse and Its Environs,* 3 vols. (New York, 1924), II, 817; Herbert S. Weet, "The Development of Public Education in Rochester 1900–1910," Rochester Historical Society *Publications* 17:183–186, 188–189, 230–231 (1939).

had a single head with such powers as were here proposed. Whatever doubt remained in the governor's mind was dispelled when Platt wired: "Upon reflection think your original views concerning Troy School bill are wisest advise veto." [14]

The amendment to the Poughkeepsie charter which replaced the twelve elective commissioners with seven men appointed by the then-Republican mayor, on the other hand, satisfied Roosevelt's political scruples. This change was in line with current development in school systems and had the support of State Superintendent of Public Instruction Charles R. Skinner and Poughkeepsie reformer Robert F. Wilkinson. The old board, furthermore, had clearly been remiss in management. Roosevelt finally agreed to sign the bill, but only after he had exacted the mayor's promise to consult with Wilkinson on the prospective candidates. [15]

The need for state intervention in New York City schools arose out of the city government's resistance to teachers' demands for higher salaries. At Albany in 1899 the Teachers' Association backed Senator Ahearn's proposal to force the board of estimate and apportionment to allot increased and more equitably distributed funds for elementary school salaries. The board of education opposed this measure, which would deprive them of part of their supervisory power. So, too, at first did Roosevelt, who believed that New York City should take care of the matter itself and that the provision which allowed "time service" alone to govern promotions was most objectionable. However, City Superintendent of Schools Maxwell and Nicholas Murray Butler not only convinced

[14] Roosevelt to Black, to James Russell Parsons (secretary of the regents), April 20, 1900, TR MSS.; *Albany Argus*, April 24, 1900; Platt to Roosevelt, April 23, 1900, TR MSS. (LC); *Public Papers* (1900), pp. 124–125.

[15] Gaius C. Bolin to Roosevelt, April 11, 1900, TR MSS. (LC). Roosevelt to Bolin, April 12, 1900; to Parsons, April 20, 1900; both TR MSS. Poughkeepsie Board of Education, *Fifty-Fifth Annual Report* (1898), pp. 21–34; Roosevelt to R. F. Wilkinson, April 23, 1900, TR MSS.

the governor that state action was necessary but also framed an amendment which would consider "merit" as well as length of service for advancement. Further conferences with Maxwell and the teachers resulted in an acceptable compromise which even Mayor Van Wyck subsequently approved.[16]

The establishment of a $600 annual minimum and specific increases by the end of 10 and 15 years service made "the salaries of teachers in the City of New York higher . . . than those paid to teachers in elementary schools in any other city in the world." Still the funds provided by the board of estimate and apportionment were insufficient to pay the mandatory increases and keep up other salaries and services. Hundreds of pay reductions resulted, some instructors had to be discharged, and new developments in kindergartens and high schools, in cooking, sewing, and manual training classes were cut off. Hardest hit of all were the principals and teachers in Queens and Richmond, to whom no money whatever was paid during October, November, and December 1899. Though the state legislature relieved their desperate plight in February 1900, the Teachers' Association agitated anew for more effective statutory protection.[17]

At Albany the Republican majority responded with a bill to free teachers from the board of estimate by providing a local tax for school salary purposes of 4 mills to the dollar of assessed valuation. At the same time the bill broadened, extended, and made uniform

[16] New York Tribune, January 25, February 24, March 5, 9, 25, 29, 30, and April 4, 5, 23, 1899. Roosevelt to W. A. Sinclair, February 24, 1899; to Nicholas Murray Butler, March 10, 1899; both TR MSS. Low to Roosevelt, March 18, 1899, Low MSS. Roosevelt to Low, March 21, 1899; to Butler, March 24, 1899; both TR MSS. New York Evening Post, March 21, 1899.

[17] [New York] City Superintendent of Schools, First Annual Report (July 31, 1899), pp. 148–149; Educational Review 20:99–100 (June 1900); [New York] City Superintendent of Schools, Second Annual Report (July 31, 1900), pp. 61–65; New York Evening Post, April 5, 1900.

throughout the boroughs the salary standards set for the elementary schools alone in the Ahearn law. Objection to the centralizing effect and the increased costs caused the mayor, the city comptroller, the borough boards of education of Manhattan and Brooklyn, and such papers as the *New York Tribune* and *Brooklyn Eagle* to oppose the bill. When the legislature refused to heed their protests, they turned to the governor to urge him not to sign "a concededly slovenly and half-digested measure." [18]

While admitting that it was "clumsily drawn on one or two points," however, Roosevelt declared that the "general purpose . . . is admirable, and the best educators, the men most interested in seeing the public schools of the Greater New York put upon a thoroughly efficient basis and absolutely removed from the domain of politics, most earnestly favor the measure." Attorney General Davies and the auditor of the school board had assured him that the fears of a three to seven million dollar added expense were exaggerated. The claim that salary increments would continue even after the supposed maximum was reached also appeared unfounded. This and other ambiguous points, Roosevelt concluded, were not serious enough to warrant the veto of such a progressive step in public education. [19]

The governor's decision delighted New York educators as much as it disappointed the "home rule" Brooklynites who had spearheaded the opposition. The *Brooklyn Eagle* continued to assert that Roosevelt had subordinated statesmanship to partisanship, but Superintendent of Schools Maxwell, Henry W. Taft, and such dissimilar editors as William Randolph Hearst and Horace White all approved. From Nicholas Murray Butler, whose influence had

[18] New York *Evening Post,* April 5, 1900; *New York Tribune,* March 31, 1900; *Brooklyn Eagle,* April 8, 15, 1900 (RS).

[19] *Public Papers* (1900), pp. 130–132. See also Roosevelt to Bishop, May 2, 1900, TR MSS.

weighed more heavily than any other's in Roosevelt's decision, came high praise for this "epoch-making" law, which "sets free the teachers from all dependence upon local school politicians, and puts them in a position where simply professional zeal and professional ambition will count." [20]

Roosevelt's most ambitious educational project—unification of the department of public instruction and the University of the State of New York—was generally acknowledged to be an urgent need. The corporation known as "The Regents of the University of the State of New York" claimed by reason of an 1853 law that its province extended to the state's 523 public secondary schools as well as to academies, universities, museums, and libraries. The state superintendent of public instruction, on the other hand, maintained that the high schools belonged with the elementary grades under his sole jurisdiction. As a result there was continual friction over examinations, inspection, and the licensing of teachers. Both conducted examinations, for example, "but the Regents will not credit a person with examinations passed in obtaining a teacher's certificate, nor will the department of instruction credit those who are seeking licenses to teach with any subject passed under the Regents." It was "plainly the duty of our legislature," concluded one Normal College president, "to put an end to this unfortunate condition of affairs." [21]

A bill was introduced at the 1899 session to vest control of all tax-supported schools in a new official nominated by the governor and confirmed by the senate for a six-year term. In opposing this,

[20] *Brooklyn Eagle,* May 27, 1900 (RS); *New York Tribune,* May 5, 6, 1900; *New York Journal,* May 4, 1900 (RS); New York *Evening Post,* April 5, 1900; William H. Maxwell, "New York Public Schools," *Municipal Affairs* 4:747–749 (December 1900); Butler to Roosevelt, May 1, 1900, TR MSS. (LC); *Educational Review* 21:99–101 (June 1900).

[21] *Educational Review* 18:71 (June 1899).

the regents reasoned that their own body, constitutional since 1894 and representing "no party, no sect, no section, no duty and no aspiration save that for the best education of the greatest number," was the proper place in which to lodge such control. Elected for life by joint ballot of the legislature, they prided themselves on their removal from politics; this new bill, they argued, would simply expose educational administration to party strife and patronage. In its stead they advocated a measure empowering them to appoint the state superintendent and hence to coordinate all branches within the system.[22]

So widespread was the opposition, however, that consolidation under the board of regents as then constituted reportedly "would not receive ten votes in either branch of the legislature." Most opponents objected to the way in which the board was set up: the number of regents was excessive, and tenure for life was undemocratic. Some also found fault with the educational theories of the University, arguing that it "has perverted the whole system of education so far as it has gained power to do so, by making the academic course a strife for percentage of markings, a cramming process for examinations rather than for true educational purposes." Even Roosevelt admitted to "the gravest kind of doubts" about the board's methods. "I very thoroughly feel that there has been a tendency among some of the best educators recently to divert from mechanical trades people who ought for their sake to keep in at the mechanical trades," he wrote his sister Corinne,

[22] University of the State of New York, *113th Annual Report* (1899), p. 226; *New York Tribune*, April 18, 1899; *Educational Review* 18:56 (June 1899). Among the more prominent of the nineteen elective regents were Whitelaw Reid (*New York Tribune*), St. Clair McKelway (*Brooklyn Eagle*), Senator Chauncey Depew, Chester S. Lord (managing editor, New York *Sun*), and Episcopal Bishop William C. Doane of Albany. Roosevelt and three other state officials were *ex officio* members. See Charles E. Fitch, ed., *Official New York from Cleveland to Hughes*, 4 vols. (New York, 1911), II, 85–86.

"and I am not at all sure that Parsons [director of the high school division for the regents] and those for whom he stands are working along the right lines; or . . . that there is any point in my telling them I think so, when they with such sincerity and zeal believe in their work."[23]

When the 1899 session adjourned without resolving the issue, the governor himself took a hand. He agreed with the regents that popular election of their members would be unwise and that under a proper plan of unification they should be the ones to appoint the state superintendent. Nevertheless the legislature "will not turn over the public schools to the regents as now constituted," Roosevelt warned; "Before you can be given this power you must submit to reorganization upon a different basis." At its June convocation the university board responded by requesting the governor to appoint a special body to "consider ways and means of unifying the present educational systems." So Roosevelt in October 1899 appointed a nonlegislative commission headed by Frederick W. Holls of Yonkers, the chairman of the committee on education at the Constitutional Convention of 1894, to find a solution.[24]

The seven members of this commission, whom Roosevelt with the advice of Holls and Nicholas Murray Butler had carefully selected to represent both sides of the dispute, were unable to compose their differences. They did approve establishment of a department of education with a single executive head (a chancellor) removable for cause by the university board, but otherwise they split down political lines. Holls and the three other Republi-

[23] *Educational Review* 18:59, 61, 63–64, 66, 77 (June 1899); *Watertown Times,* April 11, 1899 (RS); Rochester *Post Express,* April 18, 1899; Rochester *Democrat and Chronicle,* April 10, 14, 1899; Roosevelt to Corinne Robinson, May 25, 1899, TR MSS.

[24] *New York Tribune,* April 25, 1899; University of the State of New York, *113th Annual Report* (1899), p. 276; *New York Tribune,* October 24, 1899.

cans wanted the first chancellor to be appointed by the governor with the consent of the senate, the second and succeeding ones by the regents or by the governor with the consent of the regents. The secretary of the university and the two Democratic members held out for selection by the regents or by the governor with the consent of the regents. The Republican majority also desired to change the university board by reducing its membership, setting 70 as the retirement age, and providing for the choice of new regents through regular gubernatorial appointment. The minority advocated instead "the retention of the board of regents as at present constituted, and without age limit." [25]

Though Roosevelt endorsed the majority report in his annual message to the legislature, behind the scenes he sought further compromise. He found, however, that the G.O.P. legislative leaders thought Holls had already made too many concessions to the regents. To keep the people's hold on the common schools, they argued, the legislature should elect the chancellor just as it did the regents. And in this stand they had the support of State Chairman Odell, who was manifestly concerned that the chancellor should not be antagonistic to the Republican organization.[26]

The attitude of the Republican leaders dashed whatever hope Roosevelt had of working out an acceptable formula. As he surveyed the wreckage, the governor realized that it had been unrealistic to try to take this question out of politics by appointing a non-legislative commission. He also saw that the majority report had

[25] New York State Department of Public Instruction, *Forty-Sixth Annual Report* (April 5, 1900), p. 17.

[26] *Public Papers* (1900), p. 51; Roosevelt to Holls, January 3, 5, 1900, TR MSS.; Butler to Roosevelt, January 13, 1900, TR MSS. (LC); Roosevelt to St. Clair McKelway, February 2, 1900, TR MSS.; *New York Tribune* and New York *Sun* (RS), January 31, 1900; Roosevelt to Butler, February 15, 1900, TR MSS.

shown slight regard for the realities of the situation: to vest the governor with the power to appoint the first chancellor might be wise administratively, but it was certain to antagonize the organization and the legislature. What impressed Roosevelt most, though, was the intensity of the dispute; there had never been a time, said one authority, when "so much personal abuse, vilification and impeachment of motives had been injected into the discussion of a great educational question." Not until 1904, and then over the dogged resistance of the Democrats and many of the regents, did a bill finally provide for a commissioner of education.[27]

Political considerations intruded also into the third area in which Roosevelt sought to promote the general welfare: conservation. An occasional bill such as the one creating the Palisades commission received bipartisan endorsement, but this was seldom so with legislation affecting municipal water supply or sewage disposal or the state forests. In one instance, at least, politics led the governor to a poor decision, but in general he evidenced the enlightened approach that was to characterize his Presidency.

By 1899 the movement for the preservation of the Palisades, where quarrying for construction purposes had already despoiled the cliffs in the vicinity of Bull's Ferry, had progressed to the point of interstate cooperation with New Jersey authorities. When the 1899 legislature failed to appropriate funds for an official delegation, the governor asked Andrew H. Green of the Society for the

[27] New York State Department of Public Instruction, *Forty-Sixth Annual Report* (April 5, 1900), p. 23; *New York Tribune,* February 15, 16, 17, 18, 1904. Roosevelt also supported Senator Nathaniel Elsberg's bill to put an end to segregation of Negro children in New York schools, sending up an emergency message to speed it through the legislature. This bill attracted almost no attention at the time. It had a statewide application but was aimed principally at Long Island. See Roosevelt to Elsberg, March 20, 1900; to Ellsworth, March 20, 1900; both TR MSS. *Senate Journal* (1900), pp. 1464–65; Chapter 492, *Laws of New York* (1900).

Preservation of Scenic and Historic Objects to organize an informal committee to represent New York. The report of the interstate group, recommending the establishment of a 700-acre park from Fort Lee to Piermont, led with Roosevelt's strong endorsement to the legislature's unanimous approval in 1900 of a Palisades commission appointed by the governor and empowered to expend $10,000 toward this purpose. To head up the body he appointed a man whom he had known only slightly before F. W. Holls' recommendation, but who was destined for an important part in his later career, George W. Perkins of the New York Life Insurance Company.[28]

Upstate another problem associated with urban and industrial growth—water supply—occasioned further appeals to the state government. To Albany came complaints against high rates and inadequate service of some of the private companies that still supplied about half the communities. From the municipally owned systems in the larger cities came requests for bonding authority for improvements and extensions. And from riverside towns, often offenders themselves, came protests against the dumping of sewage and refuse upstream.

In line with his stand in the annual message of 1900, Roosevelt approved those changes to municipal ownership that the legislature sent to the executive chamber. Over Democratic opposition he

---

[28] Roosevelt to Green, June 17, 1899, TR MSS.; *Public Papers* (1900), p. 28; *New York Tribune*, January 18 and February 2, 16, 1900; Chapter 170, *Laws of New York* (1900); Roosevelt to F. W. Holls, March 15, 1900, TR MSS.; Holls to Roosevelt, March 16, 26, 1900, Holls MSS., CUL; Roosevelt to Perkins, May 18, 1900, TR MSS. On Roosevelt's earlier meeting with Perkins, relative to a bill limiting the amount of life insurance that one insurance company could have in force, see Theodore Roosevelt, *Theodore Roosevelt: An Autobiography* (New York, 1913), pp. 318–320, and John A. Garraty, *Right-Hand Man: The Life of George W. Perkins* (New York, 1957), pp. 74–78.

also signed bills authorizing Rochester to purchase additional lands around Hemlock Lake to protect its supply, and Troy to build a new $1,250,000 gravity system. It was only when the bill authorizing Gloversville to channel its sewage into Cayudutta Creek came before him that the governor failed to strike a blow for reform. He knew the dangers of stream pollution. At the hearing on the Gloversville bill, moreover, the arguments of the downstream communities against it impressed him favorably. The sole reason he signed it was political: an antimachine ally, United States Representative Lucius N. Littauer, the "boss of Gloversville," was emphatically for the measure, and Roosevelt, perhaps for support in his fight against a draft as McKinley's running mate, felt obliged to abide by Littauer's wishes.[29]

But the Gloversville case faded into insignificance before the controversy that arose in 1900 over the water supply of the Greater City. This dispute went back to August 16, 1899, when the municipal board of public improvements first voted on a 40-year contract with the Ramapo Water Company to furnish New York City (beginning in 1902) 200,000,000 gallons of water daily at the city limits at a pressure equivalent to a 300-foot elevation for a price of seventy dollars per million gallons. Commissioner of Water Supply William Dalton, an ex-butcher put into this post by Tammany, had vouched for the necessity of this contract to avert impending shortages, the fire underwriters advocated the increased pressure, and Corporation Counsel Whalen had just affirmed the propriety

[29] Chapter 645, *Laws of New York* (1899); Chapter 368, *Laws of New York* (1900); Rochester *Post Express*, April 26, 28, 1899; *Troy Times*, December 2, 1899; Chapter 370, *Laws of New York* (1900); *Albany Argus*, May 1, 1900; Roosevelt to Littauer, March 24 and May 1, 1900, TR MSS.; Chapter 754, *Laws of New York* (1900). See G. W. Chessman, "Theodore Roosevelt's Campaign Against the Vice-Presidency," *The Historian* 14:173–190 (Spring 1952).

of the action. But Comptroller Coler and five other officials voted against this exorbitant private contract and finally secured a two-week postponement for further consideration.[30]

Publication of the forestalled contract created a sensation overnight. At once the New York *World* obtained a temporary injunction against further steps by the city authorities. William Randolph Hearst and the Vigilance League followed that up with an application to the attorney general for dissolution of the Ramapo Water Company on the grounds that it was a paper organization holding little more than some options across the Hudson in the Esopus watershed. Investigation meantime revealed that prominent Republican politicians had also taken an interest in Ramapo: back in 1895 Ed Lauterbach and Assemblyman Nixon had successfully promoted the bill that gave the company the right to acquire lands by the same condemnation proceedings used by railroads, to accumulate and sell water to any cities, and to lay pipes under any navigable waters in the state. Benjamin F. Tracy had urged Governor Morton to approve this valuable grant. Since 1897 another Republican, Silas B. Dutcher of Brooklyn, had been the firm's president, and its stock continued to be held by men of both parties.[31]

The coincidence of Republican backing with Tammany's eagerness for a water contract provided "satisfactory proof" for the New York *Evening Post* "that Croker and Platt have resumed the deal business." That opinion gained strength at Albany in 1900, where

[30] Merchants' Association of New York, *An Inquiry into the Conditions Relating to the Water Supply of the City of New York* (New York, 1900), pp. xxiii–xxvii; *New York Tribune*, August 17, 1899; New York *World*, August 22, 23, 24, 1899; *Mazet Investigation*, pp. 2684–2701, 2829, 2988–3014.

[31] New York *World*, August 22, 23, 1899; *New York Tribune*, August 20, 25, September 8 and November 2, 1899; *Mazet Investigation*, pp. 2792–94, 3043, 3222, 3231; also 2928–33, 3014–27, 3028–29, 3306–07, 4633–47.

three bills all aimed at the Ramapo "water steal" ran up against "powerful covert opposition." The most summary one was Demarest's of Rockland County, which would have repealed the 1895 act that had "defined" the company's charter in such a favorable fashion. Another measure, introduced for the Merchants' Association by Assemblyman Morgan of Kings, would have lifted the charter restriction that prevented the City of New York from going into other counties for water supply, thus furnishing an alternative to a contract with a private company. Still a third proposal, sponsored by Assemblyman Fallows of New York, would simply have given an absolute veto on any contract to that outspoken opponent of the Ramapo scheme, Comptroller Bird S. Coler.[32]

March came and the assembly committee on cities still had not reported any one of these three bills. In the committee's defense it was said that the Demarest proposal was unconstitutional, while the other two were being held up pending investigations into the supply situation by Comptroller Coler and the Merchants' Association. New York's more independent editors scoffed at such arguments and belabored the legislature for its inaction. The New York *World* queried whether the time for "strenuous" effort by the governor was not at hand, to which the *Tribune* replied in a bitter and taunting affirmative. "A year ago he rushed into the arena," said Reid's organ of Roosevelt,

a perfect hero, to prevent the same band of jobbers from strangling franchise taxation. It cannot be that he is less opposed to such methods now. It cannot be that he lacks courage for such a fight.[33]

[32] New York *Evening Post*, August 18, 1899; Merchants' Association of New York, *Inquiry*, pp. xxx–xxxi; *New York Tribune*, February 7, 12, 16, 24, 1900.

[33] New York *Evening Post*, March 6, 1900; *New York Tribune*, February 18 and March 2, 7, 1900.

It was true that Roosevelt had done little to influence the course of the controversy since his annual message, where he had asserted that "New York must own its own water supply" and "legislation permitting private ownership should be annulled." As he explained to Seth Low on March 7, "I have been reluctant to thrust myself into another [fight] in which theoretically I ought not to be required to act save as I have already acted." To Cabot Lodge five days later he further described the ways in which the Ramapo jobbers had tried to keep him from becoming involved. They wanted to cut Comptroller Coler out of the Fallows bill, "saying that he may be my successful opponent for the Governorship on the democratic ticket if I now build him up," Roosevelt reported, but he was "taking measures to see that he is left in." "They also want to pass the bill so late that the Mayor can veto it after the legislature has adjourned and thereby to shift the responsibility on him," added the governor, concluding that "with their queer shortsightedness in great matters like this, they fail to understand the interest of the people." [34]

At his conference with Platt and Odell in mid-March Roosevelt "finally got the Organization all straight on the Ramapo business, but it took blood to do it." The governor agreed to sacrifice repeal of the company's 1895 charter in the face of the "honest difference of opinion" about its constitutionality. Similarly he as much as gave up on the Morgan bill (to which rural areas upstate objected) in order to be sure that he obtained the Fallows measure with its veto power for the comptroller. Roosevelt considered this the most important safeguard against consummation of the Ramapo deal and so refused to bargain it away. As he told the Merchants' Asso-

[34] *Public Papers* (1900), p. 19. Roosevelt to Low, March 7, 1900; to Lodge, March 12, 1900; both TR MSS.

ciation, he had tried to get through their proposal also—the Morgan bill—but had "been utterly unable to unless I would agree to substitute it for the Fallows bill, in which case I would have had the support of all the Ramapo jobbers." [35]

Although the anti-Platt press remained critical of the governor's course, he believed himself vindicated on April 3 when Mayor Van Wyck vetoed the Fallows bill. The Republican majority at once took up and repassed it over Tammany's opposition, but the fate that awaited the Morgan bill was so certain that in the knowledge that the legislature would not then be in session to reapprove it the Merchants' Association ordered it withdrawn. For Roosevelt, Van Wyck's action was a "complete justification" of his course at Albany. "Had I tried any more I would have simply gotten nothing," he wrote Lyman Abbott of *Outlook*. "I could not have exercised one additional pound of pressure," Roosevelt assured the Rev. Mr. Slicer on April 6; "to have done so would have been to court disaster." [36]

The event justified Roosevelt's belief that the Fallows bill would be an effective stopgap until a proper and permanent solution could be found. At the governor's explicit request the Merchants' Association resolved to keep on with its investigation—its surveys were not completed until August 1900—and to cooperate with the newly appointed New York City charter commission to this end. Such action led in 1901 to the passage of bills to repeal the 1895

[35] *New York Tribune*, March 14, 1900. Roosevelt to Lodge, March 14, 1900; to Frederick B. DeBerard of the Merchants' Association, March 13, 1900; to William F. King of the Merchants' Association, March 14, 1900; all TR MSS.

[36] *New York Tribune*, April 4, 1900; Roosevelt to Abbott, April 3, 1900, TR MSS.; *Outlook* 64:760–762 (April 7, 1900); Roosevelt to Slicer, April 6, 1900, TR MSS.

charter of the Ramapo Company (as Demarest had originally proposed), to extend the city's power of eminent domain (as the Merchants' Association had intended in the Morgan bill), and to exempt water bonds from the debt limit imposed by the charter.[37]

More important yet, the surveys made by the comptroller and the Merchants' Association stimulated public discussion of the larger problem: the future sources of a water supply for Greater New York. It was this aspect that had particularly interested Roosevelt, who declared that "we should build a water system, not for one summer but for half a century to come—a system that shall once for all meet the needs of the future city and be capable of almost automatic expansion as these needs increase." By 1907 New York had begun to implement that aim through the construction of the famed Catskill Aqueduct from the Ashokan Reservoir, a tremendous municipal undertaking that took 10 years and over $150,000,000 to complete.[38]

The most significant project which Roosevelt took on in the field of conservation, however, was the reform of the forest, fish, and game commission. So many complaints about the inefficiency of this five-man board had come to his attention that it could be assumed that when the terms of all the members expired in 1900 he would try to replace them with better appointees. But Roosevelt had a more ambitious aim, for he hoped to replace them with a single commissioner. In his view, and in the estimate of the plan's sponsor, the Boone and Crockett Club, centralization of authority

[37] Roosevelt to DeBerard of the Merchants' Association of New York, April 6, 1900, TR MSS.; *New York Tribune*, May 5, 1900; Merchants' Association of New York, *Inquiry*, pp. xxxviii–xxxix, 23–24; *New York Tribune*, March 1, 5, 9, 13, 15, 20, 1901.

[38] Roosevelt to DeBerard of the Merchants' Association of New York, April 6, 1900, TR MSS.

would inhibit political influences and improve administration. Beyond that, it would make it easier to obtain a more constructive program for New York timber resources.[39]

For Gifford Pinchot, Chief Forester of the United States and member of the Boone and Crockett Club, this last consideration constituted the main purpose of the whole proposal. As he saw it, the Constitutional Convention of 1894 had taken an unprogressive step when it approved a provision that the state preserves should "forever be kept as wild forest lands. They shall not be leased, sold or exchanged, or be taken by any corporation, public or private, nor shall the timber thereon be sold, removed or destroyed." At that time, he recognized, this "Gibraltar of Forestry" had been thought necessary to prevent further raids by the lumber interests, but Pinchot argued that "conservative lumbering" carried on under careful supervision would not only profit the state financially but actually would improve the forests. Hence he advocated the commission's reconstruction to prepare the way for introduction of scientific methods of professional forestry in New York's 1,300,000-acre preserve.[40]

Though Pinchot's ideas did not enjoy great popularity among New York conservationists, the governor was most impressed. Two of Roosevelt's closest advisers in this field, C. Grant La Farge and James MacNaughton, were Pinchot supporters, as was Colonel William F. Fox, the capable superintendent of the New York state

[39] Roosevelt to the Forest, Fish, and Game Commission, November 28 and December 1, 1899, TR MSS.; *Buffalo Express*, December 3, 1899; Gifford Pinchot to Roosevelt [n.d.], cited in *New York Times*, March 11, 1900 (RS). Roosevelt had been the first president of Boone and Crockett, which was organized at his home in 1887.

[40] Alfred L. Donaldson, *The History of the Adirondacks*, 2 vols. (New York, 1921), II, 187–196; Gifford Pinchot, "Working Plans for the New York Forest Preserve," *Outing* 36:89–90 (April 1900); Pinchot to Roosevelt [n.d.], *New York Times*, March 11, 1900 (RS).

forests. It was Pinchot, at La Farge's suggestion, to whom Roosevelt turned for advice on the forestry section of his annual message. "We need to have our system of forestry gradually developed and conducted along scientific principles," the governor accordingly declared.

When this has been done it will be possible to allow marketable timber to be cut everywhere without damage to the forests—indeed, with positive advantages to them; but until lumbering is thus conducted, on strictly scientific principles no less than upon principles of the strictest honesty towards the State, we cannot afford to suffer it at all in the State forests.[41]

A "thorough reorganization of the work of the commission" was thus the first requirement. It would surely produce an improvement in the quality of wardens, some of whom were so inept that they had to hire guides to go into the woods. It would protect the forests from despoilation while permitting scientific cutting. And it would accomplish all this, Roosevelt implied, by vesting one qualified official with the authority exercised by the cumbersome, ineffective five-man board. "Ultimately the administration of the State lands must be so centralized as to enable us definitely to place responsibility in respect to everything concerning them," declared the governor, "and to demand the highest degree of trained intelligence in their use." [42]

So indifferent was the response of press and public to this proposal that Roosevelt feared he would be unable to convince Platt

[41] Gifford Pinchot, *Breaking New Ground* (New York, 1947), pp. 144–145, 385; La Farge to Roosevelt, November 10, 1899, TR MSS. (LC); MacNaughton's article in *New York Times,* March 11, 1900 (RS); Roosevelt to La Farge, December 12, 1899, TR MSS.; *Public Papers* (1900), p. 35. MacNaughton represented the MacIntyre Iron Association, which owned 90,000 acres of Adirondacks land.

[42] *Public Papers* (1900), pp. 35–37.

and Odell of its wisdom. He nevertheless urged his friends to drum up popular support for the single-commissioner bill so that he might at least have a bargaining point, to convince the machine leaders of the need for a complete change in the commission's personnel. These tactics paid off, for though Boss Platt was most reluctant to make a clean sweep, he and Odell agreed in February 1900 to support the appointment of five new members.[43]

Since the senate would still have to confirm his nominees, political considerations weighed equally with competence in Roosevelt's subsequent selection. In at least one case, moreover, his choice later proved faulty. Still the new board represented a definite improvement, if only because it was headed by W. Austin Wadsworth of Livingston County, gentleman landowner and sportsman, president of Boone and Crockett Club, and member of a family already prominent in Republican politics. Under Wadsworth's leadership the activities of the forest, fish, and game divisions received closer attention. And in cooperation with the United States forestry service the new commission began the preparation of working plans for constructive development of the state forests.[44]

The work to which Roosevelt had gone to reconstitute the commission went largely for naught, for the next year the legislature consolidated the forest preserve board with the forest, fish, and game commission, reduced the new body to three members, and provided that by 1903 a single commissioner should head the whole department. Worthy as this reform might be, however, it was only as good as the spirit that animated it. Motivated chiefly by his

[43] Roosevelt to Grant La Farge, January 29 and February 9, 16, 1900, TR MSS.; New York *Sun*, February 21, 25, 1900; *New York Times*, March 11, 1900 (RS); *Forest and Stream* 54:161 (March 3, 1900); Roosevelt to George Bird Grinnell, March 14, 1900, TR MSS.; *Outing* 36:92–93 (April 1900).
[44] Pinchot, *Breaking New Ground*, p. 182; Forest Commission, *Annual Report, 1900*, pp. 22–24, 157–236.

desire for economy and for control over patronage, Governor Odell failed to carry forward the constructive policy which Roosevelt had advocated. The preparation of working plans for forest development came to a halt. So too did the addition to the state's timber holdings through annual purchases. Official laxness came to characterize the administration of the forest preserve.[45]

Such a result would never have ensued under Roosevelt. When Grant La Farge warned him about a bill which would permit a railroad running through the state forest to use coal-burning engines, the governor acted to stop it. Again Roosevelt sided with Superintendent of Forests Fox against Odell on a measure which would have permitted the Utica Electric Light Company to acquire lands owned by private individuals within the Adirondacks Park. Consistently an upholder of the public over the private interest, Theodore Roosevelt ably indicated the path he was later to follow on national conservation.[46]

[45] Donaldson, *History of the Adirondacks,* II, 208–209, 217–219.

[46] La Farge to Roosevelt, November 10, 1899, TR MSS. (LC). Roosevelt to William F. Fox, to Odell, to La Farge, January 31, 1900; to La Farge, February 6, 1900; to Odell, March 24, 1900; to Lucius Littauer, April 24, 1900; all TR MSS. Odell to Roosevelt, March 25, 1900, TR MSS. (LC); *Public Papers* (1900), p. 138. See also Roosevelt to Frank M. Chapman, May 8, 1900, TR MSS., relative to Roosevelt's approval of the Hallock bill regulating the killing and capture of birds in New York State.

CHAPTER XII **Administrative Reform**

Governor Roosevelt brought the same zeal for improvement to the general administration of state departments and institutions that he had brought to canal operations and labor relations. It was not his object to effect a sweeping governmental reorganization. Nor did he expect to best the machine on every point of conflict. He aimed, wherever opportunity arose, to make New York officialdom responsible to the public interest. The officer who was corrupt or inefficient, or who put party above the people, should be turned out if at all possible. Where methods were out-of-date and unprogressive, they should be brought into line with the best thought of the day. Only thus, Roosevelt believed, would the government discharge its duty to promote the general welfare.

Lack of opportunity to effect changes, of course, limited the scope of any governor's activity. The board of railroad commissioners, for example, was practically an independent body; all three members had appointments extending beyond 1900, and Roosevelt never had to concern himself about their work. The same was true of Excise Commissioner Henry H. Lyman and Superintendent of State Prisons Cornelius V. Collins. On one occasion Roosevelt had Lyman send a special agent to investigate Billy McGlory's at the insistence of the Rev. A. P. Doyle of the Paulist Fathers. But when numerous individuals besought the governor to stop Collins' removal of Sing Sing's warden, Roosevelt begged off because he did not want to request anything of an adherent of Lou Payn. It would have taken some act of official misconduct to bring the governor into such a case as this.[1]

The direction of reform interest further restricted Roosevelt's endeavors. Except in that other incident connected with Lou Payn —the State Trust affair—the governor never felt called upon to intervene in Superintendent of Banking Kilburn's field. Nor did agricultural matters arouse concern among the independents; Commissioner Charles A. Wieting's endorsement by Platt and by the various farm organizations was sufficient for reappointment, and thereafter the executive chamber paid no attention to that department.

But Roosevelt had been at Albany only a short time before he began to run up against inefficiency. He discovered defects in the construction of the capitol, and the repairs cost an exorbitant amount. Then he found that while there was a disused power plant in the capitol basement, the state purchased electricity at an expensive rate from a private company. The accounts of the treasurer's office and the departments of public works and public buildings were seriously depleted, he learned, by expenditures in advance of appropriations. And several boards were paying large fees to outside lawyers instead of assigning their legal work to the attorney general.

To the extent that he was able, the new governor remedied these practices. He removed the capitol commissioner and with Platt's aid secured senate confirmation of the well-known New York architect George Lewis Heins as a successor, his function being broadened by law into that of state architect with supervision over state

[1] Roosevelt to the Rev. A. P. Doyle, *The Catholic World*, December 11, 1899; to Rabbi Gustav Gottheil, January 16, 1899; to J. B. Bishop, February 16, 1899; all TR MSS.

construction wherever located. A bill to reactivate the state electric-light plant ran afoul of the local utility's opposition, but Roosevelt and the other capitol trustees secured a substantial reduction in the cost of future service. To check the practice of anticipating appropriations, the governor approved a measure compelling state officials to stay within their allotted funds. The legislature also adopted his recommendation that the attorney general's office at least should take over the legal work of the lunacy commission.[2]

Roosevelt took particular care also to raise the efficiency of the national guard. The military code was revised, and actual field tests were instituted at the summer encampment. Requests were made to the federal government to equip New York's troops with the same rifle used in the regular army, and to provide two vessels for the naval militia. At Roosevelt's urging the federal government undertook an investigation of the relation of reserve and regular military organizations abroad. In every way he sought to coordinate Empire State forces with those of the nation, an especially desirable aim when so many volunteers were going off to fight in the Philippines.[3]

In view of the improvements effected in the guard, it was the more regrettable that the investigation into the alleged cowardice of the Seventy-First Regiment at the battle of San Juan engendered such bitterness. This closed-doors probe had been in progress before Roosevelt came to Albany and ordered a "full and complete

[2] *New York Tribune*, January 11, 31, February 1, 11, 23, March 1, 2 and May 17, 1899; Chapter 566, *Laws of New York* (1899).

[3] *Public Papers* (1900), pp. 31–34; *Watertown Daily Times*, May 6, 1899 (RS). Roosevelt to the Secretary of the Navy, February 2, 1899; to William Cary Sanger, January 27, 1900; both TR MSS. Avery D. Andrews, "Theodore Roosevelt," unpub. MS., Roosevelt Collection, 2 vols. (1945), II, 213–218, 226.

inquiry" into the matter; the colonel and the major whose failure had been most serious had resigned, moreover, before the board of inquiry released its finding. The second in command, Lieutenant Colonel Clinton H. Smith, did not resign, however, nor did he accept the board's recommendation (approved by Roosevelt since neglect of duty appeared "clearly established" though "not so sharply cut") that he be sent up before a "Bouncing Board." In and out of the civil courts Smith waged a protracted fight against the "course of oppression" he claimed was being pursued against him; it was even charged that Roosevelt was biased because he had wanted originally to go into the Seventy-First as a major but couldn't because the two majors already there—one of whom was Smith—had desired to remain. It is most unlikely that this fact had influenced the governor, but before the review board in June 1900 finally discharged him, Smith and his legal counsel had stirred up the regiment and the public press to a degree unfortunate for the good of the guard.[4]

As Roosevelt turned to the management of state institutions, he found that inefficiency was usually intertwined with a second general problem—the subordination of state to local interests. Boards of managers were often dominated by members living in the immediate area. They were therefore prone to favor local business at the cost of economical operation. And they tended to resent state supervision of their activities, whether by the comptroller or by the state board of charities, a conscientious body of public-

[4] A. D. Andrews to Major General Roe, January 4, 1899, printed in *New York Tribune*, January 5, 1899; *Public Papers* (1899), pp. 81–87; *New York Press*, May 10, 1899 (RS); *New York Tribune*, May 18, 19, 1899; *New York Press*, July 21, 1899, June 7, 1900 (both RS); Roosevelt to A. D. Andrews, June 12, 1900, TR MSS.; William G. Bates to Roosevelt, June 9, 1900, TR MSS. (LC).

spirited citizens empowered under the constitution to "visit and inspect all institutions . . . of a charitable, eleemosynary, correctional or reformatory nature." [5]

Because of his long relation with work in the charities field, first through his father and then through his reform activities, Roosevelt was naturally disposed to align himself with the state board's efforts. As a spirited defender of the commonweal, moreover, it was characteristic of him to declare, as he did in his annual message of 1899, that boards of managers should realize that "administration should always be simply in the interest of the State at large." [6]

Where the reform attack centered on financial matters the initiative usually remained with the comptroller's office and the charities board, which together launched a lively campaign against the idea that "had quite generally prevailed in the neighborhood of public institutions that they present legitimate plunder for the locality." When Comptroller Morgan put a stop to purchases of coal by the Batavia School for the Blind at fifty cents a ton above the going rate, one manager resigned in protest. The entire board at the Western House of Refuge quit in reaction against increased state regulation of their affairs. This more stringent supervision sprang in part from Chapter 383 of the Laws of 1899, which ordered the comptroller and the president of the state board of charities to classify and fix the salaries and wages of "the officers and employees of the various charitable and reformatory institutions required by

---

[5] Except reformatories in which adult males convicted of felony were confined and institutions for the care and treatment of the insane. See New York State Charities Aid Association, *Twenty-Eighth Annual Report* (1900), pp. 103–104.

[6] *Public Papers* (1899), p. 26; *New York Tribune*, January 6, 1899; Charities Board, *Annual Report, 1899*, pp. 197–198; Comptroller, *Annual Report, 1898*, pp. xxvi–xxxvii.

law to report to the comptroller." But it was also a consequence of Morgan's determination to effect economies, a determination so zealous as to appear unreasonable to unsalaried managers.[7]

In his general appointment policy Roosevelt backed up the charities board, at times against the persistent opposition of influential politicians, but in no instance did he intervene more actively than in the case of the New York State Soldiers' and Sailors' Home at Bath in Steuben County. The governor's own involvement in military affairs undoubtedly sharpened his concern for the 1,400 pensioned veterans who lived at the home under the benevolent rule of Colonel C. O. Shepard. But the conflict of state and local interests in the management was so heated that as an *ex officio* board member he could hardly have avoided participation. This conflict had split the nine-man board of trustees into two factions. The majority group, headed by two politicians resident in Bath—Democratic State Committee Chairman Frank Campbell and Otis H. Smith, an adherent of the Republican county machine—was favorable to the locality and critical of the conduct of the superintendent. Against this political "ring" were ranged Generals King of Brooklyn and Sickles of New York and Colonel Shoemaker of Elmira, who championed Shepard for his insistence that the institution serve primarily the veterans and the state.[8]

Sympathetic to the minority yet hesitant to pick a fight with the Republican organization, Roosevelt at first tried to restore harmony by compromise. He would have liked to replace Otis H. Smith when that trustee's term expired—a step which would have affronted Judge John F. Parkhurst, editor of the *Steuben Courier*

[7] *New York Tribune*, July 7, 8, 1899; file of correspondence dated April–July 1899 between the Albion managers and the state board, in TR MSS., Private (LC).

[8] *Syracuse Herald*, March 12, 1899; *Buffalo Express*, February 9, 1899.

and leader of the Republican county machine—but the governor was willing to reappoint him if the board would approve the substitution of a permanent chaplain (as Shepard and the minority desired) for the old system under which four local clergymen shared the ministerial duties at the home. In the midst of a February blizzard Roosevelt unexpectedly turned up at a board meeting in Bath and obtained the trustees' approval of a resident chaplain. Five days later the names of Smith and Shoemaker went to the senate for confirmation.[9]

Although Roosevelt's visit lifted the veterans' morale and brought a period of peace to affairs there, in August 1899 by a vote of 6 to 5 the trustees asked that Shepard resign. As superintendent, charged the majority, he had mishandled state funds and services, was "addicted to excessive use of intoxicants" and had held drinking parties in the chapel, was "irritable and impatient, and frequently abuses the inmates of the Home and has slandered his subordinates." The charge of intemperance most alarmed Roosevelt, for he had once seen the superintendent under the influence of liquor and had then issued a warning. As recently as July 31, however, he had defended Shepard to Platt as a "much finer" man than those who would "divvy up not merely the patronage, but the money benefits of the institution equally between republican and democratic organizations in Bath." So the governor agreed with General Sickles that unless evidence that would satisfy an "honest and disinterested man" was presented, Shepard should remain.[10]

Determined to get at the facts, the governor on August 19, 1899,

---

[9] *Steuben Courier,* December 2, 1898; Roosevelt to Odell, January 16, 24, 1899, TR MSS.; *Buffalo Express,* February 9, 1899; Charities Board, *Annual Report, 1900,* pp. 333, 379.

[10] *New York Tribune,* August 12, 1899. Roosevelt to General King, August 14, 1899; to General Sickles, August 16, 20, 1899; to Platt, July 31, 1899; all TR MSS.

directed the state board of charities to open an investigation into
the management of the Soldiers' Home. He suspended that order
shortly thereafter, as the board of trustees agreed that Shepard
could remain in office until February 1900, but once the fall elections were past Roosevelt requested the charities board to reopen
its inquiry. By that action he may have intended to afford Shepard
a fair hearing, but the protests of Judge Parkhurst's *Steuben
Courier* clearly indicated much more than that. Whether he could
save Shepard or not, Roosevelt wanted ammunition with which to
effect a sweeping change on the board of trustees.[11]

Eventually the state board was to conclude that the charges
against the superintendent had not been proven and that "had
Mr. Shepard been more subservient to the demands of those who
sought to use the home to their own advantage no charge would
have been presented against him." But that verdict only came in
May 1900; the previous February, at the meeting of the Bath
board, it had been insisted that Shepard resign as agreed, that is,
if a majority so desired, and without charges being preferred.
With Roosevelt's support the minority had unsuccessfully tried to
delay a vote until the inquiry was completed. Then even the governor had refused to countenance a "very improper scheme" to
keep Shepard in office for another year by means of a court
injunction. With their coup scotched, King, Sickles, and Shoemaker
had surrendered their trusteeships in a futile protest. On February
10 the six remaining trustees had voted unanimously to suspend
the superintendent.[12]

But against all opposition, ranging from a "clean bill of health"
for the old board from an assembly committee of visitation, to a

[11] *Steuben Courier,* December 8, 1899 and January 12, 1900; Charities
Board, *Annual Report, 1900,* pp. 273, 430–432.

[12] *Albany Evening Journal,* February 8–10, 1900. Roosevelt to Generals
Sickles and King, February 5, 1900; to Slicer, February 22, 1900; all TR MSS.

personal plea for trustee Finch from Boss Platt, the governor carried through his plan to supplant the trustees whose terms were expiring (or who had resigned) with eight new men, all veterans and representative of the entire state. For Roosevelt had enough evidence, more fully detailed later by the charities board investigators, to gain his way. Over one hundred thousand dollars in annual pensions had been deposited without interest or bond in the bank owned by Campbell and Parkhurst, the state board reported, and the veterans' posthumous funds had been similarly mismanaged. At the same time the Post Exchange had supplied free liquor and cigars to the trustees, exploitation of the veterans in saloons outside the home had proceeded unchecked, and the purchasing of supplies had favored local interests to the detriment of administrative economy and efficiency. Armed with facts such as these, a soft-speaking Roosevelt would be heard, and heeded.[13]

The revengeful Parkhurst-Campbell faction salvaged something from this defeat. It had ousted Shepard upon charges that the charities board investigators later concluded had not been proved. It escaped punishment for the trustee misconduct revealed by the inquiry. It even managed to put through the legislature a bill exempting the Soldiers' Home from the "management and control" of the state board of charities. Since that body had never possessed such power, the effect of this measure was negligible; it nevertheless disturbed the state board, which had just suffered a severe setback in a legal battle with the Society for the Prevention of Cruelty to Children, and so resented any slight upon its authority.[14]

[13] Charities Board, *Annual Report, 1900,* pp. 404ff. See also *Steuben Courier,* February 16, March 23, 30, 1900; *Rochester Union and Advertiser,* March 16, 27, 1900; *Albany Argus,* February 13, 1900; Roosevelt to Platt, March 22, 1900, TR MSS.

[14] Charities Board, *Annual Report, 1900,* pp. 390ff.; Roosevelt to Sickles, April 9, 1900, TR MSS.; D. M. Schneider and Albert Deutsch, *The History of Public Welfare in New York State, 1867–1940* (Chicago, 1941), pp. 133–135.

In signing this measure, Roosevelt realized that he would further antagonize the reform element that had sided with Shepard. The governor discounted the bill's effect upon the state board, however, and argued that it would soothe the feelings of the elderly veterans at the home: they did not want to be regarded as "charitable" cases, and 1,415 of them had petitioned him to remove them entirely from the supervision of the state board. All things considered, Roosevelt was content. He had successfully attacked the corrupt syndicate at Bath. By his appointments he had made it clear that local interests were no longer to be dominant there. He had taken the essential steps toward re-establishment of good administration at the Soldiers' and Sailors' Home.[15]

As he shifted attention to the state reformatories, the governor came up against the third general problem of state institutions: the harsh and "unprogressive" methods often followed there. President William Rhinelander Stewart and his colleagues on the charities board were particularly exercised at the continued practice of corporal punishment, which for lack of a legal prohibition they were determined to eliminate by administrative surveillance. Where such harsh methods prevailed, moreover, it was likely that managers had lost sight of their true purpose, which according to the progressive "pedagogical penology" of the day was to reform rather than punish, to fit inmates in the best possible way for return to society. And that was just what had happened at the House of Refuge for Women at Hudson in Columbia County, one of New York's two reformatories for female misdemeanants of fifteen to thirty years of age.[16]

In its wish to eliminate all "prison" aspects, to classify inmates

---

[15] *Buffalo Express,* March 17, 1900; *Public Papers* (1900), pp. 133–134; *Buffalo Courier,* May 7, 1900; Roosevelt to Bishop, May 2, 1900, TR MSS.

[16] New York *Evening Post,* July 10, 1899; Comptroller, *Annual Report, 1899,* pp. xlii–xliii; Blake McKelvey, *American Prisons: A Study in Social History Prior to 1915* (Chicago, 1936), pp. 93–118, 143, 169–170.

and establish a suitable program of industrial and domestic training, the state board of charities had long despaired of the Hudson
example. The difficulty there arose partly from the physical plant,
as the lack of small cottages made necessary the continued use
of the old central prison building for housing many of the 300
young women. Yet former boards of managers had done little to
alter this; indeed, they had "tenaciously maintained" the *"prison*
features of the institution." What was more, Hudson continued to
evidence "an unsympathetic system of repressive discipline; the
lack of systematic classification of inmates; the neglect of . . . their
individual study and treatment; too limited systems of technical
instruction." A change of superintendents in 1898 had produced
only "a temporary appearance of improvement"; what was really
needed, concluded the state board, was a reform of the board of
managers.[17]

When the terms of two Hudson managers expired in the spring
of 1899, Roosevelt acted on William Rhinelander Stewart's advice
to name Vassar professor Herbert E. Mills and Dr. Christian Herter
of New York to succeed. Soon three other board members, all
Black appointees from the immediate vicinity of Hudson, took
this latest sample of charities board "interference" as sufficient
provocation for submission of their own resignations. After the
governor had filled these vacancies with Stewart's selections from
Syracuse, Ghent, and New York, the six-man board had quite a
changed complexion.[18]

That summer the new administrators initiated a few improvements as they dismissed the superintendent, curbed lax methods
of supervisors and guards, and abolished the strap and cold shower

[17] Charities Board, *Annual Report, 1898,* p. 253; *ibid., 1899,* p. 66.
[18] *New York Tribune,* May 19, 1899. Roosevelt to Appointment Clerk New-
comb, July 19, 1899; to Platt, November 6, 1899; both TR MSS.

in favor of solitary confinement as a means of discipline. Still there were too few of the homelike cottages that facilitated classification, and too many inmates necessarily lodged in the prisonlike central building. Worse yet, a good percentage of the women were found to be felons committed there, under an 1896 amendment to the penal code, for sentences of one year or less. Reform techniques were ill adapted to these "hardened vicious women who had been living abandoned, criminal lives for years," and whose presence had undoubtedly contributed to the old board's difficulties.[19]

The new managers had had no opportunity to cope with these more deep-seated problems before a "riot" occurred at the reformatory. The trouble began in the central prison one October weekend when Kate McCormick, "one of the worst characters in the institution," turned a fire hose on the attendants; in the ensuing meleé, 100 inmates caused damage of $2,000 to fixtures, furniture, and windows. At once the Democratic press fixed the blame for the "insurrection" on the governor and the state board of charities. The situation at Hudson had been "ideal," declared the *Albany Argus,* until Roosevelt disrupted the old board of managers; the new appointees knew so little about discipline that Professor Mills had even told the assembled inmates that he intended to treat them just as he did his Vassar students. Most Republican organs devoted little attention to the affair, but the influential New York *Sun* agreed with the *Argus* that the "silly and harmful policy" of moral suasion without corporal punishment was responsible for the disturbance of an institution which had been "a State pride" up to a year before.[20]

---

[19] *New York Tribune,* October 12, 1899; New York *Evening Post,* July 11, 13, 1899; New York *World,* July 15, 16, 1899; Comptroller, *Annual Report, 1899,* p. xlii; Prisons Commission, *Annual Report, 1899,* p. 75.

[20] *New York Tribune,* October 10, 1899; *Albany Argus,* October 11, 1899;

Ever concerned over the political effect of happenings in New York, Thomas Collier Platt was considerably disturbed. Not only was an election close at hand, but Hudson was in Lou Payn's bailiwick, and in the interests of harmony the Boss was currently solicitous of his lieutenant's welfare. "I understand the course pursued by some of the State employees with reference to this institution has caused great embarrassment and has rendered the election of our member of the Assembly very doubtful in Columbia County," Platt wrote the governor on November 4, as he forwarded the clippings from the *Albany Argus*. Ordinarily the work of the state board of charities did not concern the Boss, but he had a low opinion of some of the reformers' ideas. "I should think the attempt to adopt a policy, such as I am told has been tried there," concluded Platt, "of governing these conscienceless women by kindness and treating them as 'Vassar girls,' is a serious blunder." [21]

From Oyster Bay the governor replied that the *Argus* gave "but a fraction of the truth." Admitting that he was "not altogether satisfied" with the new managers, Roosevelt thought "the main trouble . . . comes from the utter demoralization left behind by the old board." If Mills had actually made the "Vassar girls" remark it was "infinite folly," the governor added, "but it has been stoutly denied." He would take the matter up again when he returned to Albany.[22]

The immediate effect of the Hudson riot was to instill more caution in the administration of reformatories. Not content to act solely on the advice of the state board of charities, on November 11 Roosevelt asked Speaker Ellsworth to write him "as soon as

---

New York *Sun,* October 15, 1899 (RS). Also *Valatie Rough Notes,* October 13, 1899; *Utica Observer,* October 16, 1899 (both RS).

[21] Platt to Roosevelt, November 4, 1899, TR MSS. (LC).

[22] Roosevelt to Platt, November 6, 1899, TR MSS.

possible about those Western House of Refuge appointments": "I am so afraid some outbreak or other will occur." The authorities at Hudson were equally fearful. Putting to one side for the moment their plans for a more homelike reform atmosphere, the board went so far as to have the inmates of the prison building locked in their cells at mealtime "in such a way that not more than six seemed to be together at one time." As the visitor from the state commission on prisons observed in May 1900, "The management seems to dread above everything another outbreak." [23]

The October disturbance at Hudson nevertheless speeded the establishment of permanent reforms. Four insane inmates were quickly sent to the Matteawan State Hospital, and at the next legislative session the objectionable section of the penal code was amended to close the House of Refuge to women twice convicted of felonies. The managers obtained the services of a capable superintendent, a building apart from the central prison was opened for the reception of new inmates, and skilled instructors took over the industrial training program. By December 1900, the state prison commission inspectors found the fears of "smashing-out" abated and only five women in solitary confinement. The next year the commission heartily commended the management on the reformatory's condition.[24]

The inception of new methods at Hudson did not provoke nearly as much controversy as it did at the state reformatory at Elmira. For Elmira was more than just another state reformatory. From the time of its founding in 1877, this institution had been a model in advanced penology for the entire nation. And inseparably asso-

[23] Roosevelt to Ellsworth, November 11, 1899, TR MSS.; Prisons Commission, *Annual Report, 1900*, pp. 103–105.

[24] Chapter 1114, *Laws of New York* (1900); Prisons Commission, *Annual Report, 1900*, pp. 105–106; *ibid., 1901*, pp. 95–98.

ciated with its fame was Zebulon R. Brockway, the first and in 1899 still the active superintendent. His practical genius had been responsible for the success of the Elmira experiment, and the techniques he had developed—a grading and marking system joined to intelligent application of the indeterminate sentence, instruction in industrial trades, military drill and callisthenic exercise, and constant effort at intellectual stimulation—had exerted a powerful influence upon prison reform everywhere.[25]

Brockway's regime had never been without its critics, but not until the 1890's had the protests attained considerable volume. Paradoxically, Brockway's very success was partly responsible, for in the late 1880's magistrates began to sentence more and more young men convicted of their first felony to the "College on the Hill." Since expansion of facilities did not keep pace with commitments, overcrowding became the rule. The elaborate reform discipline, so effective with the 500 or so prisoners from 1880 to 1885, became increasingly difficult to apply when numbers rose to well over 1,000 after 1889. The superintendent had to resort more frequently to corporal punishment, and the incidence of "spanking" (or more accurately "paddling," since a leather paddle soaked in water was commonly used) inclined upward at a higher rate than did the prison population.[26]

Chiefly as a result of a newspaper campaign led by the New York *World* against "Paddler" Brockway during the year 1893, the affairs of the reformatory had undergone several investigations. The first of these, conducted by the state board of charities, found that overcrowding was largely responsible for the "cruelty and inhumanity" unearthed, but that Brockway had paddled for the

---

[25] McKelvey, *American Prisons*, pp. 114–118.
[26] Elmira Reformatory, *Yearbook, 1895*, pp. 30–31.

"slightest cause," without a doctor being present, and in a "very brutal and inhumane manner." When the Elmira managers refused to remove Brockway on the basis of this "illegal, untrue, and unjust" report, Governor Hill named a special commission to make a second investigation. A majority of this body decided that the punishments meted out by Brockway had not been "excessive in number and in severity, and therefore . . . cruel," whereupon Hill ruled that though the Elmira managers did "deserve criticism, as do their subordinates, they are not guilty of permitting gross abuses in the infliction of punishment, or in the management of the institution." [27]

When Roosevelt took over the governorship, Brockway still ruled at Elmira. Three of the five managers who had supported him in 1894 remained in office, and the two more recent appointees were not hostile to his methods. The 71-year-old superintendent seemed more firmly seated than ever, for by constitutional amendment the state board of charities had had to give over supervision of the reformatory to the new state commission on prisons.[28]

Yet signs of dissatisfaction with the originator of the Elmira system persisted. In New York the *World* and the *Herald* were as critical of him as ever. And at Albany in 1899 the legislature passed a bill designed to curb Brockway's power by abolishing the indeterminate sentence. Quite properly the governor refused to approve such a step, which would have destroyed an indispensable part of the reform penology. But when Roosevelt determined to broaden

[27] "Report and Proceedings of the State Board of Charities Relative to the Management of the State Reformatory at Elmira," *Assembly Documents*, vol. XV, no. 89 (1894), I, x, xiii, xv–xxii, xxv; Zebulon R. Brockway, *Fifty Years of Prison Service: An Autobiography* (New York, 1912), pp. 282–283, 333–335; Elmira Reformatory, *Yearbook, 1895*, pp. 3–4, 9, 13.

[28] Brockway, *Autobiography*, p. 348.

the representation on the five-man board by supplanting three retiring members, all residents of the immediate area, with able citizens from Buffalo, Rochester, and New York, he unwittingly aided Brockway's opponents. In combatting the evil of localism, in other words, Roosevelt really began a shakeup at Elmira.[29]

In contrast to the former managers, who had left Brockway largely to his own devices, the reconstituted board held monthly meetings, each of several days' duration, and "familiarized itself, as deeply as possible . . . with the system and needs of the Reformatory and its inmates." The new president of the board, Thomas D. Sturgis of New York City, a former civil service commissioner and fire commissioner under the reform administration of Mayor Strong, soon revealed an earnest opposition to the superintendent's practices. Under his leadership the Elmira board adopted the policy that "nothing which is not truly reformative in its nature and its effects shall be permitted to continue a part of the system," that "methods of discipline" should conform to this rule or be forbidden, and that prisoners unsuited to reform should be transferred elsewhere. Then Sturgis carried a vote for the abolition of the paddle.[30]

This controversial action precipitated a critical disagreement between Sturgis and another Roosevelt appointee, Ansley Wilcox, a Gold Democrat from Buffalo, who took his case to the governor. Roosevelt was inclined at first to side with Wilcox, to whom he replied that

what you describe is just about what I anticipated would happen. I have never felt the horror of corporal punishment for criminals. Personally, I

[29] *Watertown Times,* April 25 and May 3, 1899 (RS); New York *Sun,* April 20, 1899 (RS); *New York Tribune,* April 20, 21, 1899; Rochester *Evening Times* and *Auburn Bulletin,* April 20, 1899 (RS); *New York Herald,* April 18, 1899 (RS); New York *World,* April 21, 1899; *New York Tribune,* May 3, 1899.

[30] Elmira Reformatory, *Yearbook, 1899,* pp. 11–12.

should be heartily glad to see the whipping post used for wife beaters and abusers of children.

Roosevelt went so far as to prepare a letter recommending a relaxation of the paddling prohibition, only to have Sturgis present "a large number of facts with the purpose of showing me that it [corporal punishment] is not necessary and that order can be guaranteed without a return to the old methods." Sturgis' "very strong opinions" influenced Roosevelt (who after the Hudson riot was clearly intent on "order") to withhold the recommendation.[31]

As the news soon leaked out, the governor defended his decision as a matter of expediency: he denied the *Brooklyn Eagle's* charge that he had "taken the side of the sentimentalists," and assured Wilcox that "I have never stated I was against corporal punishment . . . If best results can be obtained through corporal punishment, then I want it; otherwise not." [32]

Nonetheless, his action did lend support to those who opposed Brockway's methods as a matter of principle. Ansley Wilcox soon tendered his resignation, and thereafter the breach between the managers and the reformatory superintendent steadily widened. Zebulon Brockway may have approved some of the reforms initiated by Sturgis and his colleagues, such as the transfer of the insane and the incorrigibles to Matteawan and Auburn, but the old superintendent was quite out of sympathy with the general policy. What galled him most was the sight of one hundred or so "recalcitrant" prisoners restricted to their cells for "punishment." In his view, these men were soon more pampered than penalized; the only thing that kept their example from infecting the whole population, con-

---

[31] *Ibid.,* p. 12; *New York Press,* July 28, 1899 (RS); Roosevelt to Wilcox, October 9 and November 9, 1899, TR MSS.

[32] Roosevelt to Wilcox, November 15, 1899, TR MSS. See New York *World, New York Journal,* and *Brooklyn Eagle,* November 14, 1899 (RS).

cluded Brockway, was the "prevailing powerful moral control" which his methods had achieved for the orderly men.[33]

Brockway's impatience with the new administration finally found release in an extraordinary punishment inflicted on half a hundred "noisy and troublesome" prisoners. He had them placed four and five together in six-foot by eight-foot triangular cells, raised the temperature therein to 95 degrees, and then subjected the area to whistle-blowing and pan-beating for three days. The noise and heat then stopped, but the men were kept incarcerated for seven more days. As a result, Roosevelt wrote Paul Dana of the *Sun* on July 25, 1900, twelve of the men were under surveillance as insane, and two-thirds of the rest had not yet recovered. The "somewhat diabolical ingenuity" of the whole incident, as Roosevelt put it, was that never a paddle had been used.[34]

This was the last straw for the Elmira board, which by this time was entirely sympathetic to Sturgis' position. When Platt urged Roosevelt to have action on Brockway deferred until after the November election, the governor replied that to his own previous request for delay the managers had said that they "would not be responsible and would not stay in if they had to longer keep quiet." On July 31, 1900, Zebulon Brockway submitted his resignation peaceably, as Roosevelt had hoped he would, and the man who one authority has said "stands without rival as the greatest warden America has produced" went quietly into retirement in nearby Elmira.[35]

While legitimate disagreement may exist as to whether Brock-

[33] Elmira Reformatory, *Yearbook, 1900,* pp. 12, 14ff.; Comptroller, *Annual Report, 1899,* pp. xliii, xlvi–xlvii, xlix; Brockway, *Autobiography,* pp. 363–373.
[34] Roosevelt to Dana, July 25, 1900, TR MSS.
[35] Platt to Roosevelt, July 26, 1900, in *Barnes* v. *Roosevelt,* pp. 2490–91; Roosevelt to Platt, July 29, 1900, TR MSS.; McKelvey, *American Prisons,* p. 144.

way or the "sentimentalists" had the right position on corporal punishment, Roosevelt's action had the merit of consistency.[36] He had not set out from the first to "get" the superintendent, but rather to secure a better board of managers. Once the opposing views of Sturgis and Wilcox had appeared, the governor had chosen the one he favored, and thereafter had named men sympathetic to that view to the vacancies that occurred. By the end of his term, harmony had been reestablished on the Elmira board and the transition to the new discipline was well underway.[37]

Although politics were ever a consideration in the administration of state institutions, no single appointment caused Roosevelt more embarrassment than the replacement of Truman J. Backus, a former president of Vassar College, as a manager on the Long Island State Hospital board. No one incident—unless it be the Lou Payn affair—better illustrated the pitfalls confronting an "independent organization man" like Roosevelt. No other action put the governor so on the defensive, forcing him to construct a reasoned review of his whole administrative career.

When the question of Backus' reappointment first arose, in January 1900, it appeared to be a routine renomination, for strong endorsements had come in from Alexander E. Orr, another member of the Long Island State Hospital board, and many others. Since Odell had certain adverse information, however, the governor sought the approval of the state lunacy commission, a three-man board composed of a "non-political" president, Dr. Peter M. Wise;

[36] Philip Klein, *Prison Methods in New York*, Columbia University Studies in History, Economics and Public Law, no. 205 (New York, 1920), p. 228; Elmira Reformatory, *Yearbook, 1900*, pp. 33–34; Roosevelt to Paul Dana, July 25, 1900, TR MSS.

[37] Klein, *Prison Methods*, p. 228; Elmira Reformatory, *Yearbook, 1904*, pp. 13–15; *ibid., 1908*, pp. 17–19. These later reports show that the new discipline, though often difficult to apply, was retained at Elmira.

a Republican member, William L. Parkhurst, brother-in-law of
State Senator John Raines; and the Democratic member, William
Church Osborn, son-in-law of wealthy William E. Dodge and a
Princeton and Harvard Law graduate, whom Roosevelt had named
to the post in April 1899 as a replacement for Albany lawyer
Goodwin Brown. And at this point a misunderstanding occurred.[38]

Because of protests from the Republican member, Parkhurst,
Osborn requested Roosevelt to hold Backus' nomination in abeyance a few days. Subsequently Osborn and Dr. Wise agreed that
Backus should be named, but thinking that the governor would so
act they did not inform him of their decision. Parkhurst, meantime,
had carried his objections to the executive chamber, and Roosevelt
erroneously took these views to be those of the whole commission.
Already under pressure from Odell, the governor altered his intention. Without notifying Osborn, Orr, or any of Backus' supporters
of this change, he proceeded to send in the name of wealthy, cul-
tured Bradish Johnson, by general consent an excellent man for the
position.[39]

"The failure to reappoint Dr. Backus has caused a veritable
storm!" exclaimed Roosevelt as he forwarded Odell clippings from
the *Brooklyn Eagle* and the *New York Tribune* and letters from
Orr and Silas B. Dutcher, the prominent Brooklyn Republican who
also served on the hospital board. The protestors all asserted that
Senator Raines was the main influence behind the appointment:
he had simply sought revenge for his son-in-law, Dr. Sylvester,
whom Backus, as president of the board of managers, had forced
out of the hospital superintendency in a recent investigation. And

[38] Roosevelt to Odell, January 4, 1900; to William Church Osborn, January
5, 1900; both TR MSS.

[39] Statements by Roosevelt and Osborn in *New York Tribune*, February 13,
1900; Roosevelt to Odell, January 29, 1900, TR MSS.; *New York Tribune*,
February 13, 1900.

when Roosevelt learned that the objection to Backus on the state board had come from Parkhurst alone, he saw that Raines (acting through another son-in-law, Parkhurst) indeed might have been instrumental. Yet the governor knew there was more to the case than this, for it did not explain Odell's opposition.[40]

Odell's animus against Backus stemmed from the latter's resistance to the replacement of Goodwin Brown on the lunacy commission the previous year. For after the governor had decided that Goodwin Brown was "not straight" and would have to go, it was Odell's candidate, William VanAmee of Newburgh, who got the recommendation as Brown's successor. And it was Backus, through his brother-in-law—an editor on the *New York Tribune*—who then allegedly had furnished the material for the *Tribune's* attacks upon the VanAmee appointment. In particular, the *Tribune* had divulged the fact that VanAmee had been a prominent supporter of Isaac H. Maynard, whose association with the infamous "Senate steal" of 1893 still rankled in Republican breasts. As a result chiefly of this revelation, Odell and Roosevelt had soon agreed that confirmation was impossible. VanAmee's name had been withdrawn, and after a careful screening ("find out from him *for my own use only* if he voted *against* Maynard," he had cautioned Douglas Robinson) the governor had finally sent up William Church Osborn's name.[41]

---

[40] Roosevelt to Odell, February 3, 1900, TR MSS.; *Binghamton Herald*, February 6, 1900; New York *Evening Post*, February 5, 1900; *Brooklyn Eagle*, February 6, 1900 (RS); New York *Sun*, February 7, 1900 (RS). Roosevelt to Alexander E. Orr, to William Church Osborn, February 3, 1900; to William L. Parkhurst, February 8, 1900; both TR MSS.

[41] Roosevelt to Orr, February 7, 1900, TR MSS. On the VanAmee affair, see Roosevelt to Bishop, April 8, 17, 1899, TR MSS.; *New York Tribune*, April 4, 5, 8, 13, 1899; *Albany Argus* and New York *Evening Post* (RS), April 6, 1899. See also Roosevelt to Platt, April 4, 1899; to Douglas Robinson, April 6, 1899; to Bishop, April 18, 1899; all TR MSS.

Although Roosevelt denied that knowledge of Backus' part in the Goodwin Brown-VanAmee dispute had influenced his own decision, to one correspondent he did admit that it had made him "unwilling to go into a disagreeable fight which might hurt the institution without benefiting anyone." The speed with which Roosevelt notified Odell of the outcry at dropping Backus indicated the true source of the governor's concern. More than likely Odell had argued that Backus should not be rewarded for his part in the VanAmee episode, and that if he were, there might be complications in the confirmation of Hendricks as Lou Payn's successor. But whatever the exact reasoning, it was Odell's advice that had been heeded.[42]

Despite the quick confirmation of Bradish Johnson, Roosevelt remained touchy about the whole affair. When the Long Island Hospital managers, with Johnson abstaining, published a resolution assuming responsibility for each and all of Backus' official acts and censuring the governor's "methods of procedure" in the case, Roosevelt informed Orr that such a public pronouncement was "scandalous, and at once removed any doubt I might have had as to the wisdom of my previous action." When the *Evening Post* continued to maintain that the executive had had full knowledge in advance of the attitude of Osborn and Wise, Roosevelt was pleased that Osborn set the matter straight with a letter to that journal. And after investigating carefully the charges later brought against Backus by Senator Raines, the governor notified the board of managers on November 15, 1900, that if Backus were still in office he would have to be removed. But since it would only be harmful to publish that, Roosevelt merely reprimanded the other managers for their unequivocal support of their former colleague.[43]

[42] Roosevelt to Orr, to Dr. E. F. Smith, February 7, 1900, TR MSS.
[43] *New York Tribune*, February 25, 1900; Roosevelt to Orr, March 2, 1900, TR MSS.; New York *Evening Post*, March 7, 8, 10, 1900; Roosevelt to

The way in which Roosevelt pursued the Backus case reflected his bad conscience over the initial decision. At various times he had admitted two errors on his part—he should have notified Orr of the change in plans, and he should have had a "full understanding" with William Church Osborn. But though these oversights might be excused, as Roosevelt suggested, because of the need for haste in covering the vast amount of work he had had in January 1900, such was not the case with Odell's influence. Indeed, the arguments which the state chairman had advanced against Backus would only have irritated the reformers further. Roosevelt as much as acknowledged that to Josephine Shaw Lowell when he wrote that "since Dr. Backus was a sufficiently good man it was a mistake (merely from the standpoint of policy) to give to the malignant liars of the Evening Post and kindred papers the chance by their unscrupulous mendacity to mislead people like yourself." [44]

The New York *Evening Post* did not miss such a glorious chance to trace "a steady depreciation in the morale of Mr. Roosevelt and a marked growth of machinism in his action and in his ideas." But the *Brooklyn Eagle* struck closer to the truth when it observed that Roosevelt "was not a large enough man, publicly, to admit that he had done wrong, though we believe he is still a good enough man, to realize that he did." The closest Roosevelt came to a public confession of an error in the replacement of Backus was—of all times!—on Washington's Birthday in a speech at the Saturn Club of Buffalo. There he acknowledged that those who "strive in practical fashion" for righteousness were going to make mistakes, even as he had done. "I do not mean the mistake is to be excused," he

Osborn, March 15, 1900, TR MSS.; *New York Tribune*, April 3, 1900. Roosevelt to Orr, April 10, 1900; to Raines, April 18, 1900; to Bishop, May 26, 1900; to Board of Managers, Long Island State Hospital, November 15, 1900; to Orr, December 3, 1900; all TR MSS.

[44] Roosevelt to Orr, March 2, 1900; to Osborn, March 15, 1900; to Josephine Shaw Lowell, February 20, 27, 1900; all TR MSS.

then added, "only it is to be given its proper place in estimating the aggregate of the work done . . ." [45]

In "the aggregate of the work done," Roosevelt firmly believed, his record as an administrator was superior to that of any other governor of New York in at least two decades. So when Josephine Shaw Lowell gave him a "very trite little sermon" about how disappointed she and others "who are trying to help on the City in practical ways" were in his performance, the governor asked for a catalogue of their complaints. Her list included the failure to reappoint Backus, the Hornellsville speech, the inefficiency of the factory inspector's department, the proposal to appoint unsalaried inspectors instead of removing the inefficiency, the appointment to a quarantine commissionership of "a man with a dishonest past," the interference in the Bath Old Soldiers' Home affairs, and the frequent conferences with Platt. In a six-page reply, Roosevelt defended himself on all counts. [46]

His only real errors, Roosevelt maintained, had been in the canal speech at Hornellsville, where he had left himself open to a misconstruction he had since corrected, and in regard to the factory inspectors ("but there never was a mistake made which sprung from more honest sincerity of purpose"). As for the interviews with Platt, these were simply the means to "clean and efficient administration" and conformed with his policy to see and consult "every man with whom I could work to some purpose." Judged by the *"aggregate"* of his deeds, asserted the governor, his

[45] New York *Evening Post* [n.d.], cited in *Brooklyn Eagle,* February 14, 1900; *Brooklyn Eagle,* February 14, 1900; *Buffalo Express,* February 23, 1900 (all RS).

[46] Lowell to Roosevelt, February 11, 1900, TR MSS. (LC); Roosevelt to Lowell, February 20, 1900, TR MSS. The *Evening Post* had bitterly denounced the appointment of the Republican leader of Richmond County, Hugh McRoberts, to a quarantine commissionership, but Roosevelt had investigated the charges against him carefully before allowing the senate to take up the matter.

record compared favorably with Cleveland's, who had failed to remove the indicted Sheriff Davidson and had vetoed the controversial tenure of office bill because of an amendment *"put in at his special request."* [47]

Cleveland had labored under a set of conditions so different that a fair verdict was impossible, yet the significant thing was that Roosevelt felt called to draw the comparison. Psychological necessity dictated his attitude in some degree, but he was also responding to the criticisms of the reformers, whose approval he coveted above that of any other group. Conscious of the similarity of his aims and theirs, and at the same time forced into compromise, he naturally assumed a posture of defense. This reaction made him at times appear vain and egotistical. In other instances it led him to minimize the extent of his compromises. And inevitably it caused him to assign more virtue to the machine, and more mendacity to the independent element, than the facts warranted. [48]

Still Roosevelt could and did put up a sturdy defense for his course as a public servant. He had compromised, yes, but so must anyone in politics. To the Constitutional Convention, to Washington and Lincoln he appealed for support of the thesis that common sense was equally as necessary as virtue, that the "hodge-podge of the ideal and the practicable" sneered at by a man like the Rev. Parkhurst was in reality nothing but statesmanship. Speaking of the "little knots of fantastic extremists who loudly proclaim that they are striving for righteousness," Roosevelt declared that

the typical extremist . . . differs from the practical reformer, from the public man who strives in practical fashion for decency, not at all in superior morality, but in inferior sense. He is not more virtuous; he is

[47] Cf. Allan Nevins, *Grover Cleveland: A Study in Courage* (New York, 1932), pp. 142–143; Alexander, *Political History,* IV, 18–19.

[48] For one reformer's criticism on this score, see James C. Carter to Roosevelt, March 9, 17, 1900, TR MSS. (LC).

less virtuous. He is merely more foolish. When Wendell Phillips denounced Abraham Lincoln as "the slave-hound of Illinois," he did not
show himself more virtuous than Lincoln, but more foolish. Neither did
he advance the cause of freedom.[49]

In words that summoned up images of his past critics, Roosevelt
inveighed bitterly against the "cloistered virtue which timidly
shrinks from all contact with the rough world of actual life, and
the uneasy, self-conscious vanity which misnames itself virtue, and
which declines to cooperate with whatever does not adopt its own
fantastic standard." For by their stand these idealists "tend to rob
the forces of good of elements on which they ought to be able to
count in the ceaseless contest with the forces of evil." At times, he
was willing to admit,

a man must cut loose from his associates, and stand alone for a great
cause; but the necessity for such action is almost as rare as the necessity
for a revolution; and to take such ground continually, in season and out
of season, is the sign of an unhealthy nature.

In the proper sense, compromise "merely means agreement," he
concluded, and "opportunism should merely mean doing the best
possible with actual conditions as they exist." For evidence that
he had done that, Roosevelt would stand on his record.[50]

[49] Roosevelt, "Latitude and Longitude among Reformers," *Century Magazine* 60:211–216 (June 1900) reprinted in Theodore Roosevelt, *The Strenuous
Life* (New York, 1900), pp. 41–62.
[50] *Ibid.*, pp. 44–45.

CHAPTER XIII

Parting Shots

Had Theodore Roosevelt had his way, he would have gone on to consolidate this record over the next two or even four years as governor, but that June of 1900 at Philadelphia Boss Platt and the Republican National Convention willed otherwise. And once involved in the November race as McKinley's running mate, Roosevelt found himself increasingly removed from New York's affairs. The state convention did endorse the major measures of his administration, but it was Platt's man, not Roosevelt's, that the G.O.P. nominated for governor. It was the Republican organization, too, that chiefly determined his handling of the charges against Mayor Van Wyck in the Ice Trust dispute. Only in the final acts of his term of office—the removal of Tammany's Asa Bird Gardiner as district attorney of New York County and the appointment of reform Democrat Eugene A. Philbin as his successor—did the governor at last assert his independence. He might bow to expediency when an election demanded, but he was still a Rough Rider.

His campaign to avoid the Vice-Presidential nomination had less effect upon his conduct of the governorship in 1900 than the independents often charged. In his desire to gain Platt's endorsement for a second term Roosevelt was indeed more cautious during his second year in office, exhibiting a greater reluctance to take up and push some measures, a greater willingness to postpone others until the next year. Yet it was easy to exaggerate the extent to which he acted solely out of regard for the senator's goodwill. One thing that discouraged Roosevelt from interference in the legislature's work was the complaint that in 1899 he had transgressed too often the theoretical limits set upon the executive by the state constitution. Again, a certain amount of political expediency was legitimate, for he shared his party's concern over the November election. In fact, the remarkable thing was not that he did so little but that he attempted so much in 1900 that was impolitic from his own and from the party's standpoint.[1]

And in June 1900 he received a kind of reward when the national convention drafted him, over Mark Hanna's protests, as the Republican candidate for Vice-President in the fall election. It was Roosevelt's popularity in the West as much as boss rule in the East that determined that verdict, yet no doubt Platt had decided long before —perhaps after the franchise tax—to work toward this end. He had only taken on the colonel originally because of the desperate situation in New York; now that the organization had recovered its standing there, it could safely turn to a more trustworthy if less popular figure. Roosevelt had served his purpose: it was the perfect time to "elevate him to a higher position." [2]

The first indication of the consequent change in Roosevelt's position in New York was the report that Boss Platt wanted to scuttle the plan to have Francis Vinton Greene succeed Quigg as chairman of the New York County Republican committee. Since Greene was an independent Republican and was known to have the governor's support for the place, Platt's action seemed to show a resurgent disregard for the reformers now that their champion had been pushed into the Vice-Presidential candidacy. Roosevelt immediately notified the senator that "the proposed turning down

[1] On complaints regarding the constitution, see *New York Press*, November 23, 1899; interview of State Senator Brackett by J. H. French (RHP). Roosevelt to Butler, February 17, 1900; to Low, March 7, 1900; both TR MSS. See also G. W. Chessman, "Theodore Roosevelt's Campaign Against the Vice-Presidency," *The Historian* 14:173–190 (Spring, 1952).

[2] *Ibid.*, pp. 185–188.

of General Greene . . . would . . . be not only a cruel injustice to him and the bitterest possible affront to me but would result in united damage to our cause this year." This and other representations caused Platt to desist from the scheme, but the brief flurry presaged a harder struggle over the selection of the next gubernatorial candidate.[3]

In Platt's view, the logical man to succeed Roosevelt was Benjamin B. Odell. He was a straight Republican, trusted by the machine leaders. His successful term as state chairman and his Newburgh residence found favor in country districts, while his business background and his important connection with E. H. Harriman commended him to the financial community. The only difficulty was that Odell refused to have his name considered since state office would interfere with his real aim—to succeed Platt as party leader in New York.[4]

Odell's resistance afforded Roosevelt the opportunity to advocate a candidate less intimately associated with the organization. Odell was the best of the regulars mentioned, opined Roosevelt, but "as yet" he had not "shaken himself as entirely free as I would desire from machine influences, and, above all, I do not believe that the independent republicans, not to speak of the independents generally, would recognize that he was not merely Mr. Platt's candidate." The support of these elements would be particularly hard to obtain if the Democrats nominated as upright a man as Comptroller Bird S. Coler. So with Odell's concurrence Roosevelt favored someone on the order of Seth Low, Elihu Root, or Francis Vinton Greene.[5]

[3] Roosevelt to Platt, June 24, 1900, TR MSS.; Platt to Roosevelt, June 25, 1900, in *Barnes v. Roosevelt*, p. 2489; Roosevelt to Platt, June 26, 1900, TR MSS.; *New York Tribune*, June 24, 27, 1900 (RS).

[4] See Roosevelt to Low, August 3, 1900, TR MSS.; Alexander, *Political History*, IV, 336.

[5] Roosevelt to Low, August 3, 1900; to Platt, August 9, 1900; to Odell, August 10, 1900; to Platt, August 15, 20, 1900; all TR MSS.

But Odell's refusal had caused Platt to look in quite another direction—to Lieutenant Governor Woodruff, or Speaker Nixon, or senate majority leader Ellsworth. "I do not believe we are going to lose a great many votes by reason of taking a man who is known as a straight Republican and will carry out the wishes of the organization," Platt assured the governor. An Independent, on the other hand, could not possibly be elected because the "rank and file would demur and would not support him." "If we are to lower the standard and nominate some such man as you talk about," the senator concluded, "we might as well die first as last." [6]

To this Roosevelt sharply retorted that "to speak of . . . lowering the standard is an utter misuse of words" and that "to have it publicly known that the candidate, whoever he may be, 'will carry out the wishes of the organization' would insure his defeat." Still he was without effective means to alter Platt's intention. When McKinley also objected to consideration of Root's candidacy, the governor confessed to friends that "I feel a little hopeless." [7]

On August 23 Odell finally agreed to run, a decision more difficult for Roosevelt to endorse after the publicity given his differences with Platt. But reasoning that in the interests of the national election the reform Republicans had to go along with the machine, the governor soon reconciled himself to the result. He balked at Platt's suggestion that he make the nominating speech at the state convention, but once the unanimous verdict was recorded he addressed the delegates in praise of the entire ticket and especially of Odell, his "close and staunch friend," a "trusted helper and adviser in every crisis," the "irresistible" candidate.[8]

[6] Platt to Roosevelt, August 16, 1900, TR MSS. (LC). See Roosevelt to Low, August 25, 1900, TR MSS.

[7] Roosevelt to Platt, August 20, 1900; to F. V. Greene, August 22, 1900; to Butler, August 24, 1900; all TR MSS.

[8] *Albany Argus,* August 1, 1900; New York *Commercial Advertiser,* August

Such a tribute was not as gross and self-stultifying as some critics made out. Except where it hedged on the canal issue, the Republican platform took Roosevelt's view on such major issues as civil-service reform, the franchise tax, and municipal ownership of New York City's water supply. And not only had Odell reportedly insisted upon the endorsement of the franchise tax, but in his acceptance speech he lashed out at the Ramapo Company, whose charter he pledged to repeal at the next legislative session. Odell had "entirely abandoned the theory that, if [he were] governor, Senator Platt and not he himself should have the final say," Roosevelt had earlier confided to Seth Low. Benjamin B. Odell was a better candidate than many Platt might have selected.[9]

Propulsion into the thick of national affairs presented Roosevelt with another problem of adjustment: to what extent should he take the stump outside New York? His three-week stint in the fall of 1898 had been such a strain that three days more and his voice would have given out. Then, too, whistle-stop appearances would detract from his dignity, even as Chauncey Depew had done at Philadelphia with his impromptu remarks seconding " 'Teddy' . . . the child of Fifth Avenue . . . the child of the clubs . . . the child of the exclusiveness of Harvard College . . . the dude [who] had become a cowboy." Though his executive duties were not heavy during these months, his enemies would set up a regular "howl"

2, 1900; *New York Press*, August 7, 1900; *Buffalo Express* and *New York Herald*, August 13, 1900 (all RS). Roosevelt to Low, August 25, 1900; to Butler, August 24, 1900; both TR MSS. *New York Herald, New York Press* and *New York World*, August 28, 1900 (RS); New York *Evening Post*, September 5, 1900.

[9] According to the *Buffalo Express*, September 4, 1900, Odell won out against Frank H. Platt over whether endorsement of the franchise-tax law should go into the platform. See also New York *Evening Post*, September 5, 1900; New York *World* and *Utica Observer*, September 7, 1900 (RS); *Watertown Times*, September 7, 8, 1900 (RS).

at his protracted absence. Already some editors were suggesting that he resign the governorship if he expected to undertake a "Bryanite" campaign and make a great many speeches across the nation.[10]

Since a Rough Rider had been forced upon him, however, Mark Hanna intended to make all possible use of him. McKinley was the one whose position would be protected; except for a few speeches he would limit his activities to his front porch in Canton, Ohio. The burden of the canvass would fall on the governor of New York, who if he wanted to preserve his dignity should show more care in his dress, get rid of his slouch hat. "We will send him all over the country," remarked Hanna after Roosevelt had conferred with him at his country estate near Cleveland in early July. "He will be the star attraction of the performance." [11]

His objections put aside to the needs of the hour, Roosevelt did his best to fulfill that rather sardonic prediction. A veritable "steam engine in trousers," he matched the Silver Knight speech for speech the nation over. He even relaxed vigorously: ROOSEVELT GALLOPS THROUGH DAY OF REST announced the New York *World* on October 15. Before he was through over three million Americans had glimpsed the flashing grin, the bespectacled squinting eyes, the smashing fist on palm. With over 600 appearances and 20,000 miles behind him, Roosevelt concluded that "after McKinley and

[10] Twelfth Republican National Convention, *Official Proceedings* (Philadelphia, 1900), pp. 134–135; Roosevelt to Low, June 23, 1900, TR MSS.; New York *Sun*, July 8, 1900 (RS); Roosevelt to Hanna, June 27, 1900, TR MSS. For press discussion of the resignation question, see *Brooklyn Eagle*, June 22, 1900; *Troy Press*, June 25, 1900; *New York Times*, July 11, 1900 (all RS).

[11] New York *World*, July 7, 1900 (RS). The New York *Sun* (July 7, 1900 [RS]) confirmed the *World's* report of this fantastic interview, in which Hanna not only lectured Roosevelt on his clothes but advised him to speak without effort—as McKinley had learned to do—if he wanted to save his voice.

Hanna, I feel that I did as much as anyone in bringing about the result—though after all it was Bryan himself who did most." [12]

Much of the alarm expressed in the Democratic press in New York over all this activity was of a purely partisan nature, as when the *Rochester Herald* stirred itself into an "absurd frenzy" over the absent governor's signature on a proclamation issued at Albany in September for the relief of the Galveston storm victims. It became more serious when, upon the death of State Comptroller Morgan, the lieutenant governor would not assume responsibility for the interim appointment. But the most telling blows were directed at the delay in the investigation of Mayor Van Wyck's connection with the Ice Trust.[13]

This probe had been touched off back in May, when the American Ice Company revealed its intention to boost the price of delivered ice from 30 to 60 cents a hundred pounds. A lean winter harvest was given as the excuse, but those who had watched this company's systematic campaign to drive independent dealers out of New York City through underselling and control of the ice piers on the North and East Rivers were at once up in arms. With Tammany's aid, they declared, American Ice simply intended to exploit its monopolistic power: had not the city dock board leased most of the available piers to a subsidiary of the American Ice Company, had not Van Wyck vetoed a bill providing for more docks, and had not the mayor and Croker's chief political lieutenant just been on a tour of the firm's ice houses in Maine? Before one could say "Tammany Ice Trust" the *New York Journal* petitioned the state attorney general to institute proceedings against American Ice under the Donnelly antitrust law of 1899. Shortly thereafter the

[12] Roosevelt to Lodge, November 9, 1900, TR MSS.; Henry F. Pringle, *Theodore Roosevelt: A Biography* (New York, 1931), p. 225.
[13] *Buffalo Express,* September 16, 1900; *New York Tribune,* September 9, 11, 1900; Davies to Roosevelt, October 4, 1900, TR MSS. (LC).

New York *World,* having obtained evidence that Van Wyck was a stockholder in American Ice, brought charges with the governor to have the mayor removed from office.[14]

The antitrust proceedings soon bogged down in what looked to be a lengthy legal battle over the constitutionality of the Donnelly law, but Roosevelt's principal concern was the *World's* attack upon Van Wyck. The lawyers retained by that yellow journal argued that on the basis of their petition filed on June 2, 1900, the mayor should be immediately suspended from office and a commissioner named to take evidence. Attorney General Davies, on the other hand, was not fully satisfied on the facts: his plan called for the petitioners to present their claims, the mayor to have an opportunity to present an answer, and then the governor to decide whether further action was necessary. Davies' plan was the standard procedure in removals of elected officials, and preferring the *World's* needling to the risk that Van Wyck might be made to appear a martyr, Roosevelt adopted it. This was to be a "judicial proceeding," he declared on June 4, and no personal or political factors were going to influence the final result.[15]

The *World* of course had a political motive: the quicker Van Wyck's corruptness was proved, the better the chance that the Democrats would fall in with David B. Hill's design to make Comptroller Coler the gubernatorial candidate. Pulitzer's organ did not want to bother to find out whether the charter provision forbidding an official to be interested in a corporation doing business with the city meant simple stock ownership or something more. It was enough for this sensational journal that in Judge Gaynor's courtroom on June 9 Van Wyck testified that having been told it was

[14] *New York Tribune,* May 25, August 17 and December 12, 1899; March 16, May 8, 9, 14, 24, 25, 26 and June 5, 1900.
[15] Roosevelt to Lodge, June 9, 1900, TR MSS.; Lodge to Roosevelt, June 5, 1900, in Lodge, ed., *Selections,* I, 463; *New York Tribune,* June 5, 1900 (RS).

"a good thing" he had acquired $250,000 worth of American Ice stock at the "rock bottom" price of $50 a share, paying $50,000 in cash and the rest through "time notes" with the Garfield National Bank. Even when Gaynor ruled that this evidence was "incompetent" for removal proceedings, bringing a long delay while Pulitzer's counsel prepared a new set of charges finally submitted on July 27, the *World* continued to berate Roosevelt for dilatory tactics. This badgering went on through August and into September—indeed, until it became clear that Coler would not be nominated, whereupon the services of its lawyers in the Van Wyck case were abruptly terminated and the prosecution dropped.[16]

The length of time Davies allowed **Van Wyck** in which to file an answer—from August 17 until September 27—indicated that the Republicans, too, had a political interest in the case. But their hopes that the affair would supply timely campaign material suffered a setback upon receipt of the mayor's reply. Van Wyck had indeed become a stockholder in American Ice on April 11, 1899, but he denied knowledge of or implication in the company's price policy or pier leases and asserted that as soon as the exposures of May 1900 had revealed these things he had begun and had since completed the divestment of his holdings. Except for the purchase of $200,000 of the stock by promissory note to the ice firm's president, which of itself was "not sufficient evidence of criminal intent," this answer was in Davies' opinion "very complete and satisfactory." Unless the *World* reconsidered its withdrawal and presented

---

[16] *New York Tribune,* June 10, 1900; New York *World,* June 29 and July 9–11, 1900 (all RS). J. Noble Hayes to Roosevelt, November 17, 1900, TR MSS. (LC); "Memorandum of the Charges against the Mayor in Connection with the Ice Trust," TR MSS. (LC), a document evidently prepared by Attorney General Davies to be published on November 19, 1900; New York *World,* August 23, 29, 31, September 30 and October 1, 1900 (RS); The *World* to Hayes, September 21, 1900, in Hayes to Roosevelt, November 17, 1900, TR MSS. (LC).

new evidence which by itself would justify removal, Davies opined, there was no cause to proceed further against Van Wyck.[17]

Roosevelt, meantime, had become more and more anxious about the matter out on the campaign trail, where Bryan was beginning to chide him for inaction against the Ice Trust. The first of October came and passed without the scheduled publication of the mayor's answer and the appointment of Tracy C. Becker of Buffalo as commissioner to hear the case. Then a telegraphed request from Roosevelt for information brought an unsatisfactory reply from Davies: "unforeseen complications" had arisen due to the *World's* withdrawal and the attorney general would keep him informed. On October 2 the governor wired back that "there should be no unnecessary delay in Ice Trust matter" and outlined his plans for the appointment of a commissioner to take testimony. To that he received the following telegram:

Oct. 3rd, Newburgh, N.Y.—Have talked with Attorney General. Any action by you now would be unwise you can better afford to delay than to do anything or give out any interviews until your return on twentieth. This is important and imperative. Wire answer Newburgh. (signed) B. B. Odell, Jr.

Still befuddled as to why Davies and the party leaders objected to publication of the mayor's answer, Roosevelt agreed not to give out any interview but demanded a letter of explanation. That was at last forthcoming, for on October 4 Billy Youngs took a copy of the answer, with Davies' opinion attached, and boarded a westbound train.[18]

[17] Davies submitted the charges to Van Wyck on August 17; Van Wyck asked for and received two extensions of the 15 days originally allotted for his reply. See "Memorandum of the Charges," TR MSS. (LC); New York *World,* September 30, 1900 (RS); Davies to Roosevelt, October 4, 1900, in "Memorandum of the Charges," TR MSS. (LC).

[18] New York *World,* September 19, 1900 (RS); *New York Press,* September 30 and October 3, 15, 1900 (RS); Roosevelt to Davies, October 1, 2, 1900,

Upon Youngs' arrival Roosevelt realized what troubled the G.O.P. strategists. Standing by itself the answer did not justify removal. Nor was the appointment of a commissioner warranted, since the *World* apparently would not present additional evidence. The only possible alternatives were to publish the answer and hold the formal clearance of the mayor in abeyance, to publish both answer and decision at the same time, or to postpone action. Of these the first would be least advantageous to the Republicans, whereas the second raised the objections that Roosevelt could not so act while outside the state and the mere fact that Van Wyck would be formally "cleared" would improve Tammany's position. Hence the governor wrote Platt on October 7 that "I shall do nothing until I get back and can go over the whole business with Davies." [19]

The trouble with this course was that the *New York Journal* and the rest of the Democratic press could claim that the Van Wyck answer was being withheld because it assailed the G.O.P. as the party of trusts. And by October 28, back in New York, Roosevelt became convinced that publication would be less harmful than these continued attacks. But that same day Odell wired him at Binghamton that Van Wyck also desired no publicity.[20]

"Senator has read reply of V and agrees that it would be danger-ous and might lose an effect that we have with us and which V and his friends are willing we should have," read Odell's message. "If after this you desire to take the responsibility of course I have

---

TR MSS. (LC); Davies to Roosevelt, October 2, 1900, Davies MSS., NYRL; Odell to Roosevelt, October 3, 1900, and Roosevelt to Odell, October 4, 1900, TR MSS. (LC); Roosevelt to Platt, October 7, 1900, in *Barnes v. Roosevelt*, p. 2494.

[19] *Ibid.*

[20] New York *World* and *Brooklyn Citizen,* October 23, 1900; New York *Sun,* October 1, 1900; *New York Times,* October 25, 1900; *Albany Argus,* October 27, 1900 (all RS).

nothing further to say except that I would hesitate to do it if I were in your place." [21]

Whatever motives influenced Van Wyck, the governor accepted this advice, for he here discerned a solution short of publication. On October 29 Roosevelt informed the press that he had planned to give out the mayor's answer when he released his decision, but that Van Wyck was free to publish it himself at any time. This announcement effectively combatted the charges of the Democratic press until after the election. [22]

On November 9 the *World* reopened the case with its publication of the Van Wyck answer, the attorney general's opinion of October 4, and a wire allegedly sent by Odell to Roosevelt on September 26, antedating by one day the mayor's answer. The Odell telegram read:

Theodore Roosevelt, Governor of New York, Cripple Creek, Colorado: Wire Attorney-General Davies to be sure not to give out to the reporters the Van Wyck answer at this time. It must be held until after the election is over. This would imperil our chances and get us into a useless wrangle. I have also wired Davies. B. B. Odell.

Here, charged the *World*, was ample proof that the Republicans had played politics in the affair right along; they, and not the *World*, were responsible for any delay. [23]

No one questioned the authenticity of the first two documents, but the Cripple Creek telegram drew immediate fire. Odell pointed out that "B. B. Odell" was his father, whereupon the next edition of the *World* appended a "Jr." to the signature! Roosevelt declared that the message was "an absolute fake" and that he would get the telegraph company to prove it. Meantime one Republican

[21] Odell to Roosevelt, October 28, 1900, TR MSS. (LC).
[22] *Brooklyn Eagle*, October 29, 1900 (RS). See Roosevelt to Odell, October 28, 29, 1900, TR MSS. (LC).
[23] New York *World*, November 9, 1900 (RS).

journal observed that whether genuine or not the Odell wire meant little, because Van Wyck had been free to disclose his answer and had obviously preferred not to do so.[24]

Though a search through his files finally turned up the real Odell telegram of October 3, Roosevelt never publicly exposed the fake. In a way it would have been to his advantage to do so, for the original was by no means as bald a statement. But the *World's* version was so shrewd an approximation that it was politically expedient to continue to deny its authenticity without presentation of proof. Odell did not desire to make the true facts public, so Roosevelt had to be content to reveal them only to trusted friends.[25]

The election over, the Van Wyck case moved to a speedy conclusion. In a reversal of its stand of late September, the *World* again retained J. Noble Hayes as counsel and evidenced a desire to pursue the prosecution before a commissioner. The brief Hayes submitted, however, contained no additional testimony or indication where it could be obtained, so Davies held to his original opinion that guilty knowledge had not been proved. Roosevelt concurred and on November 23 dismissed the case, leaving only the *post mortems* of the party press as to who had been responsible for the long delay.[26]

In this continuing debate the Republican papers had the advantage, for on November 19 Roosevelt published a long memorandum prepared by Davies which set forth all the devious tactics of the *World* but omitted the Odell telegrams. Had these wires been included it would have been apparent that Van Wyck, the *World,*

[24] New York *World,* November 9, 10, 1900; New York *Sun, New York Tribune* and *Utica Observer,* November 10, 1900; *New York Tribune,* November 14, 1900 (all RS except the last).

[25] Roosevelt to Bishop, November 14, 20, 1900; to Paul Dana, November 22, 1900, TR MSS.

[26] *Public Papers* (1900), p. 192; Davies to Roosevelt, November 23, 1900, TR MSS. (LC).

and the Republican leaders had all contributed to the postponement in various ways and for different purposes. In this curious conjunction of aims the governor had not been immune to political considerations. Yet among the principals his course had been the least objectionable, and that primarily because his regard for the New York independents moved him to seek the just balance between the *World's* recklessness and the machine's partisanship.[27]

An abiding fear of the reform forces in New York City was that the removal of an elective Tammany official would turn him into a "martyr" and thus endanger their chances of victory in the mayoralty election of 1901. For that reason they approved the way in which Roosevelt had leaned over backwards to be fair to Van Wyck. Suspicious and morally objectionable as the mayor's conduct had been, it was better in the absence of clear proof of "wilful violation of law" to leave the remedy to the voters.[28]

The same reasoning applied with even greater force to the removal proceedings against the offensively partisan Asa Bird Gardiner, district attorney of New York County. Had Van Wyck been found guilty another Tammany man, the president of the council, would have succeeded, but if Gardiner was removed for misconduct in the fall election of 1900 then the governor would have the chance to appoint a Republican to fill the place until another could be elected. The possible political advantage thus made caution doubly imperative.

In September 1900 it had appeared that Gardiner would survive the criticism of those who had called him, in the *New York Times'* phrase, "an impossible, an inconceivable, District Attorney." The

---

[27] Cf. *Brooklyn Times* and Rochester *Post Express,* November 19, 1900; *Utica Observer,* November 19, 26, 1900 (all RS).

[28] *New York Times,* November 25, 1900; *Brooklyn Eagle,* November 24, 1900 (both RS).

City Club had brought charges against him the year before, alleging in a 500-page brief that he had manipulated indictments to favor his friends and his party, failed to account for $183,900 in forfeited bail bonds, shielded criminals from prosecution, and in general mishandled his considerable powers. Gardiner's insolent 61-page reply had been so unsatisfactory that Roosevelt had appointed Ansley Wilcox commissioner to take testimony. With "more than judicial indulgence and almost grandmotherly kindness" Wilcox had permitted the hearings "to be spread over a great variety of subjects and over an inordinate length of time," the *Brooklyn Eagle* had observed approvingly, until in July 1900 he had given the opinion that since the prosecution had not proved the specific counts of malfeasance and misfeasance, the only reason for removal would be Gardiner's "mental and moral unfitness for the office." That would have been justification enough for Platt and Odell, providing a Republican was appointed in his stead, but Roosevelt had feared the consequences among Gold Democrats and independents too much to replace Gardiner with a Republican. On September 13 he had dismissed the City Club's charges, concluding that "the moral conviction that a public servant is unfit, or the fact that his conduct has caused great and justifiable dissatisfaction to conscientious citizens is quite distinct from legal proof of shortcomings so serious as to warrant his removal from the office to which he has been elected by the people." [29]

There the matter would have rested had not Tammany committed a blunder just before election day. The burdens of Bryanism,

[29] *New York Tribune*, October 31, 1899; *New York Times*, November 1, 22, 1899 (RS); New York *Evening Post*, November 20, 1899 (RS); Roosevelt to Slicer, December 1, 1899, TR MSS.; *Brooklyn Eagle*, December 2, 4, 1899, and May 26, August 5, 1900 (all RS); Roosevelt to Ansley Wilcox, July 13, 1900, TR MSS.; F. V. Greene to Roosevelt, July 13, 1900, TR MSS. (LC); Roosevelt to Odell, July 14, 1900, TR MSS.; *Public Papers* (1900), p. 188.

the Ice Trust scandal, and the Van Wyck investigation made Boss Croker exceptionally truculent that fall. It was not enough for him to denounce the opposition as the party of trusts, imperialism, and "that wild man" Roosevelt: toward the end of October he began to charge that the Republicans intended if possible to count his party out at the polls. "My advice to democratic voters the country over is to congregate about the polling places on the evening of election day," Croker asserted, "count noses, and then if the election returns for Bryan do not tally with their count, to go into the polling places and throw those fellows in charge of the returns out into the street."

Shown the statement on October 13, the governor denounced "this incitement to riot and violence at the polls," but Croker reportedly chuckled as he replied that there would be a riot if Bryan was cheated out of his election, "as I know they are trying to do." [30]

Croker's immediate object was merely to direct attention to the Metropolitan District Elections Act under which the state-imposed, bipartisan force of deputies headed by Republican John McCullagh superintended registration and voting in Greater New York. But at 5:20 P.M. on Sunday, November 4, Police Chief "Big Bill" Devery warned all commanders by special order against "tactics and methods of intimidation, perpetrated upon respectable citizens . . . who are legal voters, by John McCullagh, Superintendent of Elections"; the city police were to be instructed "to use all means within their power to protect the honest right and franchise of all citizens on election day." [31]

The G.O.P. was quick to counter this "senseless and incendiary order." The next day, Monday, November 5, Odell suggested that

[30] *New York Herald*, October 31, 1900 (RS).
[31] New York *Sun*, November 6, 1900 (RS).

Roosevelt make Van Wyck as head of the city government responsible for any "breach of the peace, intimidation, or crimes against the election laws" resulting from the Devery edict. The governor, who several days before had made secret arrangements "so that in the event of need I could have any regiment of the National Guard out at once," now notified not only Van Wyck but also the sheriff and the district attorney of the County of New York of their "duty to assist in the orderly enforcement of the law." At the same time John Henry Hammond, special deputy to McCullagh for the prosecution of cases in violation of the election law, obtained a Grand Jury indictment of Chief Devery.[32]

The Devery indictment infuriated Asa Bird Gardiner: it was an "outrage," the *Press* and the *Sun* reported him saying, it wouldn't stand up, the district attorney's signature was a "forgery," and the grand jury foreman was "a bastard reformer." Elsewhere Tammany beat a hasty retreat. Van Wyck received the governor's message at the Democratic Club on election eve, conferred with Boss Croker immediately, and then told Devery to rescind the order. Devery complied, and the next day the election proceeded without disturbance.[33]

A little over a month later, special deputy Hammond preferred charges for "malfeasance and misconduct in office" against the district attorney: Gardiner and his aides had failed to aid the state's prosecution of election law violations, Hammond complained, and in the case of the Devery indictment they had "wil-

[32] New York *Evening Post,* November 6, 1900 (RS); Odell to Roosevelt, November 5, 1900, TR MSS. (LC). Roosevelt to Davies, November 1, 1900; to John Hay, November 10, 1900; to the Mayor of the City of New York, to the Sheriff of the County of New York, to the District Attorney of the County of New York, November 5, 1900; all TR MSS.

[33] New York *Sun* and *New York Press,* November 6, 1900 (RS); New York *Evening Post,* November 6, 1900.

fully and unlawfully delayed, interfered with and hindered the Attorney General and your petitioner." In a flippant answer Gardiner denied every contention, whereupon Roosevelt summoned both parties to a hearing in the executive chamber.[34]

There Gardiner contended that he had not known his remarks were to newspapermen and that in speaking of an "outrage" he had referred to the unauthorized use of his name by Hammond, not to the indictment of Devery. But the governor pointed out that if Gardiner had not intended to uphold the chief of police he should have published a denial of the newspaper stories. And even if the district attorney had not received the governor's message "before election," concluded Roosevelt, he should have replied as the mayor and the sheriff had done.[35]

For these reasons the governor could not believe Gardiner innocent of the charges. Since "crime against the ballot box" was the most serious one against the state in time of peace, the district attorney's action was not to be regarded lightly. Nor did Gardiner's well-known personal shortcomings excuse his failure to do his duty. "It is impossible again to accept the plea that acts like these are to be excused on the ground that they spring from folly, rather than from intent to do wrong," declared Roosevelt. On December 23, 1900, he removed Gardiner and appointed reform Democrat Eugene A. Philbin in his stead.[36]

Since this was the one major appointment on which he had failed to consult Platt, Roosevelt expected the Republican machine to be less than pleased. He was equally prepared for the *Evening Post* to term the action "really astounding," "erratic," "a blot on the Governor's record." What surprised him was not that journals

[34] *New York Press,* December 18, 1900 (RS).

[35] *New York Journal,* December 21, 1900; *Albany Times-Union,* December 22, 1900 (both RS).

[36] *Public Papers* (1900), pp. 202–205.

as widely divergent as the *World* and the *New York Tribune* approved, but that the *Sun* refused to endorse the removal and the *New York Times* called it "a political error of serious importance." The ex-district attorney could now pose as "a sort of martyr," reasoned the *Sun* and the *Times,* and the rise of public opinion against Tammany would be checked. However ideal the selection of Philbin, they concluded, the causes of Gardiner's displacement had been insufficient.[37]

In time these fears would prove unwarranted: Gardiner's martyrdom never developed, the Van Wyck administration sank ever lower in public esteem, and in November 1901 the ticket headed by Seth Low brought an end to Croker's effective power. As the Vice-President-elect quit New York for a western hunting trip he had no apologies. "Very few things in my official career have pleased me more than the chance of ousting Gardiner, to put in Philbin and to appoint John Proctor Clarke as Judge," he wrote his friend James R. Sheffield. Properly viewed, the last shot Roosevelt rammed home was cased in a strong sense of righteousness and charged with a spirit of independence. Gardiner had to go despite the calls for expediency from the anti-Tammany people: Philbin had to succeed regardless of the organization. Everyone was going to discover that the Colonel was still a Rough Rider.[38]

[37] New York *World, New York Herald, New York Tribune,* Rochester *Post Express, Buffalo Express, Brooklyn Times* and *New York Press,* December 24, 1900 (all RS); Wilcox to Roosevelt, December 24, 1900, TR MSS. (LC); New York *Evening Post,* December 24, 1900; *New York Times,* December 25, 1900 (RS); Roosevelt to James R. Sheffield, December 31, 1900, TR MSS.
[38] *Ibid.*

Conclusion

In retrospect, it was a favorable conjunction of events that propelled Colonel Roosevelt into the governorship in 1898. The people of New York thereby acquired a chief executive intent upon reform and good government. At the same time the Republican organization benefited as the party recovered its prestige. Most important of all, Theodore Roosevelt gained an invaluable opportunity to bring all his talents to bear for the first time as a responsible head of a government. His two years at Albany were an apprenticeship in the political guild in which he came to be a master.

The independent press testified to his achievement. Roosevelt had been "a Governor of the Cleveland, Lucius Robinson, and Marcy class," affirmed the *Brooklyn Eagle*. "He said such things and he did such things that he will be gubernatorially remembered as long as they." The unanimity with which independent Republican organs had favored his renomination bore out this appraisal. Admittedly the New York *Evening Post* professed disappointment at the results of his "heralded plan of partial and leisurely reform"; in his preference for excitement to work, claimed the *Post*, Roosevelt had allowed the state administration to suffer from "palpable neglect." But then there was a good deal of truth in Roosevelt's observation that the *Post* was "simply incapable of going right." [1]

[1] *Brooklyn Eagle* [n.d.], RHS; New York *Evening Post*, December 31, 1900; Roosevelt to James R. Sheffield, December 31, 1900, TR MSS.

If he had disregarded the Montauk Point agreement and fought with the machine, he would have satisfied the *Post*, but he would have secured few of the reforms he sought. The appointment of Partridge as superintendent of public works; repeal of the "starchless" civil-service law; the ouster of Lou Payn; inauguration of a canal survey; renovation of the forest, fish, and game commission; the Fallows measure to stop the Ramapo scheme—all these and more were obtained with Platt's cooperation. The Ford franchise tax was the prominent exception, but the aroused state of public opinion had made that an unusual case. The failure of the Jenks bill for greater publicity of corporate affairs demonstrated what usually happened to measures of which Boss Platt disapproved.

Though Roosevelt did not accomplish all that he would have liked in each instance, and sometimes gained nothing whatsoever, in the great majority of cases what was done represented his desire. "I don't know whether you have realized how entirely during my administration I have had the kernel [*sic*] and Mr. Platt the husk," the governor wrote Seth Low. ". . . Throughout these two years in both legislation and administration I have carried my point nine times out of ten." Somewhat more accurately the *Brooklyn Eagle* concluded that four times out of five the machine had done Roosevelt's bidding; in the fifth, as a rule, he had done what it wanted.[2]

Roosevelt owed his success in some part to his caution, tact, and willingness to compromise. He avoided commitment to candidates or programs that would antagonize Platt outright. He recognized the boss, consulted with him, and made every effort to enable him to put a good face on things publicly. Where he felt he legitimately could, as with the inheritance-tax appraisers bill and numerous appointments, he accepted the machine's request. Where insistence

[2] Roosevelt to Low, August 3, 1900, TR MSS.; *Brooklyn Eagle*, March 31, 1900 (RS).

upon the ultimate would lead to complete failure, as with the barge-canal proposal, he settled for something less.[3]

Boss Platt did not relish many of the concessions he made, yet he too had to be tactful. The governor's veto inspired caution. More than that, if driven far enough Roosevelt might institute an open fight for his case, as he came near doing over the franchise-tax bill. Despite his dominance in the organization and the legislature, Platt knew that he could not trifle with a politician who possessed so firm a hold on the popular confidence.

The immediate satisfaction Platt derived from the gubernatorial term was clear enough. In 1898 the party had been divided and discredited, his prestige at a low point. Roosevelt's administration altered that. The G.O.P. came back into repute, the justification for independent political organization grew ever more tenuous. To the *Evening Post's* irritation Platt became more respectable, his hold on the party stronger. No wonder the Easy Boss thought that an organization man would suffice for the 1900 election; his position was such that he could afford to be somewhat careless about the views of the antimachine element.[4]

Yet Roosevelt had sown seeds of independence within the party. His example had impressed his successor, Odell, who was responsive to public opinion and determined to exercise his own judgment in the executive chambers. By word and deed, Roosevelt had encouraged the more promising young politicians to resist machine dictation. "If you choose to be cattle I must consult your driver," he told two assemblymen, "Be men and I want your advice." In the legislature he supported Slater, Cooley, Elsberg, White, Hig-

---

[3] Roosevelt to Low, August 3, 1900, TR MSS.

[4] *Oswego Times,* May 9, 1900; *Watertown Times,* May 23, 1899; *Batavia News,* March 9, 1900; New York *Evening Post,* December 14, 1899 (all RS except the last).

gins; outside it he brought forward Goddard, Greene, and other responsible citizens. The "general policy . . . I have desired that my administration should stand for," he told Seth Low, was the destruction of that servility to party "which is not consistent with self-respect and good cititzenship." [5]

As he left Albany, Roosevelt was not at all sure that this process by which "independent men are being educated to a knowledge of their rights and powers" would continue. "Very possibly, in fact, in all human probability," he wrote Francis C. Lowell, "there will be a big set-back." But that retreat was not to be as pronounced as Boss Platt imagined as he surveyed the scene at the close of 1900. And though Roosevelt was gone, he would be back in a year with increased power to keep the educative work going. [6]

For Roosevelt himself, finally, the governorship was eminently worthwhile. Before coming to Albany, he had had some responsibility as a legislator, more as an administrator; but here he was legislative planner, administrative head, and political leader—chief executive of the largest and most diverse state in the union. All the problems and duties he had ever had, and more that he had not, were at this upstate capital. It was an excellent proving ground for his ideas and abilities. It was an opportunity for political experience matched only in the White House.

The very prominence of the office made this a crucial time in his career as well. If he made good at Albany he obviously would be a Presidential contender. If he fought with Platt, however, or even if

[5] "Studies in American Character, No. 5," *Brooklyn Eagle*, June 3, 1900 (RS); Roosevelt to Low, August 3, 1900, TR MSS. When Roosevelt thanked Justin McCarthy, Jr., for the *Eagle* sketch he called him "a straight, game man, with common sense, and you can be trusted under any and all circumstances—so I am 'wid yer,' as the boys say!" Roosevelt to McCarthy, June 6, 1900, TR MSS.

[6] Roosevelt to Francis C. Lowell, March 16, 1900, TR MSS.

he was only too impetuous and radical, the G.O.P. leaders would consider their fears of his unreliability confirmed. If he was too subservient to the machine, on the other hand, his standing with the people would suffer. To a party man of his brand this last possibility was of much concern, for it has been well said that "without the popular support he received the politicians would have made short shrift of him." [7]

In some respects his pursuit of a way through these dangers fell far short of success. His administrative reforms alienated parts of the New York machine, the Ford franchise-tax law antagonized powerful members of the business community, and the uneasy Platt plotted to get rid of him. At the same time the independents were angered at his caution, at his conferences with the boss, at his compromises with the organization. In terms of his own preference for his next political post Roosevelt wound up the governorship a failure.

But in the larger view his two-year term only added to his stature within the G.O.P. In an extremely difficult situation he had blended reform and politics in such a manner as to avoid a break with the machine without losing the enthusiastic support of the bulk of the party. Had Platt not taken advantage of his popularity to force him onto the national ticket, Roosevelt's renomination would have been undeniable. As it was he remained the man to reckon with in 1904.

Those who boomed Roosevelt for the Presidency could no do better for their argument than to turn to the record of the governorship. There they found formulated his doctrine on the relation of party to the government and the people; his general theory on the role of the state in modern society; and his stand on such issues as trusts, transportation, labor, and conservation. More than that,

[7] Lewis Einstein, *Roosevelt: His Mind in Action* (Boston, 1930), p. 78.

they found these theoretical positions applied in case after case in actual practice. Roosevelt's prescriptions for politics were no idle speculations; he had put them to work under the most demanding conditions. He was a seasoned leader.

Broadly conceived in the interests of the people, the Roosevelt program rested firmly upon the concept of the square deal by a neutral state. Neither political machines, nor great corporations, nor any group or individual with a special objective endangering the general good should dictate policy. Rather the community through its elected representatives should stand above the conflict, mediating the struggle of contending factions in an even-handed fashion. Whether the issue was an appointment of a superintendent of public works or insurance, or the terms and taxation of franchises, or the degree of publicity required of chartered companies, or the disposition of the canals, or the settlement of a labor dispute, or the conservation of natural resources, or the management of New York's agencies and institutions, the same rule applied. In every instance the primary consideration was the promotion of the general welfare.

This policy had a conservative yet dynamic aspect. It was conservative in that it did not entail a sweeping change that would discriminate against a particular group or class within society. It was dynamic in that it aimed to eliminate the favoritism enjoyed by political machines when they rewarded corruption and inefficiency, or by business companies when they obtained great privileges from public authorities without assuming commensurate responsibilities. It was dynamic also in that it would accord fairer treatment to those who had been exploited previously, whether garment workers, or investors, or tenement dwellers, or teachers, or just plain citizens.

What Roosevelt offered the Republicans, in short, was a workable plan by which to move forward toward greater democracy in an era of revolutionary change. The regnant powers had resisted his program in New York, and so they would do in the nation. But the dissatisfaction that Roosevelt felt with current conditions in business and politics was widely shared within his party and the country generally. That mounting protest needed direction; it needed a policy and a leader. In September 1901 it found both in ex-Governor Theodore Roosevelt. His apprenticeship in the Empire State would not go to waste.

LIST OF ABBREVIATIONS

BIBLIOGRAPHICAL NOTE

INDEX

List of Abbreviations and
Short Titles

Alexander, *Political History*	DeAlva Stanwood Alexander, *A Political History of the State of New York,* 4 vols. (New York, 1906–1923). Volume IV is known as *Four Famous New Yorkers.*
Assembly Journal	*Journal of the Assembly of the State of New York,* 7 vols. (Albany, 1899–1900).
Barnes v. *Roosevelt*	*William Barnes, plaintiff-appellant,* v. *Theodore Roosevelt, defendant-respondent: Case on Appeal,* 4 vols. (Walton, N.Y., 1917).
BiPL	Binghamton Public Library, Binghamton, New York.
BPL	Buffalo Public Library, Buffalo, New York.
Butler MSS.	Nicholas Murray Butler MSS., Low Library, Columbia University, New York City.
Canals Committee, *Report*	The Committee on Canals of New York State, *Report, January 25, 1900* (Albany, 1900).
Charities Board, *Annual Report*	New York State Board of Charities, *Annual Report* (Albany). For the years 1898 (32nd), 1899 (33rd), and 1900 (34th).
Commerce Commission, *Report*	New York Commerce Commission, *Report, January 25, 1900,* 2 vols. (Albany, 1900).
Comptroller, *Annual Report*	New York State Comptroller, *Annual Report* (Albany). For the years 1899 and 1900.
CorUL	Cornell University Library, Ithaca, New York.
CUL	Columbia University Library, New York City.
Elmira Reformatory, *Yearbook*	New York State Reformatory at Elmira, *Yearbook* (Elmira). For the years 1894 (19th), 1899 (24th), 1900 (25th), 1904 (29th), and 1908 (33rd). In 1904 and 1908 this is entitled *Annual Report.*
Factory Inspector, *Annual Report*	New York State Factory Inspector, *Annual Report* (Albany). For the years 1899 (14th) and 1900 (15th).

Forest Commission, *Annual Report*	New York State Forest, Fish, and Game Commission, *Annual Report* (Albany). For the years 1899 and 1900.
HCL	Harvard College Library, Cambridge, Mass.
Laws of New York	*Laws of the State of New York,* 4 vols. (Albany, 1899–1900).
LC	Library of Congress, Washington, D. C.
LL	Low Library, Columbia University, New York City.
Lodge, ed., *Selections*	Henry Cabot Lodge, ed., *Selections from the Correspondence of Theodore Roosevelt and Henry Cabot Lodge, 1884–1918,* 2 vols. (New York, 1925).
Low MSS.	Seth Low MSS., Low Library, Columbia University, New York City.
Mazet Investigation	*Report of the Special Committee of the New York Assembly to Investigate the Public Offices and Departments of the City of New York,* 5 vols. (Albany, 1900).
Mediation Board, *Annual Report*	New York State Board of Mediation and Arbitration, *Annual Report* (Albany). For the years 1899 (13th) and 1900 (14th).
Morison and Blum, eds., *Letters*	Elting E. Morison and John M. Blum, eds., *The Letters of Theodore Roosevelt,* 8 vols. (Cambridge, Mass., 1951–1954).
NEDL	New England Deposit Library, Boston, Mass.
NYPL	New York Public Library, New York City.
NYRL	New York Regional Library, Cornell University, Ithaca, New York.
NYSL	New York State Library, Albany, New York.
Platt, *Autobiography*	Thomas Collier Platt, *The Autobiography of Thomas Collier Platt,* compiled and edited by Louis J. Lang (New York, 1910).
Prisons Commission, *Annual Report*	New York State Commission on Prisons, *Annual Report* (Albany). For the years 1899 (5th), 1900 (6th), and 1901 (7th).
Public Papers	*Public Papers of Theodore Roosevelt, Governor* (Albany, 1899, 1900).
Quigg MSS.	Lemuel E. Quigg MSS., Roosevelt Collection, Harvard College Library, Cambridge, Mass.
Riis MSS.	Jacob A. Riis MSS., Russell Sage Foundation, New York City.

RHP	Roosevelt House Papers, Roosevelt Collection, Harvard College Library, Cambridge, Mass.
RHS	Roosevelt House Scrapbooks, 28 East 20th Street, New York City.
RML	Rundel Memorial Library, Rochester, New York.
Roosevelt, *Autobiography*	*Theodore Roosevelt: An Autobiography* (New York, 1913).
Roosevelt Collection	Theodore Roosevelt Collection, Harvard College Library, Cambridge, Mass.
Root MSS.	Elihu Root MSS., Library of Congress, Washington, D. C.
RS	Roosevelt Scrapbooks, Roosevelt Collection, Harvard College Library, Cambridge, Mass.
Senate Journal	*Journal of the Senate of the State of New York,* 4 vols. (Albany, 1899–1900).
SPL	Syracuse Public Library, Syracuse, New York.
TR MSS.	Theodore Roosevelt MSS., Roosevelt Collection, Harvard College Library, Cambridge, Mass.
TR MSS. (LC)	Theodore Roosevelt MSS., Library of Congress, Washington, D. C.
UPL	Utica Public Library, Utica, New York.

Bibliographical Note

The Theodore Roosevelt Memorial Collection in the Harvard College Library contains the bulk of the primary and secondary sources for this study. The chief supplement to this invaluable collection assembled by the Theodore Roosevelt Memorial Association is in the manuscripts division of the Library of Congress, which houses most of Roosevelt's original incoming correspondence as well as the original copies of many of his outgoing letters. Beyond these, the most important records for this period are the documents in the New York State Library at Albany and the newspapers in various depositories in New York State.

This bibliographical note discusses mainly the primary sources, which are divided into manuscripts, both letter and other; memoirs and published letters; writings of contemporaries; documents; and periodicals, newspapers, and scrapbooks.

PRIMARY SOURCES

MANUSCRIPTS: LETTERS

Most of Roosevelt's outgoing letters, 1899–1900, are on microfilm in the Roosevelt Collection (HCL). There are 15 reels of "personal" letters and 7 reels of "executive official" letters, all arranged chronologically and indexed. There is also a reel of Roosevelt letters culled from incoming boxes at the Library of Congress, as well as a reel of letters to his sister and brother-in-law, Corinne and Douglas Robinson, which is particularly valuable in the 1898 period not covered in the Roosevelt press-letter books. On microfilm also, and of some use, are letters to *Review of Reviews* editor Albert Shaw (originals in NYPL); the correspondence of Francis Vinton Greene (originals in NYPL), touching upon the national guard, state politics, and the canals; the correspondence of Nicholas Murray Butler (originals in LL); letters to Anna Roosevelt Cowles, most of which are in *Letters from Theodore Roosevelt to Anna Roosevelt Cowles, 1870–1918* (New York, 1924) or have duplicates elsewhere in the Roosevelt Collection; and letters from the papers of Joseph Benson Foraker (LC), John Hay (LC), Brander Matthews (CUL), and Carl Schurz (LC), none of them of much value to this study. Important Roosevelt letters of 1898 are in the papers of Seth Low (LL) and Lemuel E. Quigg (microfilmed in Roosevelt Collection).

The Library of Congress has 7 boxes of incoming letters, 1882–1900, of which 5 boxes cover the governorship period. To supplement this most important single source of letters to Roosevelt, there are the John C. Davies letter books (NYRL), which deal mainly with administrative detail of the attorney general's office in 1900; the Frederick William Holls papers (CUL) that have two volumes of letters to various parties, 1898–1900; the letters from Low to Roosevelt in several boxes of miscellaneous correspondence (1897–1900) in the Seth Low papers (LL); the letters from Riis to Roosevelt in a file drawer of assorted notes and records (1899–1900) in the Jacob A. Riis papers, Russell Sage Foundation, New York City; and several letters from Root to Roosevelt in the letter books (July 1899–1900) in the Elihu Root papers (LC). The Lemuel E. Quigg letters (1894–1913) on microfilm in the Roosevelt Collection have important communications from Quigg to Roosevelt, especially in 1898–1899 and 1913.

A few other letter collections touch upon the governorship. The papers of John Jay Chapman, in the Houghton Library of Harvard University, have valuable material (August–October 1898), not all of which is in Howe's biography of Chapman. The papers of Jonas Van Duzer (NYRL) have a folder on Roosevelt and state politics (1898–1900); and the Charles Scribner's Sons collection, microfilmed in the Roosevelt Collection, contains miscellaneous letters on the 1898 nomination and campaign. Few of the personal letters in the Joseph Hodges Choate papers (1898–LC) deal with state politics, while the box of correspondence (1897–1898) in the papers of George Washington Aldridge (RML) treats only canal affairs. There is pertinent data in the box of correspondence (1899–1900) of the New York Civil Service Reform Association (NYRL), and the incoming boxes of Elihu Root (LC) have important items on the State Trust affair (1900).

MANUSCRIPTS: OTHER

The Roosevelt Collection (HCL) contains a number of other manuscripts relating to the governorship. J. H. French's interviews of men who knew and worked with Roosevelt, in the Roosevelt House Papers of the collection, are especially valuable, although the facts recalled long after the event can be unreliable. William J. Youngs, secretary to Governor Roosevelt, has some interesting detail in "A Short Resumé of the Administration of Theodore Roosevelt" (1904). Avery D. Andrews, a participant in national-guard reform and the State Trust investigation, has useful sidelights in a two-volume unpublished essay, "Theodore Roosevelt" (1945). John Proctor Clarke, "Random Recollections of Campaigning with Col. Roosevelt," dated September 14, 1917, lends color to the 1898 campaign, for which the manuscript "Speeches of Col. Theodore Roosevelt" are also available in the Roosevelt Collection.

The New York Public Library has the Richard Ward Greene Welling diary, 1896–1907, which records the reactions of a young Independent to the 1898 nominations and campaign, but in "The Story of My Life" (NYPL) Gherardi Davis ignores his years in the legislative assembly. The Roosevelt papers in the Library of Congress contain the useful "Memorandum of the Charges against the Mayor in Connection with the Ice Trust," which was probably prepared by Attorney General John C. Davies, in November 1900.

MEMOIRS AND PUBLISHED LETTERS

The memoirs most valuable for this work are Thomas Collier Platt, *The Autobiography of Thomas Collier Platt,* compiled and edited by Louis J. Lang (New York, 1910), which speaks frankly of the Easy Boss's methods but not of his ideas, and Theodore Roosevelt, *Theodore Roosevelt: An Autobiography* (New York, 1913), which continues to afford the best insight into the spirit of the Roosevelt era. Of particular use on the 1898 nomination and campaign are Joseph I. C. Clarke, *My Life and Memories* (New York, 1925); Chauncey M. Depew, *My Memories of Fifty Years* (New York, 1922); William Dudley Foulke, *A Hoosier Autobiography* (New York, 1922); and Lincoln Steffens, *The Autobiography of Lincoln Steffens* (New York, 1931). For one who was Roosevelt's adviser on educational matters, Nicholas Murray Butler says remarkably little about the governorship in *Across the Busy Years,* 2 vols. (New York, 1939), but there are useful details on Elmira Reformatory in Zebulon R. Brockway, *Fifty Years of Prison Service: An Autobiography* (New York, 1912), on forest conservation in Gifford Pinchot, *Breaking*

New Ground (New York, 1947), and on labor in Samuel Gompers, *Seventy Years of Life and Labor: An Autobiography*, 2 vols. (New York, 1925).

An invaluable source, despite bowdlerization, is Henry Cabot Lodge, ed., *Selections from the Correspondence of Theodore Roosevelt and Henry Cabot Lodge, 1884–1918*, 2 vols. (New York, 1925). I have preferred, wherever possible, to use the copies of letters to Lodge in Roosevelt's own files, but in 1898 there was usually no text other than Lodge's.

WRITINGS OF CONTEMPORARIES

Anecdotal material on Roosevelt is in *Theodore Roosevelt: The Man as I Knew Him* (New York, 1919), by Ferdinand Cowle Iglehart, an upstate minister who interested himself in Roosevelt's career and reform legislation; Jacob A. Riis's enthusiastic *Theodore Roosevelt The Citizen* (New York, 1904); and Corinne Roosevelt Robinson, *My Brother Theodore Roosevelt* (New York, 1921), which gives revealing glimpses of Roosevelt's gubernatorial campaign and conferences with Boss Platt.

Theodore Roosevelt advances his views vigorously in *American Ideals and Other Essays Social and Political* (New York, 1897); *The Rough Riders* (New York, 1899); and *The Strenuous Life* (New York, 1900). The complete edition of Roosevelt's writings is by Hermann Hagedorn, ed., *The Works of Theodore Roosevelt*, 20 vols., National Edition (New York, 1925).

John Ford's debunking "Theodore Roosevelt's Feet of Clay," *Current History* 34:678–685 (August 1931) has important information on the franchise tax, as do his "The Taxation of Public Franchises," *North American Review* 168:730–738 (June 1899); John DeWitt Warner, "The Ford Act: Taxation of Local Franchises," *Municipal Affairs* 3:269–298 (June 1899); and especially E. R. A. Seligman, "The Franchise Tax Law in New York," *Quarterly Journal of Economics* 13:445–452 (July 1899).

Other legislative measures have particular studies of value. The barge-canal project has Francis Vinton Greene, "The Inception of the Barge Canal Project," and Thomas W. Symons, "The United States Government and the New York State Canals," both in Buffalo Historical Society *Publications* 13:109–120, 121–134 (1909). The Jenks antitrust bill has Jeremiah W. Jenks' *The Trust Problem* (New York, 1900) and "Publicity: A Remedy for the Evils of Trusts," *Review of Reviews* 21:445–

449 (April 1900). The police legislation has Frank Moss, "State Oversight of Police," *Municipal Affairs* 3:264–268 (June 1899), while Gifford Pinchot, "Working Plans for the New York Forest Preserve," *Outing* 36:89–90 (April 1900) testifies on conservation plans.

DOCUMENTS

The documents basic to this study are *Laws of the State of New York*, 4 vols. (Albany, 1899–1900); *Journal of the Assembly of the State of New York*, 7 vols. (Albany, 1899–1900); *Journal of the Senate of the State of New York*, 4 vols. (Albany, 1899–1900); and *Public Papers of Theodore Roosevelt, Governor*, 2 vols. (Albany, 1899–1900).

Of especial importance also are the *Report of the Special Committee of the New York Assembly to Investigate the Public Offices and Departments of the City of New York*, 5 vols. (Albany, 1900), herein entitled the *Mazet Investigation*, a Platt-inspired project that casts much light on Tammany's operations; and *William Barnes, plaintiff-appellant, v. Theodore Roosevelt, defendant-respondent: Case on Appeal*, 4 vols. (Walton, N. Y., 1917), herein entitled *Barnes v. Roosevelt*, a celebrated court case which explores Roosevelt's relationship with the Republican machine. *Barnes v. Roosevelt* is a major source for Boss Platt's letters, copies of which (according to the senator's grandson, Livingston Platt of New York City) were probably destroyed upon his death.

The *Annual Reports* of various state officers and boards are valuable. Particularly useful on state institutions are the annual reports of the comptroller, the state board of charities, the commission on prisons, and Elmira Reformatory; on labor relations, the annual reports of the factory inspector and the board of mediation and arbitration; on education, the annual reports of the University of the State of New York, the state department of public instruction, and the New York City superintendent of schools; and on conservation, the annual reports of the forest, fish, and game commission.

Useful, too, are the *Annual Reports* of a number of private organizations for the years 1899 and 1900: The Charity Organization Society of the City of New York, The Consumers' League of the City of New York, the executive committee of the Civil Service Reform Association of New York, and the New York State Charities Aid Association.

Two special reports clarify the canal problem: Committee on Canals of New York State, *Report, January 25, 1900* (Albany, 1900), and the New York Commerce Commission, *Report, January 25, 1900,* 2 vols. (Albany, 1900). On New York City's water supply, The Merchants' Association of New York, *An Inquiry into the Conditions Relating to the Water Supply of the City of New York* (New York, 1900) is useful, as is the *Mazet Investigation.* The best analysis of New York's tax situation in 1899–1900 is *Report to the Legislature of New York by the Joint Committe on Taxation, January 15, 1900* (Albany, 1900). There is relevant data on labor conditions in vol. VII of the Industrial Commission, *Report,* 19 vols. (Washington, 1899–1902) and on trusts in the Chicago Conference on Trusts, *Speeches, Debates, Resolutions . . . September 13–16, 1899* (Chicago, 1900).

PERIODICALS, NEWSPAPERS, SCRAPBOOKS

The most useful general periodicals—the dates indicating the period covered—are *Nation* (1898–1900); *American Monthly Review of Reviews* (1899–1900), edited by Albert Shaw; and *Outlook* (1899–1900), edited by Lyman Abbott. *The Nursery* (1897–1900, entitled *The Political Nursery* after September 1898), edited by John Jay Chapman, is particularly valuable on Roosevelt's relation with the Independents and the machine. *Gunton's Magazine* (1898–1900), edited by George Gunton, treats problems of capital and labor, while *Outing* (January–April 1900) and *Forest and Stream* (January–April 1900) touch upon conservation. *Harper's Weekly* (1898–1900) and *Rural New Yorker* (1899–1900) yielded little, but *Educational Review* (1899–1901), edited by Nicholas Murray Butler, was quite rewarding in its special area.

Newspapers are an indispensable primary source. I relied especially on the *New York Tribune* (1898–1900: HCL), New York *Evening Post* (1898–1900: NEDL) and New York *World* (1898–1900: NEDL). But most useful also were the *Albany Argus* (1898–1900: NYSL), *Buffalo Courier* (1898–1900: BPL) and *Rochester Union and Advertiser* (1898–1900: RML) for the Democratic party press; the *Albany Evening Journal* (1898–1899: NYSL; 1900: LC), *Troy Times* (1898–1900: NYSL) and *Utica Herald* (1899–1900: UPL) for the Republican party press; and the *Binghamton Herald* (October 1898–1900: BiPL), *Buffalo Express* (1898–1900: BPL), *Syracuse Herald* (1898–1900: SPL), *Utica*

Press (1898–1899: UPL), Rochester *Democrat and Chronicle* (1898–1899: RML), and Rochester *Post Express* (1900: RML) for the more or less independent Republican journals. For the period of the nomination and campaign, from July to November 1898, I consulted several other Republican papers—*Buffalo Commercial* (BPL), *Ithaca Journal* (CorUL) and *Syracuse Journal* (SPL)—and several other independent Republican papers, namely, the *Auburn Advertiser* (CorUL), *Binghamton Weekly Herald* (BiPL), New York *Commercial Advertiser* (NYPL), New York *Mail and Express* (NYPL) and *New York Press* (NYPL). Among the weeklies, the *Binghamton Weekly Leader* (September 1898–May 1899: BiPL) gave the Democratic viewpoint, but the *Prattsburgh News* (1899: CorUL) and *Utica Globe* (1898–1899: UPL) were not nearly as useful as the *Steuben Courier* (1898–1900: CorUL), which was quite informative on the New York State Soldiers' and Sailors' Home.

The Theodore Roosevelt Scrapbooks (herein denoted by the symbol RS) in the Roosevelt Collection (HCL) are an invaluable supplement to the regular newspaper files. For the years 1898 through 1900, there are 9 large volumes of clippings, covering most aspects of Roosevelt's activities, and representative of the New York press. I found relatively little use for the Roosevelt House Scrapbooks, 28 East 20th Street, New York City; nor did I gain much from the scrapbooks of George Washington Aldridge (1898–1899: RML) and James T. Rogers (1899–1900: in possession of James T. Rogers, Jr., of Ridgewood, N. J.).

SECONDARY SOURCES

This bibliographical note does not essay a complete listing of the secondary sources utilized in this study. Most of these already have full references in the footnotes. Here, therefore, there is mention only of the more significant histories and interpretations.

The most knowledgeable general political history of this era in New York is still in DeAlva Stanwood Alexander, *A Political History of the State of New York,* 4 vols. (New York, 1909–1923), but Harold F. Gosnell supplies a valuable study of *Boss Platt and His New York Machine: A Study of the Political Leadership of Thomas C. Platt, Theodore Roosevelt, and Others* (Chicago, 1924). M. A. DeWolfe Howe sheds light on the Independent nomination of 1898 in his *John Jay*

Chapman and His Letters (Boston, 1937), but the best interpretation of that episode is Elting E. Morison's in Appendix II of the second volume of Elting E. Morison and John M. Blum, eds., *The Letters of Theodore Roosevelt*, 8 vols. (Cambridge, Mass., 1951–1954). Henry F. Pringle's study of the governorship in *Theodore Roosevelt: A Biography* (New York, 1931) is superficial; the best brief survey is in William H. Harbaugh, *Power and Responsibility: The Life and Times of Theodore Roosevelt* (New York, 1961). Among the older interpretations of Theodore Roosevelt, Lewis Einstein, *Roosevelt: His Mind in Action* (Boston, 1930) is particularly discerning.

Beyond Roosevelt's relation with Platt and the G.O.P. machine, no aspect of the governorship has been investigated more closely than its labor policy. Howard L. Hurwitz, *Theodore Roosevelt and Labor in New York State, 1880–1900*, Columbia University Studies in History, Economics and Public Law, no. 500 (New York, 1943) is a thorough study, but too unappreciative of the political dimension of labor relations. As might be expected, the graduate school of Columbia University has produced many of the other pertinent works in its series of Columbia University Studies in History, Economics and Public Law: Elizabeth F. Baker, *Protective Labor Legislation with Special Reference to Women in the State of New York* (New York, 1925); Harry J. Carman, *The Street Surface Railway Franchises of New York City* (New York, 1919); Philip Klein, *Prison Methods in New York* (New York, 1920); Harold C. Syrett, *The City of Brooklyn, 1865–1898: A Political History* (New York, 1944); and Mabel H. Willett, *The Employment of Women in the Clothing Trade* (New York, 1944).

The other most useful biographies are Donald Barr Chidsey, *The Gentleman from New York: A Life of Roscoe Conkling* (New Haven, 1935); Mark D. Hirsch, *William C. Whitney: Modern Warwick* (New York, 1948); Philip C. Jessup, *Elihu Root*, 2 vols. (New York, 1938); and Louise Ware, *Jacob A. Riis* (New York, 1938).

Index

Steffens, Lincoln, 42, 43n
Stetson, Francis Lynde, 175
Steuben County, 183, 259–263
Steuben Courier, 259, 261
Steward, Ira, 201
Stewart, James L., 74
Stewart, William Rhinelander, 263, 264
Stillman, James, 121
Stokes, I. N. Phelps, 232n
Stranahan, Nevada N., 124
Strong, William L., 13, 44, 270
Sturgis, Thomas D., 270, 271, 272, 273
Subway, *see* Rapid-Transit Bill; Tunnel Bill
Sullivan, Timothy D., 126, 229, 231
Sunday Law, *see* Raines Liquor Law
Swayne, Wager, 19, 44
Swayne-Brookfield faction, 19, 26
Sweatshops, 55, 203, 209, 212; Roosevelt's program for, 203, 210
Symons, Thomas W., 189
Syracuse: and education, 234; and gas bill, 113; Hendricks from, 72, 95; Independents in, 36; police of, 85; prize fights in, 228; White from, 78

Taft, Henry W., 90, 237
Taft, William Howard, 128
Tammany Hall: and Brady, 123; and corporations, 115, 123, 125, 287; criticism of, 83–84, 299; and Daly, 56–59; and election of 1894, 13–14; and election of 1898, 50, 52, 56–59; and election of 1900, 291, 295–297; and eligibility question, 46, 47; and legislation, 89, 121, 125, 227–228, 230–231; and police, 82, 84, 87; and Ramapo water steal, 244, 245, 248; and strikes, 220, 222; "Tammany Annex," 77, 83, 126, 231; and taxation, 138, 140, 150; and trusts, 159, 287. *See*

also Democrats; Croker, Richard
Taxation: dodging, 49, 56, 133–134; of franchises, 5, 125, 133, 137, 138, 139, 150; joint committee on, 133, 138, 140, 156–157; in annual message of 1899, 131–132; in annual message of 1900, 167; of mortgages, 156–157; system, 133, 134, 136; Tax Commissoners, State Board of, 134, 152
Taylor, Buck, 64, 65
Teachers' Association, 235, 236
Tenement Housing: agitation over, 231–232; bill introduced, 232; building-codes commission, 231; Roosevelt supports bill, 232–233; state commission of 1894, 231
Ten-Hour day, 202–203, 218, 220
Thimme, Edward, 205
Third Avenue Company, 114, 115, 116, 117n, 127, 147
Thurber, F. B., 165
Tilden, Samuel J., 21
Tillinghast, C. Whitney, 53
Tracy, Benjamin F., 14, 245
Trimble, Merritt, 119
Troy, 12, 60, 67, 85, 118, 234–235
Troy Times: and Astoria Gas, 123, 124; in election of 1898, 60; opposes constabulary, 86; supports Black, 17; supports Payn, 97, 106
Trusts: annual message on, 166–168; Chicago Conference, 164–165; companies, 100, 103; growth, 158–159; ice, 287, 290, 296; New York laws, 159; opinions on, 23, 162, 164–166, 172; publicity and, 5, 6, 164–165, 172, 176; Republicans and, 165–166; Roosevelt's plan for, 162–164, 176; worry Roosevelt, 160–161
Tucker, Preble, 39, 44
Tunnel Bill, 120, 124, 131; Roosevelt on, 124–125, 127–128
Tweed, William, 58, 59